A Practical Guide to Museum Ethics

A Practical Guide to Museum Ethics

Sally Yerkovich

ROWMAN & LITTLEFIELD
Lanham • Boulder • New York • London

Published by Rowman & Littlefield International, Ltd.
A wholly owned subsidiary of The Rowman & Littlefield Publishing Group, Inc.
4501 Forbes Boulevard, Suite 200, Lanham, Maryland 20706
www.rowman.com

Unit A, Whitacre Mews, 26-34 Stannary Street, London SE11 4AB

British Library Cataloguing in Publication Data

Library of Congress Cataloging-in-Publication Data
Names: Yerkovich, Sally.
Title: A practical guide to museum ethics/Sally Yerkovich.
Description: Lanham : Rowman & Littlefield, 2016. | Includes bibliographical
    references and index.
Identifiers: LCCN 2015046137 (print) | LCCN 2016005674 (ebook) |
    ISBN 9781442231627 (cloth : alkaline paper) | ISBN 9781442231634
    (paperback : alkaline paper) | ISBN 9781442231641 (Electronic)
Subjects: LCSH: Museums—Moral and ethical aspects—Handbooks, manuals,
    etc. | Museums—Moral and ethical aspects—Case studies. | Museum curators—
    Professional ethics—Handbooks, manuals, etc. | Museum directors—Professional
    ethics—Handbooks, manuals, etc. | Museums—Employees—Professional ethics—
    Handbooks, manuals, etc. | Museums—Standards—Handbooks, manuals, etc. |
    Professional ethics—Handbooks, manuals, etc.
Classification: LCC AM7 .Y37 2016 (print) | LCC AM7 (ebook) | DDC 174/.9069—
    dc23 LC record available at http://lccn.loc.gov/2015046137

Printed in the United States of America

Contents

Acknowledgments

This book would not have been possible without the encouragement of Jim Gardner of the National Archives, Bob Beatty at the American Association of State and Local History, and Charles Harmon, my editor at Rowman & Littlefield. I was fortunate to be in residence in the Frederick Lewis Allen Room in the Stephen A. Schwarzman Building of the New York Public Library during the writing of this book. Jay Barksdale, Carolyn Broomhead, and Melanie Locay, Research Study Liaisons, went out of their way to help ensure that the library's incomparable resources were readily available.

My students at Columbia, Seton Hall, and the Bank Street College of Education demonstrated that discussions about ethical problems can be lively and filled with enthusiasm. I am especially grateful to the help of Lillian Diep, Dawn Eshelman, Laurel Fehrenbach, Jessimi Jones, Leslie Martinez, Karen McCree, Bonnie Naugle, Cathy Saunders, Jodi Snyder, Daniel Zeiger, and other students in the Museum Leadership Program at the Bank Street College of Education. They clarified for me some of the ethical issues that museum professionals face and helped me understand how much confusion can be caused by not having adequate policies and procedures relating to museum ethics.

Discussions and correspondence with colleagues and friends including Sheila Biddle, Julie Hart, Bonnie Naugle, Debra Hess Norris, Bruno Pouliot, Ellen Snyder-Grenier, and Glenn Wharton were enormously beneficial. In addition, special thanks must go to those willing to read drafts of the book's chapters and give me their helpful thoughts and valued advice: Patty Gerstenblith, Martha Graham, Lyndel King, Heather Stephens Kuruvilla, Claudia Ocello, Kathy Dwyer Southern, Isabelle Tokumaru, Diana Wall, and Philip Zimmerman.

Last and most importantly, two people lent their support to this project, and without them it would not have come to fruition. My colleague and friend Janet Rassweiler was the first reader of each chapter and sometimes also the last. Her abilities as both an educator and effective communicator and her thorough professionalism contributed enormously. My husband Lew Smoley's unstinting support, encouragement, and understanding enrich my life every day and they contributed immensely to this project from beginning to end.

Introduction and Framework for Approaching Ethical Problems

On February 27, 1972, "Very Quiet and Very Dangerous," an article by John Canaday in *The New York Times*, raised questions about the propriety of the Metropolitan Museum of Art's sale of four Redon paintings and took issue with the practice of "de-accessioning." Parenthetically noting that *de-accession* is the "polite word for 'sold,'" he observed, "All of this is perfectly legal when the works have been acquired without restrictions against sale. But are these sales always strictly ethical—or, if a museum doesn't worry about that, are they wise?"[1] This article is perhaps the first time that the word *deaccessioning* appeared in newsprint; yet it is certainly not the first time that museum ethics made headlines. In fact as early as December 29, 1902, *The New York Times* published "Museum Ethics," an article in which it called into question the practice of selling items from a museum collection. At that time, the Pennsylvania Academy's 1898 sale of some of its paintings was being challenged in court by the son of one of the people who originally bequeathed the works to the museum. The *Times* article asked, "What are the ethics of museums, anyhow?" and while the article admitted that some collections could benefit from careful evaluation and pruning, it concluded that if a museum chooses to sell works from its collection, it "should do it openly and above board, giving everybody a chance to discuss the wisdom of the sale."[2] These examples speak to just one area of museum practice about which ethical issues have been raised, but they demonstrate the long-standing concern about how museums operate and how they carry out their responsibilities in the public interest.

Today the media routinely raise ethical arguments about virtually every aspect of a museum's activities and operations. To respond to the lack of guidance in ferreting out and dealing with ethical concerns, the American Alliance of Museums (AAM) promulgated its "Code of Ethics for Museums" in 1994 (revised in 2000). Yet neither this code nor the current literature offers a practical methodology for approaching these problems. *A Practical Guide to Museum Ethics* was written to fill that void by creating a resource for dealing with ethical problems that arise in museums.

Museums, whether privately or publically funded, have a primary moral responsibility to the public to function ethically. Each of the ten chapters of this book deals with an area of museum practice in which ethical problems have arisen and are likely to continue to be troublesome. Principles of conduct from professional codes of ethics are discussed as they relate to the topic of each chapter. Applicable provisions from the "Code of Ethics for Museums" of the AAM and that of the International Council of Museums (ICOM) are basic points of reference and are supplemented by the American Association of State and Local History's "AASLH Statement of Professional Standards and Ethics" and the Association of Art Museum Directors' (AAMD) "Professional Practices in Art Museums."

Hypothetical and actual case histories are included in each chapter under the heading "Ethics in Action" to illustrate issues faced by museums today. Correct solutions are not provided, for the cases also demonstrate how the resolution of ethical problems can vary depending upon a museum's mission as well as upon the specific circumstances in which the problems arise and the people involved, both within and outside the museum. "Ethics in Action" gives the reader an opportunity to apply the suggested problem-solving framework and come up with his or her own resolutions. It also alerts the reader to the kinds of policies and procedures that might help avoid unnecessary ethical tangles.

Chapter 1, "Mission, Principles and Ethics," provides the foundation for the remaining chapters. It discusses a museum's mission, the fundamental statement of the institution's purpose, which the museum has an ethical obligation to fulfill. Implicit in the mission are values that can be expressed as principles of conduct, defining how the mission should be carried out. These principles form the basis for what might become a museum's code of ethics.

"Distinguishing Ethical Issues from Operational and Management Problems," chapter 2, focuses upon how a museum's policies and procedures support the mission statement and guide staff members in carrying out their various responsibilities. Documents like an institutional code of ethics, disaster and strategic plans, collections management policy and personnel handbook help provide consistency, maintain professionalism, and obviate ethical problems. A collection management policy, for example, establishes the parameters for acquiring, caring for, exhibiting, and disposing of items in a museum's collection. Without this document, decisions about a museum's holdings might be made arbitrarily, allowing for possible confusion about appropriate procedures to follow and possibly creating future problems.

The ethical responsibility of ensuring that a museum has the necessary policies and resources—human, financial, and operational—rests with the museum's governing body. "The Ethics of Museum Governance and Leadership," chapter 3, underscores the ethical aspects of governance and explores some of the conflicts that can arise both for board members and for museum staff in fulfilling their duties.

The next three chapters—"The Ethics of Acquiring and Managing Collections," "The Ethics of Caring for and Conserving Collections," and "Ethical Dilemmas of Deaccessioning"—deal with some of the fundamental ethical issues raised by museum collections—their acquisition, management, preservation and conservation, and, in some cases, their deaccessioning and disposal.

Chapters 7 and 8 raise some of the most controversial and confusing issues that face museums today—how museums deal with outside forces that seek to influence the content of their exhibitions and programs. "Ethical Problems Related to Fundraising and Other Income-Producing Activities" looks at the ethical challenges that raising money in a highly competitive environment generates for museums. Increasingly reliant upon support from fewer and fewer wealthy individuals and private foundations, museums can find the integrity of their programs and exhibitions challenged by donors. "Controversy and Censorship," chapter 8, treats instances where both political and financial pressures inside and outside the museum challenge its integrity as an unbiased educational institution.

Chapter 9, "Restitution, Repatriation, or Retention? The Ethics of Cultural Heritage," deals with three major issues relating to a museum's ownership of cultural property. By discussing actual instances in which a museum's ownership of an object or objects was challenged, this chapter illustrates the complexity of ethical considerations surrounding archaeological objects and ancient art, art confiscated during World War II, and Native American material addressed in the Native American Graves Protection and Repatriation Act (NAGPRA).

"Museum Visitors: Ethical Issues Concerning Diversity and Access," chapter 10, discusses ethical issues related to welcoming visitors and providing access to a museum's collections while ensuring that they are preserved for future generations.

FRAMEWORK FOR APPROACHING ETHICAL PROBLEMS

Although every problematic situation has its own distinctive features, resolving an ethical dilemma can be divided into two phases:

1. Phase One: Formulating the Problem
   a. Collect all of the facts. Ethical problems include both soft and hard facts. Soft facts are the feelings, attitudes, and beliefs or opinions of the people involved in the problem, whereas hard facts are the established or demonstrable details. Be as objective as possible.
   b. Distinguish between pertinent and irrelevant facts. Eliminate what is irrelevant.
   c. Identify the people and institutions who are involved, both internal and external to the museum, and their respective roles and perspectives. These could include, for example, museum members, community groups, the media, governmental agencies, donors and funders, and experts, depending upon the circumstances. Consider any possible conflicts of interest that they might have.
   d. Based upon the above information, formulate the ethical problem.
   e. Consult the provisions of relevant codes of ethics to see if they apply and consult with other museums or organizations that have faced similar problems to learn from their experience.
2. Phase Two: Establishing Possible Solutions and Actions
   a. Formulate possible options for resolving the problem.
   b. Consult any related laws as well as codes of ethics to make sure that your proposed solutions pass muster.
   c. Consider potential consequences of the decision (both internal and external) for the museum, identifying the best and worst case scenarios. Consider possible responses to the decision and developing a strategy to deal with negative responses.
   d. Obtain feedback from colleagues. Use the feedback to evaluate the decision and make corrections as necessary.

After a decision is made, enumerating appropriate and feasible action steps for its implementation helps ensure that the decision will be carried out in as straightforward a manner as possible. In all instances, stakeholders should be notified first and any negative responses be countered in a timely fashion.

This framework will provide a guide to thinking about ethical problems when real issues arise and can also be useful in considering the hypothetical cases presented in *A Practical Guide to Museum Ethics*. Ethical dilemmas in museums often evade easy solutions. They present issues that are complex, sensitive, and involve a range of people, both within and outside the institution. *A Practical Guide to Museum Ethics*, with its many hypothetical cases, seeks to make ethics approachable and worthy of both formal and informal discussion. In thinking about ethical dilemmas in museums, we have the opportunity to engage some of the more challenging issues facing the profession, to sort through the gray areas, and to be better prepared for real ethical challenges when they arise.

NOTES

1. John Canaday, "Very Quiet and Very Dangerous," *The New York Times*, Sunday, February 27, 1972, p. 175, http://timesmachine.nytimes.com/timesmachine/1972/02/27/91321031.html?pageNumber=175.

2. "Museum Ethics," *The New York Times*, December 29, 1902, p. 6, http://timesmachine.nytimes.com/timesmachine/1902/12/29/101095197.html?pageNumber=6.

Chapter 1

Mission, Principles, and Ethics

> Loyalty to the mission of the museum and to the public it serves is the essence of museum work, whether volunteer or paid. —*Code of Ethics for Museums*, American Alliance of Museums[1]

A museum's mission is one of its foundational statements. It reflects the purpose for which the museum was established, articulating how the museum is to fulfill that purpose—what it does, whom it serves, and what impact it strives to have. The mission statement is used to explain the museum's *raison d'etre* and should reflect the purpose clause in the institution's charter and bylaws in straightforward language. The Metropolitan Museum of Art, for example, notes on its website:

> The Metropolitan Museum of Art was founded on April 13, 1870, "to be located in the City of New York, for the purpose of establishing and maintaining in said city a Museum and library of art, of encouraging and developing the study of the fine arts, and the application of arts to manufacture and practical life, of advancing the general knowledge of kindred subjects, and, to that end, of furnishing popular instruction.[2]
>
> This statement of purpose has guided the Museum for over 140 years.
> On January 13, 2015, the Trustees of The Metropolitan Museum of Art reaffirmed this statement of purpose and supplemented it with the following statement of mission:
>
> *The Metropolitan Museum of Art collects, studies, conserves, and presents significant works of art across all times and cultures in order to connect people to creativity, knowledge, and ideas.[3]*

A museum's statement of purpose(s) is defined in its charter or certificate of incorporation, an official document filed with governmental authorities. Its mission statement is considered an internal document and can be changed or reworded by the governing board in keeping with stated purpose in the institution's charter or certificate of incorporation.[4] As museums have become more conscious of their responsibilities to the public, many have chosen to re-word their missions to communicate more directly the institution's basic purpose, the audiences it intends to serve and the impact it wants to make.[5]

In a 2007 lawsuit, the New York Supreme Court of Erie County made an important distinction between a museum's purpose clause in its charter and its mission statement. The Albright-Knox Art Gallery was sued after its board made a decision to deaccession 200 pieces of art in order to better address its mission of "enhancing the understanding and appreciation of contemporary and modern art."[6] The board and membership of the museum voted to sell Chinese antiquities as well as Indian, African, South American, and ancient Roman art and use the funds realized from the sale to buttress their endowment for new acquisitions. The petitioners argued that, by narrowing the focus of the museum from that stated in the museum's charter, the board had altered the purpose of the museum without amending the museum's articles of incorporation, which state, more broadly, that the museum would maintain "a collection of painting, sculpture and other works of art" and encourage "the advancement of education and cultivation of art." The court decided that only the statement of purpose in a museum's charter, not its mission statement, is enforceable as a matter of law since the board of the museum is "free to change and amend its mission [statement] . . . without amending its certificate of incorporation, so long as they do not pursue endeavors outside the stated purpose of the corporation." Thus, while the purpose clause in the museum's charter, which governs the activities of the museum, is legally enforceable, lack of adherence to its mission statement, which can be revised by its governing body, presents a purely ethical problem.[7] Nonetheless, it remains incumbent upon the museum's governors to ensure that the mission statement remains within the parameters of institution's purpose clause.

A museum's mission should be reflected in all basic policies and procedures for the institution. It is the foundation for its Collection Management Policy and scope of collections statement, as well as its strategic and interpretive plans. If departments within a museum have individual mission statements, they must directly relate how that department contributes to fulfilling the institutional mission.

Separate from but also related to the mission statement are the museum's organizational values that may be expressed in principles of conduct defining how the mission should be implemented or carried out. Establishing the organizational values, developing institutional policies consistent with the values, and creating an environment conducive to operating by the principles of conduct is the role of the museum's leadership—its governing body and director. For example in 2010, the Burke Museum of Natural History and Culture updated its mission statement to read:

> The Burke Museum creates a better understanding of the world and our place in it. The museum is responsible for Washington State collections of natural and cultural heritage and sharing the knowledge that makes them meaningful. The Burke welcomes a broad and diverse audience and provides a community gathering place that nurtures life-long learning and encourages respect, responsibility and reflection.[8]

In concert with this mission, as well as with the original statement of purpose, the Burke also endorsed the following organizational values or principles of conduct:

Integrity: Being open and truthful; adhering to the highest ethical and professional standards
Respect: Respecting each other and the objects and ideas with which we work; welcoming diverse communities and divergent points of view
Excellence: Pursuing excellence in each of our endeavors; acting as leaders in our respective fields
Stewardship: Protecting the collections and information we hold for future generations; conducting business in a sustainable way
Curiosity: Encouraging curiosity in ourselves and our visitors; posing questions and seeking answers about the world and our place in it
Relevance: Exploring critical issues involving nature, cultures, and their interconnections; being a valued resource for the communities we serve[9]

Professional codes of ethics describe standards of behavior and those standards are based, generally, upon principles upheld by the profession. Each museum in its own code of ethics should elaborate upon the professional code, articulating the principles that it holds to be important in carrying out its mission and providing general guidelines about how these principles of conduct should be followed.

The American Alliance of Museums Code of Ethics for Museums is grounded in three general principles relating to governance, collections, and programs:

Governance: Museum governance in its various forms is a public trust responsible for the institution's service to society. The governing authority protects and enhances the museum's collections and programs and its physical, human and financial resources. It ensures that all these resources support the museum's mission, respond to the pluralism of society and respect the diversity of the natural and cultural common wealth.

Collections: The distinctive character of museum ethics derives from the ownership, care and use of objects, specimens, and living collections representing the world's natural and cultural common wealth. This stewardship of collections entails the highest public trust and carries with it the presumption of rightful ownership, permanence, care, documentation, accessibility and responsible disposal.

Programs: Museums serve society by advancing an understanding and appreciation of the natural and cultural common wealth through exhibitions, research, scholarship, publications and educational activities. These programs further the museum's mission and are responsive to the concerns, interests and needs of society.[10]

The AAM Code then elaborates upon each of these principles, delineating general guidelines for professional conduct that relate to them. The Code of Ethics for Museums promulgated by the International Council of Museums is similarly structured; however, it is based upon the following eight principles of conduct:

1. Museums are responsible for the tangible and intangible natural and cultural heritage. Governing bodies and those concerned with the strategic direction and oversight of museums have a primary responsibility to protect and promote this heritage as well as the human, physical and financial resources made available for that purpose.

2. Museums have the duty to acquire, preserve and promote their collections as a contribution to safeguarding the natural, cultural and scientific heritage. Their collections are a significant public inheritance, have a special position in law and are protected by international legislation. Inherent in this public trust is the notion of stewardship that includes rightful ownership, permanence, documentation, accessibility and responsible disposal.

3. Museums have particular responsibilities to all for the care, accessibility and interpretation of primary evidence collected and held in their collections.

4. Museums have an important duty to develop their educational role and attract wider audiences from the community, locality, or group they serve. Interaction with the constituent community and promotion of their heritage is an integral part of the education role of the museum.

5. Museums utilise a wide variety of specialisms, skills and physical resources that have a far broader application than in the museum. This may lead to shared resources or the provision of services as an extension of the museum's activities. These should be organized in such a way that they do not compromise the museum's stated mission.

6. Museum collections reflect the cultural and natural heritage of the communities from which they have been derived. As such, they have a character beyond that of ordinary property, which may include strong affinities with national, regional, local, ethnic, religious or political identity. It is important therefore that museum policy is responsive to this situation.
7. Museums must conform fully to international, regional, national and local legislation and treaty obligations. In addition, the governing body should comply with any legally binding trusts or conditions relating to any aspect of the museum, its collections and operations.
8. Members of the museum profession should observe accepted standards and laws and uphold the dignity and honour of their profession. They should safeguard the public against illegal or unethical professional conduct. Every opportunity should be used to inform and educate the public about the aims, purposes, and aspirations of the profession to develop a better public understanding of the contributions of museums to society.[11]

What these two codes and other related professional codes of ethics demand is a sense of responsibility to the mission of the museum, to colleagues in the workplace and to the public that the museums serves. The guidance that they provide, while necessarily very general and malleable depending upon the specific circumstances, is essential to maintaining the public trust.

NOTES

1. American Alliance of Museums, Code of Ethics for Museums, American Alliance of Museums website, amended 2000, http://www.aam-us.org/resources/ethics-standards-and-best-practices/code-of-ethics.

2. Charter of the Metropolitan Museum of Art, State of New York, Laws of 1870, Chapter 197, passed April 13, 1870 and amended L. 1898, ch. 34; L. 1908, ch. 219.

3. Metropolitan Museum of Art, "Museum Mission Statement," Metropolitan Museum of Art website, amended January 15, 2015, http://www.metmuseum.org/about-the-museum/mission-statement.

4. Marie C. Malaro and Ildiko Pogány DeAngelis, *A Legal Primer on Managing Museum Collections*, 3rd ed. (Washington, DC: Smithsonian Books, 2012), 20.

5. See for example, Gail Anderson, ed., *Museum Mission Statements: Building a Distinct Identity*, 2nd ed. (Washington, DC: American Association of Museums, 1998).

6. Albright-Knox Art Gallery, "About the Albright-Knox," Albright-Knox Art Gallery website, accessed September 27, 2015, http://www.albrightknox.org/about-ak/.

7. Dennis v Buffalo Fine Arts Academy NY Slip Op 50520(U), accessed January 31, 2014, http://law.justia.com/cases/new-york/other-courts/2007/2007-50520.html.

8. Burke Museum, "About Us," The Burke Museum of Natural History and Culture website, updated May 2010, https://www.burkemuseum.org/info/about#mision.

9. Ibid.

10. Ibid.

11. International Council of Museums, "ICOM Code of Ethics for Museums," International Council of Museums website, revised 2004, http://icom.museum/the-vision/code-of-ethics/.

Chapter 2

Distinguishing Ethical Issues from Operational and Management Problems

Operational or management issues can have ethical ramifications when a museum does not have in place a set of policies and procedures to guide day-to-day decision-making. In order for a museum to be a good steward of the resources that it holds for the public's benefit, articulate and carry out its mission, develop programs and exhibitions that further the museum's education purpose, and operate efficiently and effectively, the museum needs to ensure that its governing board, staff, and volunteers have a shared understanding of their roles and responsibilities and the ways that they can work together as well as separately to achieve the institution's short- and long-term goals. Creating policies and procedures is key. While these guidelines cannot pretend to cover all types of situations that arise in a museum, they can establish a tone and provide general guidance that helps in problem solving and decision-making. And the absence of such guidelines can create ethical dilemmas for staff. Consider the following example in which an educator unknowingly collects a tip from a visitor who is pleased with the personal attention she and her guests received on a museum tour.

PERSONAL REMUNERATION

Neighborhood tours are part of the regularly scheduled programming for a local history museum. Education staff from the museum lead the tours and facilitate discussions among the visitors about the history of the neighborhood and make connections between this history and the personal experiences of the people on the tour. To celebrate their birthdays, a group of close friends who grew up in the museum's neighborhood took the tour together. The group was very pleased with the tour guide who personalized the experience for them. The organizer of the group attempted to give the museum guide cash as a tip, but he declined the offer, knowing that accepting the tip would be against the personnel policies of the museum. The organizer did not accept the guide's refusal, however, and, when he was distracted by another conversation, she placed a large amount of cash in the tour guide's back pocket. Later in the afternoon when he discovered the money, the tour guide was faced with a dilemma.

Would he be acting in an unethical manner if he accepted the money and said no more about it? Would his acceptance constitute unethical behavior on the part of the museum? If it would, is it because he would violate the museum's policy by keeping the money or because his conduct would be unethical in and of itself? Should the tour guide seek out the visitor and return the money? Would turning in the money to the museum resolve the ethical problem for the guide? Or would it potentially convert the problem to a managerial one? In fact, the managerial issue would be straightforward if the local history museum's personnel handbook explained that staff are not allowed to accept additional income from activities they carry out as part of their job responsibilities during work hours and that any income garnered from such situations would be considered a donation to the museum. So in this case, observing the policies and procedures of the museum obviates an ethical dilemma. And although management and ethical issues are often closely related, having appropriate management policies and procedures in place helps an institution be accountable and avoids unnecessary ethical challenges.

The following are some of the common documents that specify basic policies and general operational procedures in museums. They provide guidance for museum staff and volunteers as well as the governing body:

- An employee manual or handbook generally deals with issues related to employment at a museum, covering the recruitment, interviewing, hiring, evaluation, and termination processes; detailing how records are kept of attendance, salaries, and benefits; delineating personnel practices such as work hours, overtime, leave policy, grievance and whistle-blowing procedures, reimbursements and discounts, and training; and specifying standards for personal conduct. This handbook also defines an institution's policies related to confidentiality, conflict of interest regarding outside employment as well as personal collecting, computer and information safety, and social media and Internet use.
- A separate volunteer manual covers comparable policies for volunteers working with the museum.

As in the example of personal remuneration at the local history museum, these documents provide guidance in situations that, by themselves without appropriate policies, could create ethical problems.

The Code of Ethics for Museums of the American Alliance of Museums states that it is the role of the governing authority of a museum to ensure that professional standards and practices inform and guide museum operations, policies are articulated, and prudent oversight is practiced.[1] In addition AAM specifies that museums should have five documents that are "fundamental for basic professional museum operations and embody core museum values and practices. They codify and guide decisions and actions that promote institutional stability and viability, which in turn allows the museum to fulfill its educational role, preserve treasures for future generations and be an enduring part of its community."[2] The five are:

- Mission Statement
- Institutional Code of Ethics that "is tailored to, and developed specifically for, the museum" and "puts forth the institution's basic ethical, public trust responsibilities as a museum and nonprofit educational entity and is not solely about individual conduct (e.g., conflict of interest issues)."[3]
- Strategic Institutional Plan
- Disaster Preparedness/Emergency Response Plan
- Collections Management Policy[4] detailing all policies and procedures relevant to the acquisition, care, management, preservation, and disposal of museum collections.[5]

AAM also references a number of other ethics codes that relate to either specific kinds of museums (e.g., art, history, and natural history museums as well as zoos and aquaria) or areas of work within museums (e.g., curators, registrars, conservators, exhibition designers and developers, librarians and archivists, information technology specialists, fund raisers, and museum stores). When a museum develops its code of ethics, AAM suggests that these other codes be taken into account to avoid conflicts between the professional expectations of different staff members.[6]

In addition, AAM recommends the development of policies and procedures related to the development of business and individual donor support for museums that rely upon fundraising and earned income for their financial stability. These provide guidance concerning communicating and developing relationships with donors, acceptable types of support (e.g., will a museum accept gifts from all donors or are there some whose reputation, mission, values, or programs are inconsistent or may appear inconsistent with those of the museum), and ways of recognizing donors as well as policies concerning the confidentiality of information related to the museum's fund-raising activities.[7]

The American Association for State and Local History Statement of Professional Standards and Ethics also places the ultimate responsibility for complying with legal and ethical rules and standards on a historical organization's governing authority, which it states must establish and regularly review policies that reflect current legal, ethical, and professional practices. AASLH also acknowledges that the staff, whether paid or volunteer, must ensure that these policies are operational and that all people associated with the organization are aware of them.[8]

"Professional Practices in Art Museums" issued by the Association of Art Museum Directors adds other policies to the mandatory list, "In addition to policies regarding conflicts of interest and ethical conduct, the following . . . should be addressed: collections management; human resources; finance, audit, and investment management; and fundraising."[9]

Finally one section of the International Council of Museums' Code of Ethics is based upon the principle that "members of the museum profession should observe accepted standards and laws and uphold the dignity and honour of their profession. They should safeguard the public against illegal or unethical professional conduct. Every opportunity should be used to inform and educate the public about the aims, purposes, and aspirations of the profession to develop a better public understanding of the contributions of museums to society."[10]

Ensuring that a museum provides guidance to its staff through its established policies also allows for transparency, a clarity that inspires confidence in an organization on the part of the staff as well as on the part of the public. This transparency is critical in maintaining the public trust and fulfilling the mission of a museum. Yet even when all of the necessary policies and procedures are in place, ambiguities arise. Consulting the existing policies, discussing the issues in question with other museum staff, talking with peers in other museums and seeking guidance from local, state, regional, or national professional organizations can help formulate the various options and understand the consequences of each. The following hypothetical situations—involving the handling of money, safeguarding collections and using museum property, interacting with visitors, working with consultants, generating earned income, and concern over a museum's reputation—all revolve around the overlap between management concerns and ethical issues.

ETHICS IN ACTION

In the following scenarios, all of the names of people and institutions (except the Metropolitan Museum of Art) are fictional. All hypothetical situations are composites of real situations and actual issues faced by museums, but any resemblance to a single museum is purely coincidental.

Lecture Fees

An art museum's manager of public programs is responsible for scheduling public lectures and gallery talks for each of the museum's temporary exhibitions. Last year long after agreeing to lead several discussions, the curator of contemporary art had an unanticipated scheduling conflict and asked the manager of public programs to find a substitute for one of her lectures. The manager found a replacement—someone who had spoken at the museum previously and was happy to step in at the last minute. But because this request came long after the original schedule was drawn up, many commitments with outside speakers were already in place and the public programs manager discovered that the funds allocated for guest speakers were depleted. He approached the curator of contemporary art and explained his dilemma. Unfazed by this situation, the curator said that she would pay for a substitute speaker personally. On the day of the program, the curator wrote a personal check made out to the guest lecturer and handed it to the manager of public programs, asking him to use it to pay the substitute.

Does this situation present an ethical problem for the manager of public programs or is it simply a managerial problem? Would it be unethical for the manager to give the speaker the curator's personal check? If the manager asked the curator to take back the check and make it out to the museum, specifying that it be used to pay the guest speaker, would that resolve the problem? If so, might you conclude that the problem is purely procedural?

Use of Museum Property

A university film archive's technology department is responsible for providing equipment and qualified technicians to operate the audiovisual components of both public and private events held at the archive as well as throughout the university. As a result, they maintain a substantial amount of equipment including microphones, monitors, speakers, mixers, laptops, various kinds of projectors, MP3, and CD/DVD players. A few individuals in the department have started their own business, using the archive's equipment. They take the equipment to venues outside the university and provide audiovisual services for their clients in the evenings and on weekends. Their business is growing and they stand to make a substantial income from this sideline. The archives director discovers this "operation" during a routine inventory of the equipment.

Does this scenario present an ethical or managerial issue? Would your answer be any different if the individuals were to work at their private business during working hours? Would it be unethical for the museum to permit the workers to use the museum's equipment for personal purposes on their own time? Would the ethical issue be resolved if the museum charged the individuals for the private use of the museum's equipment?

Access to Collections

A historic house museum in a large metropolitan center interprets the history of the region through the stories of the family that owned and lived in the house from the middle of the nineteenth century until the late twentieth century. The museum maintains a small research library in the house that is accessible to the public by appointment. The library contains a miscellany of documents relating to the family, including newspaper articles, correspondence, and mementos.

One day, the museum's educator discovers that the curator has a cache of files relating to the family's history in his office, inaccessible to researchers. The files include information relating to unsavory episodes in the family's past, including an alleged murder-suicide pact between two brothers. While much of the information can be found through other means—for example, newspaper articles about the incident—the files are part of the museum's collection. The educator challenges the curator, saying that these are part of the collections that should be available to the public, but the curator defends himself, replying that the files are not central to the story that the museum tells. The curator feels that they should be kept aside from the rest of the library documents to protect the reputation of the family. The educator is astounded and feels that the materials in the curator's office should be kept with the rest of the research resources related to the family who lived in the house. The educator consults the collection management policy and discovers that it does not cover access to archival materials; yet the museum's website and mission imply that access to all of its collections is available. The educator brings the situation to the attention of her supervisor.

Would it be unethical for the museum's management to deny access to these documents in order to protect the presumed interest of the museum's founding family? Or does this situation present a purely managerial or operational issue?

Public Access

A young man of fourteen needs to use the library of his city's art museum for a school project. One Saturday his mother takes him there and because she could not make other arrangements, she also brings along her ten-year-old daughter who has autism. Saturdays are busy days at the library and the reading room is filled. The young boy readily busies himself with his assignment and the librarian generously offers help. The mother and daughter sit at a table also occupied by two other patrons. While the boy continues to work on his assignment, his sister's behavior becomes obstreperous and begins to disturb the other patrons, who alert the librarian. When the librarian approaches the woman to see if he could offer assistance, the mother refuses the offer of help, says that she has every right to stay in the museum's library with her daughter, and threatens to charge the library with violating the Americans with Disabilities Act if the librarian does anything further, thus abruptly closing the possibility of a conversation. Because it is Saturday and he has no access to a supervisor, the librarian decides to take no further action. Does the librarian's conduct raise an ethical issue or an operational problem? Or both? Would it be unethical for the librarian to ask the mother to leave with her daughter? And if so, when? What might be done to assist staff like the librarian in handling potentially difficult situations with visitors?

Work-for-Hire

A museum professional working as an independent consultant responded to a call for qualifications to work with a history museum on revamping their educational programs. The museum wanted to adapt their programs so that they would clearly address the new social science standards issued by the state. After a conversation with the history museum's education director, the consultant sent in a proposal that outlined the process she would use for the project, accompanied by a list of related projects that she had completed, information about her company, and her resume. The fee for developing the education programs would be set by the amount of support received by the museum from a local foundation, so no budget or bid was necessary. The education director found the consultant's work highly professional and was impressed with the plans she submitted. He subsequently used all of the information the consultant provided, including her resume, in the museum's application for a grant to support the project. While the consultant was not paid for the work that was submitted as part of the grant proposal, she was led to believe that, if the proposal were funded, the museum would contract with her to carry out the project.

A few months later, the consultant learned that the museum received a grant for the project. She conferred with the education director to discuss how they should proceed, the terms of the contract for her assignment, and a project timeline. Two weeks later, the education director called her to tell her that at about the same time as their last conversation, the head of the foundation supporting the project, one of the museum's board members who is close friends with the foundation head, and the museum's CEO met to discuss the project. As a result of this meeting, the museum board member, who had encouraged the foundation to support the project, decided he wanted to be involved in the selection of the consultant. The board member and the museum director asked the education director to write a job description for the project consultant. They told him that they planned to circulate this description widely to solicit interest in the project and collect resumes from which they could select the consultant to head up the project. The education director apologized to the consultant but explained that he must comply with the wishes of the museum director and board members, and he encouraged the consultant to apply for the position.

How would you describe the conduct of the museum in regard to the consultant? How could the exercise of appropriate managerial judgment forestall ethical problems in this situation?

Special Events

Karen Goldberg and Steven Frank met on a blind date at the museum and discovered their mutual love of art history and archaeology. Now they are planning their wedding and want to hold the reception at the museum where they first met. They make an appointment with Heather Simms, the museum's seasoned special events manager. Heather assures them that she has overseen a number of large fundraising galas and special events at the museum, including numerous wedding receptions. With her experience in hospitality and event coordination, she is well prepared to work with the couple to plan a very special evening for them and their guests.

"No red wine or red beverage of any kind will be permitted and we have a list of approved caterers to work with that are familiar with our specifications and the space," Heather advises Karen and Steven as they tour the museum's spaces. "We will hold the formal dinner and dancing on the sculpture court and your cocktail hour can take place in the lobby of the medieval galleries on the third floor." Karen and Steven are very pleased with the rental agreement, prices, and variety of options the museum offers. The caterer can even provide kosher meals for some of the guests. When they walk through the lobby of the medieval galleries, however, their eyes fall upon a large sculpted crucifix that hangs prominently at its center. Before committing to the rental agreement, Karen and Steven ask that the crucifix be temporarily removed or covered for their reception. They explain that their friends and family come from a variety of faiths and backgrounds and they don't want the art to make anyone uncomfortable. If the art cannot be moved or covered, Karen and Steven will have to explore other venues for their reception.

Heather is an old hand at managing special events and is familiar with the ins and outs of coordinating celebrations with the unusual restrictions of a museum, especially those with limited spaces in which to hold rental events. Karen and Steven are just one of many couples who have asked for the crucifix to be removed or covered. In fact, a significant number of potential customers decide to take their business to other locations in order to avoid the sculpted crucifix that would, for better or worse, be the centerpiece of any event held in the museum. Heather decides that it is time to approach the medieval art curator and discuss the possibility of moving the piece or asking for a screen to be made to hide the work of art during events.

Joann McCormick has been the curator of medieval art at the museum for twenty-one years. She is dedicated to the museum's collection and to creating scholarly exhibitions and programs. Under her care, the medieval collection was reinstalled to create one of the most popular galleries within the museum. Among the staff she is known to be one of the hardest working and most opinionated curators associated with the collection. When she receives Heather's message about covering the sculpted crucifix, she is both insulted and appalled. Without a second thought, Joann fires off the following e-mail to Heather copying all of the division directors and the director of the museum.

I must stridently object to your abhorrent suggestion of moving or covering the sculpted crucifix for rentals and events held at the museum. This is beneath the dignity of the museum and certainly shows a lack of understanding of our curatorial standards. I have committed years of tireless service to this collection and particularly the accuracy of its installation and interpretation. Furthermore, in the spirit of upholding the public trust and utilizing the collection to serve the many visitors we attract, it is not in the mission of any museum to change its exhibitions on demand, at the whim of the public or to accommodate a special event. I vehemently renounce any attempt to move or cover the sculpted crucifix and suggest you alert the couple that they may certainly take their business elsewhere.

Sincerely,
Joann McCormick

Heather stares at her computer in shock. While she understands the curator's commitment to the integrity of the gallery installation, the museum is losing precious rental income each year due to the fact that the crucifix is inconveniently located. The income generated from rentals and special events helps offset the skyrocketing cost of exhibitions, programming, and operations. Heather is offended that anyone on staff would assume that because her work within the museum is not scholarly it is any less valuable to the institution. She replies to Joanne's message with a reminder that the scholarly exhibitions and the publications that the curatorial division holds and produces, along with a multitude of free public programs, are all funded from the income generated by renting the space for events. She adds that the museum is in the business of serving the public, and in a service industry, "the customer is always right."

The museum's director Dr. Farfield Vulcom carefully examines the stinging e-mail exchange between Heather and Joann. He is torn. He understands the importance of providing superb customer service and knows that rental income will be the key to balancing the budget this year. At the same time, he remembers his commitment to the mission of the museum to bring art and people together for learning, discovery, and enjoyment.

Consider the ethical problems that could arise if the religious symbol is removed, covered, or otherwise hidden from view, or, conversely, if the museum refuses to take any action and the couple is told to select another venue. Would it have mattered if the object in question had no religious significance? Does the fact that the proposed use of the museum's facilities is extraneous to its primary activities have any impact upon the ethical nature of the problem? What role does the importance of raising money play here? Would the action of covering or removing the cross set a precedent? Then, would it be unethical to refuse to do the same thing in a similar future situation? Would the answer to these questions be different if the museum were asked to use the same gallery for a wedding ceremony?

Does Joann's response to Heather's request raise an ethical question? Would your answer be different if Joann also copied the governing board on her e-mail? What would your response be if Joann's assistant were to have put a copy of Joann's letter on social media or tweeted about the conflict?

How Much is Too Much?

A regional art and history museum whose mission is "to make art and history come alive for everyone" produces two major special events each year—one, a museum gala and the other, an art and antiques silent auction. These fund-raising and social events, primarily for wealthy donors and patrons, take place about three weeks apart and use all of the museum's galleries. The events require so much space that almost 75 percent of the museum's spaces—seven out of ten permanent collection galleries and its special exhibitions space—are temporarily deinstalled to make room for the event. Consequently for almost six weeks each year, the museum is reduced to displaying its collections in three permanent exhibition galleries and one family gallery. During this time, the museum remains open to the public, providing school tours and programs for students and families.

Does this situation raise an ethical issue or a managerial issue, or both? Would your answer be different if 25 percent of the museum's spaces had to be closed? Or if closing the space would be necessary for only two days?

Museum Store Sales

When the Braynard Museum of East African Traditional Art was established, the gift shop sold the traditional arts and crafts of East African cultures along with some items of dress and jewelry that were evocative of the traditional cultures. The shop focused upon genuine products and many of the objects were purchased directly from the artisans who made them so that these individuals benefited directly from museum shop sales.

Recently, however, the museum shop went through a remodeling and rebranding process. Gone are the more traditional items, replaced by more expensive objects. Many of these are "decorator" items and are not from Africa but are "African like." Lower priced items, probably targeted to the school children that come to the museum, sport "Made in China" tags. Their price stickers retain the original prices, which are several hundred times lower than the current price. The majority of the items in the shop represent the cultures that colonized the East Africa countries rather than the traditional cultures. Gin and tonic glasses with tropical themes, for example, sit on the shelves alongside croquet sets.

Is there an ethical issue here? According to the Museum Stores Association, museum stores engage in "cultural commerce" and see themselves as an important asset that can enhance the visitor's experience to a museum.[11] Generally, these stores offer for sale items that advance the museum's educational purpose.[12] Does this example violate that practice? Is a museum's store ethically obligated to demonstrate the same degree of cultural sensitivity that the museum's programs might promote?

In a related example, the Metropolitan Museum of Art recently mounted a retrospective exhibition of the work of Joel A. Rosenthal or JAR, a contemporary jewelry artist. According to the museum, the exhibition is their "first devoted to a contemporary artist of gems" and "features a selection of JAR's finest pieces."[13] For the occasion, JAR designed a number of special items to be sold both at a trunk sale and in the museum shop. Does this present an ethical problem? Would your answer be different if the proceeds from all of the items were to be given exclusively to the museum? Would it be appropriate for works from the exhibition to be offered for sale?

Serving the Public

A maritime museum prides itself in its overnight programs for scout groups, providing an opportunity for young boys and girls to gain a sense of the life on sailing schooners in the age of sail. One Monday after one of these sleepovers, the leader of one of the Girl Scout troops that has attended the program calls the local Department of Health and reports that her girls has become ill with severe vomiting and diarrhea several hours after leaving the museum. She also calls the museum to report the same. On Tuesday, another troop leader calls the museum to report that her girls have also become ill. This troop leader demands her money back. The educator who is fielding all of these calls goes to the department director who declines to refund the money. The mother is incensed and threatens that she will go to the press if she doesn't get a refund.

Is the museum ethically obligated to give a refund in this situation? If so, what is the ethical problem? If the museum decides to refund the troop's admission fees, is it admitting responsibility for the health of its visitors? Does the museum have that responsibility in any event? Would a policy or procedure about reimbursement resolve the problem?

Reputation

The Alvarez Museum of Fine Art in New Mexico is one of the state's oldest and most preeminent art institutions with deep and diverse collections. Many of the local gallery owners are supporters of the museum and frequently participate in its events. One of these, Suzi Smith, an aspiring curator, has recently contributed a sizeable portion of the funds needed to complete the creation of a Center for Innovation and Curation, a project that has long been the dream of the museum's director. The staff recently discovered that Ms. Smith, in an attempt to represent some of the better artists in the state, has been saying that she is a consulting curator at the Alvarez. If Ms. Smith is able to attract better artists, her gallery is likely to make greater profits on the sale of their artwork. Alvarez staff alert the museum director to this problem.

Does this situation present an ethical issue for the museum? Does the conduct of the gallery owner redound upon the museum? Would this be true even if the museum denies any affiliation with Suzi Smith?

FINAL THOUGHTS

Museums are public institutions with extraordinary public responsibilities. Maintaining clear and up-to-date policies and procedures helps a museum provide guidance to its staff, volunteers, and governing body and enhances its professionalism, helping create transparency in its operations and fostering public trust. These documents by no means provide the solutions to all problems that arise, but they do give consistent direction for action by all staff in situations that might otherwise generate ethical problems. They are the ground rules for carrying out one's responsibilities. For example, a mission statement that places an emphasis upon the visitor and the public benefit of the museum creates a different set of priorities for the governing body and staff than one that stresses collections care. Both are legitimate. What is important is that a museum clearly articulates these expectations through its policies and procedures. In so doing, a museum gives appropriate direction to its staff and, further, helps cultivate an understanding of the purposes as well as the aspirations of museums among the public.

NOTES

1. American Alliance of Museums, Code of Ethics for Museums, American Alliance of Museums website, amended 2000, http://www.aam-us.org/resources/ethics-standards-and-best-practices/code-of-ethics.

2. American Alliance of Museums, "Core Documents," American Alliance of Museums website, accessed September 27, 2015, http://www.aam-us.org/resources/assessment-programs/core-documents/documents.

3. Ibid.

4. AAM notes that "museums that do not own or manage collections, but borrow and use objects for exhibits, education or research" should have "custodial care and borrowing policies"; and that museums with living populations should have policies governing the plants or animals in their care. Ibid.

5. Ibid.

6. American Alliance of Museums, "What are Ethics? Relevant Ethics," American Alliance of Museums website, accessed March 6, 2014, http://www.aam-us.org/resources/ethics-standards-and-best-practices/ethics.

7. American Alliance of Museums, "Financial Stability," American Alliance of Museums website, accessed February 21, 2014, http://www.aam-us.org/resources/ethics-standards-and-best-practices/financial-stability. Alison Lonshein and Marsha S. Shaines, "Charitable Contributions 101," The American Law Institute Continuing Legal Education, Legal Issues in Museum Administration, March 19–21, 2014.

8. American Association for State and Local History, "Publication: AALH Statement of Professional Standards and Ethics," American Association for State and Local History website, updated June 2012, http://resource.aaslh.org/view/aaslh-statement-of-professional-standards-and-ethics/.

9. Association of Art Museum Directors, "Professional Practices in Art Museums," Association of Art Museum Directors website, 2011, https://aamd.org/sites/default/files/document/2011ProfessionalPracitiesinArtMuseums.pdf.

10. International Council of Museums, "ICOM Code of Ethics for Museums," International Council of Museums website, revised 2004, http://icom.museum/the-vision/code-of-ethics/.

11. Museum Store Association, "Museum Store Association Code of Ethics," Museum Store Association website, revised 2014, https://museumstoreassociation.org/code-of-ethics/.

12. Internal Revenue Service, Publication 598 (03/2012), Tax on Unrelated Business Income of Exempt Organizations, Internal Revenue Service website, accessed March 6, 2014, http://www.irs.gov/publications/p598/ch03.html.

13. Metropolitan Museum of Art, "Jewels by JAR, November 20, 2013–March 9, 2014," Metropolitan Museum of Art website, accessed March 6, 2014, http://www.metmuseum.org/exhibitions/listings/2013/jewels-by-jar.

Chapter 3

The Ethics of Museum Governance and Leadership

The ultimate responsibility for a museum's well-being rests with its governing body. Thus, it is no surprise that all professional codes of ethics for museums focus first upon the principles of conduct to which governing boards are accountable and address their obligation to safeguard each museum's assets and resources along with its reputation. The American Alliance of Museums' "Code of Ethics for Museums" states:

> Museum governance in its various forms is a public trust responsible for the institution's service to society. The governing authority protects and enhances the museum's collections and programs and its physical, human and financial resources. It ensures that all these resources support the museum's mission, respond to the pluralism of society and respect the diversity of the natural and cultural common wealth.
>
> Thus, the governing authority ensures that:
>
> - all those who work for or on behalf of a museum understand and support its mission and public trust responsibilities
> - its members understand and fulfill their trusteeship and act corporately, not as [independent] individuals
> - the museum's collections and programs and its physical, human and financial resources are protected, maintained and developed in support of the museum's mission
> - it is responsive to and represents the interests of society
> - it maintains the relationship with staff in which shared roles are recognized and separate responsibilities respected
> - working relationships among trustees, employees and volunteers are based on equity and mutual respect
> - professional standards and practices inform and guide museum operations
> - policies are articulated and prudent oversight is practiced
> - governance promotes the public good rather than individual financial gain.[1]

The International Council of Museums, Association of Art Museum Directors, and American Association of State and Local History similarly reinforce
these principles of conduct.[2]

In *Museum Governance: Mission, Ethics, Policy*, Marie C. Malaro defines
the primary duties that the law demands of members of a nonprofit governing
authority—those of care, loyalty, and obedience.[3] The duty of care requires
diligence. Like governors of other nonprofits, museum board members can be
held liable for gross negligence and fraud. But as Malaro and DeAngelis in
A Legal Primer on Managing Museum Collections point out, "The purpose of
the nonprofit is not to make money but to provide a quality product or service
(as described in its charter) to a particular segment of the public."[4] Identifying
the creation, care, and exhibition of collections as one of a museum's core
functions, Malaro and DeAngelis continue, "If there is a tendency on the
part of courts—and the public—to expect a nonprofit board to pay particular
attention to the organization's core functions, then a museum board should
give attention to the establishment and monitoring of a prudent collection
management policy for the museum."[5] One must also go further and note that
museums hold their collections for the benefit of the public; thus, governing
bodies should ensure that the institution is also fulfilling its educational role
through the creation and implementation of regular public exhibitions and
programs.

The duty of loyalty requires that board members put the museum's interests before any personal benefit. A conflict of interest policy and procedures
for regularly monitoring its implementation are essential to ensuring that
each board member has no real or apparent or implicit conflicts with the
museum. As John Henry Merryman points out, however, as straightforward
as the principle of conflict of interest may be, museums are often reluctant to
deal with it directly, preferring to take a "soft" rather than "hard" approach
to such conflict. For example, if an art museum governing board includes a
dealer who trades in the art collected by the museum, Merryman goes so far
as to question whether the disclosure of that alone absolves the museum or
the board member of an ethical problem. Unlike a banker, architect, or construction firm CEO, all of whom might recuse themselves in situations where
a potential conflict exists, Merryman points out that a dealer's work goes to
the essence of many decisions made in an art museum. He notes that in the
case of the dealer "disclosure does not make the conflict go away; it remains,
still working its harm on the conflicted trustee."[6]

In addition to conflict of interest, the duty of loyalty also precludes self-
dealing and the misuse of inside information. In the first case, trustees are
prohibited from either buying objects from the museum's collection or selling
objects or works to the museum. And in the second case, trustees are barred
from using any information gleaned from their service to a museum in manner that gives them a personal benefit.

Finally, the duty of obedience requires that a museum's governing body further the mission of the institution by judiciously setting goals and objectives for the museum and balancing the available resources with future plans. As Malaro and DeAngelis note, "although a museum board has discretion in deciding how its mission is to be accomplished, careful adherence to the duty of obedience means electing goals carefully. The question should not be merely, 'Is this goal relevant to our mission?' The harder question needs to be asked: 'Is this a wise goal in light of our anticipated resources?' "[7] This aspect of a governing board's role is essential to ensuring the museum's ability to operate well into the future. Museums are unique among nonprofits because their collections connect them to the past, oblige them to use their holdings as educational tools for a range of diverse audiences in the present, and commit them to safeguarding their collections for the use of future generations. The duty of obedience requires a governing body to consider the judicious use of its limited resources not only to create educational activities in the present and the near future but also to guarantee the institution's future well-being so that the museum can fulfill its role of conveying our collective cultural heritage from one generation to the next.

As defined in a museum's code of ethics, higher standards of care, duty, and obedience than those required by law are expected in order for museums to maintain the practices that are considered essential to the integrity of the profession. Day to day, the leadership of a museum is the joint responsibility of its governing board and its director/chief executive officer. Together they set the policies and procedures that allow the institution to operate effectively, develop the plans to give it a strategic direction, and ensure that it has the resources necessary to fulfill its mission.

Also key to a museum's effectiveness is the clear delineation of responsibilities between the governing body and the staff. Even in museums that have a small professional staff and where board members actively participate in the planning and implementation of museum activities, a clear understanding of the different roles and responsibilities is necessary. Equally important is a mutual respect for these complementary roles. It is incumbent upon the board to cultivate a respect for the staff's professionalism as well as upon the staff to appreciate the board's leadership and key connections with the larger community of which the museum is a part. Problems arise when either board or staff members do not understand and appreciate these distinctions. While this lack of understanding is not in and of itself an ethical problem, it can lead to dilemmas that become ethical or that raise ethical questions. Some of the following cases which focus upon areas of governance that have ethical dimensions—dealing with board member qualifications, conflict of interest, self-dealing, the appropriate use of museum resources—also raise issues related to distinctions between board and staff roles.

ETHICS IN ACTION

All of the names of people and institutions in the following cases are fictional. The hypothetical situations are composites of real and imaginary circumstances and reflect actual issues faced by museums. Any resemblance to a real museum is purely coincidental.

Recruiting New Board Members

Even determining who should be selected to serve on a governing board has ethical aspects. Consider the following. American Art Museum X is finishing a major capital campaign. Located in a large Midwestern city, the museum has just begun construction on a new wing that was designed by an internationally known architect; admission is projected to triple once the new wing opens, and the museum is the talk of the town. The museum director and the chairman of the museum's board of governors are taking advantage of the enthusiasm that has built up around this project to expand the board. They are pleased to find that there is no dearth of interest in being considered as a possible candidate. Most of the enthusiasts are known for their philanthropy as well as for their passion for the arts.

- Candidate A is the wife of a businessman who has just been promoted to CEO in the city's most prominent corporation and who serves as the chair of local Science Museum Board. She is active in the city's cultural and social life and knows most of the people with influence. While she is not a professional artist, she paints and likes to spend her summers in the American Southwest creating desert landscapes.
- Candidate B is the owner of the town's largest commercial art gallery and a noted collector in his own right. He is well known for his expertise in avant-garde art and his engaging lectures on the subject.
- Candidate C is the head of the town's largest construction management firm that happens to be overseeing the construction of the museum's new wing. The firm's excellent service and ability to stay on schedule in spite of inclement weather and various production delays have impressed the Board of the Museum.
- Candidate D is a public-spirited citizen who serves on several other nonprofit boards in the city, including the hospital and the library, and is known for her generosity. She is a prominent businesswoman but knows little about the art collected by the museum. Nonetheless she is a passionate collector of African art.
- Candidate E is one of the town's most prominent physicians and is singularly dedicated to his work. His practice is well established and he is widely respected in the community.

- Candidate F is an investment banker with a large firm that serves many of the area's most well-to-do citizens. Her son is an associate curator at the museum.
- Candidate F is a young hedge fund manager who has built a sizeable fortune and is interested in getting "involved in the arts." He sees the opportunity to serve on the board as a way of meeting a wide variety of civic-minded individuals and expanding his circle of acquaintances.
- Candidate G is the director of city's history museum and is actively raising funds for the expansion of her institution. She collects American art.

What are the necessary qualifications of a board member? What ethical considerations pertain? Do any of the candidates present potential ethical problems for the museum?

The Best Laid Plans

One day the director of a Western regional history museum found a large package from her new board chair in the mail. The board chair is the head of a family-owned corporation that makes packing boxes. The family firm is over one hundred years old and has created a successful business by seizing new opportunities as they have arisen over the years. What was first established as a coffin-making factory then made hatboxes and other wooden packing crates when the demand arose and began to make cardboard boxes when corrugated materials became available. It now makes containers for everything from cupcakes to shoes and uses cutting-edge computer technology. The company prides itself in its history and the flexibility that allowed it to stay healthy. For its one-hundredth anniversary, the company produced *From Coffins to Cupcakes*, a large coffee table photo book about its history, which it distributed to its best customers free of charge. A copy of that book is included in the director's package with a letter. In the letter, the board chair conveys his pleasure at taking on the reins of the organization and tells the director about one of the initiatives that he believes will be important for the museum—a publishing venture that would reprint his family history book under the imprint of the museum. Enclosed with the letter is a check for $10,000 to support this venture. The director is speechless. Several years ago, the museum discontinued its publishing efforts in a cost-saving move, so it no longer has staff that can produce publications; moreover, $10,000 would not begin to cover the costs involved in managing this project. In addition, the new strategic plan, passed by the board with the full participation of the new board chair just last year, includes no publication projects. As a result, no funds have been allocated for publications in the current annual budget.

Would it be unethical for the museum to reprint the board chair's book? Would your answer be different if the board chair were interested in re-printing a history of the region that the historical society originally published thirty years ago? What procedures might the museum have in place to deal with issues similar to the ones set forth in this example?

Board Privilege

VIP visitors (usually major donors and trustees) to the Museum of Ethnography may request private access to the Encounter Room where they can engage in hands-on activities related to other cultures. The Encounter Room is used primarily for school groups, but because its current exhibition is so engaging, a number of organizations that provide after-school programs for teens also use the room. Encounter Room staff facilitate all activities in the room and manage the groups who visit.

The wife of an Ethnography Museum trustee is an active member of the museum's community. Among other things, she has been a very effective advocate for the Encounter Room and has helped her husband raise significant financial support for it. She frequently arranges for special groups to use the room. However her enthusiasm has resulted in increased requests for special favors and workshops for her friends. In many instances, honoring her requests diverts resources away from Encounter Room programs that were designed to be free and accessible to all visitors.

Does this situation raise an ethical issue for the Ethnography Museum? Would your answer be different if the wife of the trustee suggested that another organization with which she was involved hold a benefit at the museum in the Encounter Room? What if she also offered to waive the rental fee usually charged for private events held in the room, thus depriving the Ethnography Museum of any income they might realize for this event?

New Collections, New Audiences

A small New England decorative arts center with an annual budget of around $1 million is successfully sustaining its operations due to regular support from its donors as well as grants from the state and local governments and some local foundations. They have a small but stable audience of around 15,000 visitors annually and charge no admission. Most of the people who come to the museum are from the museum's local communities; however, the museum also attracts some tourists who visit the area seasonally.

A decorative arts dealer gets in touch with the executive director to let her know of a large collection of New England quilts he is offering for sale. The director is enthusiastic, for she sees the collection as a potentially great attraction. She believes it would help bring more visibility to the museum and, as a result, both a larger audience and additional funding. The collection is selling for $1 million. The board decides that spending $1 million on this collection would be a wise investment for the center's future. In order to display the collection, they purchase a nearby former bank building and make renovations that allow them to display the quilts in an attractive and appropriate setting. While the debit incurred to purchase the quilts was paid off in a year, thanks to many individual donations, the center has to carry debt accruing from the purchase of the building and its renovation. The business plan, which the board approved when it decided to move forward with the purchase of the quilts and the building, called for paying off the debt through charging an admission fee to the substantially larger number of people expected to visit the museum once the quilts were in place. Projections placed future visitation at 75,000 annually, but these figures were based upon those of a museum in a casino at the center of a tourism hub in another part of the state rather than upon attendance at comparable institutions in the museum's immediate area.

The projected increase in attendance does not materialize. Just over 20,000 people visit the museum but not all pay admission for the quilt center. Carrying the debt for the expansion begins to have a negative impact on the museum's finances. The museum decides to open an ice cream store on the first floor of the former bank building to help attract more people to the museum and realize the goals of the business plan. Again, these efforts are for naught. There is a downturn in the economy, tourism wanes, and the grant funds regularly received from the state and local governments are cut off. Fewer than ten years later, the decorative arts center is forced to close.

Was the governing board judiciously using the resources of the museum when they made the initial decision to purchase the collection and expand? If you think that their decision was based upon poor judgment, was it also unethical?

Conservation Services

Dick Jones is appointed chairman of a mid-sized history museum. He is the retired CEO of the town's most prestigious corporation, an avid history lover, and a collector of all things related to local history. Several weeks after his appointment, Mr. Jones makes an unannounced visit to the museum and stops by the conservator's studio "just for a chat." After exchanging a few pleasantries, he asks the conservator about the projects she is working on as well as about the museum's plans for upcoming exhibitions and programs. He then asks if the conservator could stop by his office sometime to look at his collection and help him evaluate its conservation needs. Mr. Jones has a few history paintings that he believes could use some conservation attention.

Would it be unethical for the conservator to evaluate the conservation needs of Mr. Jones's collection? Would it be unethical for her to provide conservation treatment for the works in question? Would your answer be different if Mr. Jones offered to pay the museum for the use of the conservator's services? Would it be unethical for the conservator to offer her services to Mr. Jones whether for a fee or not?

Collecting

Dick Jones also has a collection of local ephemera, including postcards and baseball cards. He enjoys keeping an eye out on things available on e-Bay and often finds things to add to his collection. To coincide with the opening of a new sports arena, the history museum is planning an exhibition on city's first baseball teams. While the museum's collections contain many objects that can be used to illuminate the years when the teams first played in the city, they contain little specifically about baseball. As a result, the curator is engaging in a collecting project to strengthen the collections in this respect. As she conducts oral history interviews with some of the players, she is also requesting the loan of objects they might have, which would help in telling the exhibition's story. And she is keeping her eye on e-Bay for baseball cards and other baseball ephemera that would enhance the exhibition. One day she sees for sale a rare baseball card depicting a local player who went on to become a star in the major leagues and a baseball legend. She ends up engaging in a bidding war with another person online and ultimately is unable to secure the baseball card for the museum. A few weeks later the director of the museum attends a cocktail party at Dick Jones's house and discovers that Dick Jones had purchased the baseball card in question.

Would it be unethical for Dick Jones to keep the baseball card that he had bought? What could the museum do to remedy the ethical problem?

Collecting Silver

Suzi Peters, another history museum trustee collects silver. She knows that the museum has a fine collection of silver made by Shine-ola, a world-renowned local jewelry company, but she also knows that the museum lacks the resources to add to their collection. At a large antiques market in the county one weekend, Suzi comes across a complete early twentieth-century tea service of Shine-ola silver for sale. It is in perfect condition and is selling for a reasonable price so she immediately buys the tea service for her collection.

Would it be unethical for Suzi to keep the silver without notifying the history museum of her purchase?

Collections Management

The Z Museum of Natural History has a large research collection of ants that, after a systematic review of its entomology collections, it has determined that it is no longer useful for the research conducted at the museum. The curators determine that the ant collection is appropriate for deaccessioning and hope to sell it at public auction to another natural history museum. They plan to use the proceeds from the sale to build their collection of dragonflies that will be useful in a study of dragonfly morphology, which one of the curators will undertake in the near future. As part of the deaccessioning process, the director of research presents the sale of the ant collection to Museum Z's governing board for their review and approval. The board discusses the appropriateness of the sale, the projected amount that might be raised if the collection were sold at auction as well as the amount necessary to purchase the dragonfly collection. Ultimately they approve the deaccession, and the museum staff prepares to dispose of the collection at auction. Shortly thereafter, however, one of Museum Z's board members who had participated in the discussion about deaccessioning the ant collection approaches the head of the entomology department, offering to buy the ant collection.

Would it be unethical for the museum to sell the collection to this board member? Would your answer be different if the board member had not been privy to the deaccessioning discussion? How would it be different if the board member were bidding for the collection at a public sale?

FINAL THOUGHTS

Serving on a museum governing body has unique responsibilities. It is incumbent upon the museum's leadership to select new members carefully and to orient them to the operations and collections of the institution so that these new volunteers can appreciate and fulfill their role in maintaining and preserving the museum's holdings as well as in fulfilling the mission of this cultural and educational institution. To preserve the goodwill of the public, each member of the governing body should understand his or her legal obligations to the duty of care both to the public and to the museum and his or her duty to preserve, protect, foster, and enhance resources of the museum—its collections, facilities, staff, and financial assets—without personal conflict, making it possible for the museum to realize its mission. As important, if not more so, is cultivating an understanding and appreciation for the museum's professional code of ethics, the principles of conduct that allow a museum to maintain its reputation as a trustworthy repository and resource for all to benefit from equally.

NOTES

1. American Alliance of Museums, "Code of Ethics for Museums," American Alliance of Museums website, amended 2000, http:/www.aam-us.org/resources/ethics-standards-and-best-practices/code-of-ethics.

2. International Council of Museums, "ICOM Code of Ethics for Museums," International Council of Museums website, revised 2004, http://icom.museum/the-vision/code-of-ethics/; Association of Art Museum Directors, "Professional Practices in Art Museums," Association of Art Museum Directors website, 2011, https://aamd.org/sites/default/files/document/2011ProfessionalPracticesinArtMuseums.pdf; and American Association for State and Local History, "Publication: AALH Statement of Professional Standards and Ethics," American Association for State and Local History website, updated June 2012, http://resource.aaslh.org/view/aaslh-statement-of-professional-standards-and-ethics/.

3. Marie Malaro, *Museum Governance: Mission, Ethics, Policy* (Washington, DC: Smithsonian Institution Press, 1994), 9.

4. Marie C. Malaro and Ildiko Pogány deAngelis, *A Legal Primer on Managing Museum Collections*, 3rd ed. (Washington, DC: Smithsonian Books, 2012), 18.

5. Ibid., 18–19.

6. John Henry Merryman, "Museum Ethics," Address given at the American Law Institute—American Bar Association Continuing Legal Education ALI-ADA Course of Study, March 29–31, 2006, Legal Issues in Museum Administration, March 29–31, 2006, http://www.law.harvard.edu/faculty/martin/art_law/museum_ethics.html.

7. Malaro and DeAngelis, *A Legal Primer on Managing Museum Collections*, 20.

Chapter 4

The Ethics of Acquiring and Managing Collections

"Collections are the intellectual and spiritual capital of the museum."[1]

Collections stewardship is central to the operation of most museums today. The responsibilities of stewardship begin when a museum considers a possible acquisition and, once an object is acquired, continues in perpetuity. Even museums without collections[2] use exhibitions to communicate with and provide learning experiences for their visitors, and the proper maintenance of these installations demonstrates a museum's commitment to its educational mission. Museums that do not have their own collections but that exhibit objects from other museums and private collectors must necessarily take the same responsibility to the objects that they display as museums with their own collections.

Without their collections and exhibitions, museums would lose their distinctiveness and would not be able to fulfill their missions. Thus, all aspects of collections care—from acquisition through exhibition and interpretation, from maintenance and preservation through deaccessioning and disposition—are at the core of a museum's responsibilities, and the trustworthy care of collections is critical to maintaining an institution's reputation. In *MRM5: Museum Registration Methods*, Rebecca Buck impresses upon museum registrars and collections managers that their role is to uphold the highest ethical standards in order that their institution not be "charged with (among other things) feeding the chain of looting, selling off their collections to cover operating expenses, giving their reputations up to commercial enterprises, or becoming centers of entertainment when they should, by virtue of their missions, be educators."[3] By responsibly maintaining their collections, museums make it possible for the public to benefit from their holdings through both exhibition and study. It is no surprise, then, that all museum professional codes of ethics speak to the acquisition, maintenance, use, and care of collections in great detail.

One of the three main sections of the Code of Ethics of the American Alliance of Museums focuses upon collections:

> The distinctive character of museum ethics derives from the ownership, care and use of objects, specimens, and living collections representing the world's natural and cultural common wealth. This stewardship of collections entails the highest public trust and carries with it the presumption of rightful ownership, permanence, care, documentation, accessibility and responsible disposal.

Thus, the museum ensures that

- collections in its custody support its mission and public trust responsibilities
- collections in its custody are lawfully held, protected, secure, unencumbered, cared for and preserved
- collections in its custody are accounted for and documented
- access to the collections and related information is permitted and regulated
- acquisition, disposal, and loan activities are conducted in a manner that respects the protection and preservation of natural and cultural resources and discourages illicit trade in such materials
- acquisition, disposal, and loan activities conform to its mission and public trust responsibilities
- collections-related activities promote the public good rather than individual financial gain
- competing claims of ownership that may be asserted in connection with objects in its custody should be handled openly, seriously, responsively and with respect for the dignity of all parties involved.[4]

The American Association of State and Local History's Statement of Professional Standards and Ethics addresses the acquisition and care of historical collections:

> Historical resources—including collections, built environment, cultural landscapes, archaeological sites, and other evidence of the past, provide the tools through which we interact with the past and are the bedrock upon which the practice of history rests. In fulfillment of their public trust, historical organizations and those associated with them must be responsible stewards and advocates on behalf of the historical resources within their care and throughout their communities.
>
> A. Association members shall give priority to the care and management of the historical resources within their care and always shall act to preserve their physical and intellectual integrity.
> B. Institutions shall manage historical resources, in accord with comprehensive policies officially adopted by their governing authorities.

C. Historical resources shall not be capitalized or treated as financial assets.
D. Historical resources shall be acquired, cared for and interpreted with sensitivity to their cultural origins.
E. It is important to document the physical condition of historical resources, including past treatment of objects, and to take appropriate steps to mitigate potential hazards to people and property.

ICOM's Code of Ethics details the obligations of a museum toward its collections that are held "in trust for the benefit of society and its development."[5] The second principle of the code states:

> Museums have the duty to acquire, preserve and promote their collections as a contribution to safeguarding the natural, culture and scientific heritage. Their collections are a significant public inheritance, have a special position in law and are protected by international legislation. Inherent in this public trust is the notion of stewardship that includes rightful ownership, permanence, documentation, accessibility and responsible disposal.

Sections on acquiring collections and collections care provide further details of the ethical obligations of museums:[6]

ACQUIRING COLLECTIONS

2.1 Collections Policy
The governing body for each museum should adopt and publish a written collections policy that addresses the acquisition, care and use of collections and clarifying the position of any material that will not be catalogued, conserved, or exhibited.

2.2 Valid Title
No object or specimen should be acquired by purchase, gift, loan, bequest, or exchange unless the acquiring museum is satisfied that a valid title is held. Evidence of lawful ownership in a county is not necessarily valid title.

2.3 Provenance and Due Diligence.
Every effort must be made before acquisition to ensure that any object or specimen offered for purchase, gift, loan, bequest, or exchange has not been illegally obtained in, or exported from its country of origin or any intermediate country in which it might have been owned legally (including the museum's own country). Due diligence in this regard should establish the full history of the item since discovery or production.

2.4 Objects and Specimens from Unauthorised or Unscientific Fieldwork
Museums should not acquire objects where there is reasonable cause to believe their recovery involved unauthorized or unscientific fieldwork or intentional destruction or damage of monuments, archaeological or geological sites, or of

species and natural habitats. In the same way, acquisition should not occur if there has been a failure to disclose the find to the owner or occupier of the land, or to the proper legal or governmental authorities.

2.5 Culturally Sensitive Material

Collections of human remains and material of sacred significance should be acquired only if they can be housed securely and cared for respectfully. This must be accomplished in a manner consistent with professional standards and the interests and beliefs of members of the community, ethnic or religious groups from which the objects originated, where these are known.

2.6 Protected Biological or Geological Specimens

Museums should not acquire biological or geological specimens that have been collected, sold, or otherwise transferred in contravention of local, national, regional or international law or treaty relating to wildlife protection or natural history conservation.

2.7 Living Collections

When the collections include live botanical or zoological specimens, special consideration should be given to the natural and social environment from which they are derived as well as any local, national, regional or international law or treaty relating to wildlife protection or natural history conservation.

2.8 Working Collections

The collections policy may include special considerations for certain types of working collections where the emphasis is on preserving cultural, scientific, or technical process rather than the object, or where objects or specimens are assembled for regular handling and teaching purposes.

2.9 Acquisition Outside Collections Policy

The acquisition of objects or specimens outside the museum's stated policy should only be made in exceptional circumstances. The governing body should consider the professional opinions available to it and the view of all interested parties. Consideration will include the significance of the object or specimen, including the context in the cultural or natural heritage, and the special interest of other museums collecting such material. However, even in these circumstances, objects without a valid title should not be acquired.

2.10 Acquisitions Offered by Members of the Governing Body or Museum Personnel

Special care is required in considering any item whether for sale, as a donation, or as a tax-benefit gift from members of the governing bodies, museum personnel, or the families and close associates of these persons.

2.11 Repositories of Last Resort

Nothing in this Code of Ethics should prevent a museum from acting as an authorised repository for unprovenanced, illicitly collected or recovered specimens or objects from the territory over which it has lawful responsibility.

CARE OF COLLECTIONS

2.18 Collection Continuity

The museum should establish and apply policies to ensure that its collections (both permanent and temporary) and associated information, properly recorded, are available for current use and will be passed on to future generations in as good and safe a condition as practicable, having regard to current knowledge and resources.

2.19 Delegation of Collection Responsibility

Professional responsibilities involving the care of the collections should be assigned to persons with appropriate knowledge and skill or who are adequately supervised.

2.20 Documentation of Collections

Museum collections should be documented according to accepted professional standards. Such documentation should include a full identification and description of each item, its associations, provenance, condition, treatment and present location. Such data should be kept in a secure environment and be supported by retrieval systems providing access to the information by the museum personnel and other legitimate users.

2.21 Protection Against Disasters

Careful attention should be given to the development of policies to protect the collections during armed conflict and other human-made or natural disasters.

2.22 Security of Collection and Associated Data

The museum should exercise control to avoid disclosing sensitive personal or related information and other confidential matters when collection data is made available to the public.

[Items related to the conservation of collections will be addressed in chapter 5.]

2.26 Personal Use of Museum Collections

Museum personnel, the governing body, their families, close associates, or others should not be permitted to expropriate items from the museum collections, even temporarily, for any personal use.

In addition the ICOM Code highlights how the collections of a museum "provide opportunities for other public services and benefits" and puts forward the following principle in Section 5, "Museums utilize a wide variety of specialisms, skills and physical resources that have a far broader application than in the museum. This may lead to shared resources or the provision of services as an extension of the museum's activities. These should be organized in such a way that they do not compromise the museum's stated mission."

The Code further identifies certification services that a museum might provide:

5.1 Identification of Illegally or Illicitly Acquired Objects
Where museums provide an identification service, they should not act in any
way that could be regarded as benefiting from such activity, directly or indirectly. The identification and authentication of objects that are believed or
suspected to have been illegally or illicitly acquired, transferred, imported or
exported, should not be made public until the appropriate authorities have been
notified.

5.2 Authentication and Valuation (Appraisal)
Valuations may be made for the purposes of insurance of museum collections.
Opinions on the monetary value of other objects should only be given on official
request from other museums or competent legal, governmental or other responsible public authorities. However, when the museum itself may be the beneficiary, appraisal of an object or specimen must be undertaken independently.

Finally, "A Code of Ethics for Curators" issued by the Curators Committee
of the American Alliance of Museums (CurCom) outlines curatorial responsibilities toward the collections, specifying that

> curators must establish intellectual control of the collection under their care.
> They ensure that a record of each object in the collection is prepared at the
> time of acquisition and that the record and the object are systematically orga-
> nized and retrievable. They conduct research on and record the provenance
> of all objects in or offered to the collection, and they are responsible for the
> accuracy of the documentation, whether prepared by themselves or others.
> Curators must be aware of all applicable national and international laws and
> never knowingly acquire stolen, illegally exported or improperly collected
> objects.[7]

As noted in chapter 2 on distinguishing ethical issues from operational and
management problems, the presence of appropriate policies and procedures
can help a museum avoid ethical or resolve dilemmas. An effective collection management policy—that is, one tailored to the collections a particular
museum holds—is the first step in establishing appropriate procedures for
the acquisition and care of collections. Rigorously monitoring the policy,
the direct responsibility of the registration and/or curatorial staff (depending
upon the size and resources of the museum), can help avoid the appearance
of wrongdoing in collections-related matters. In determining the resolution of
ethical problems related to a museum's collections, the threshold question is
always whether the museum is the owner of the object. More often than not
this ownership is assumed; it is incumbent upon the museum's registration
staff to ensure that the museum has clear title for the objects in its collections.
The question of a museum's ownership is the foundation of its responsibility for collections stewardship and is integrally tied to questions of ethical
behavior with respect to its holdings.

While care for collections is the responsibility of a museum's curatorial and/or registrations or collections management staff, the well-being of the collections as a whole is an institutional responsibility and it is incumbent upon every museum to ensure that it has the resources to store, manage, and preserve its holdings. In addition, every board and staff member must share the responsibility of ensuring that their museum upholds the public trust by acquiring, caring for, displaying, and lending objects in their care transparently and without conflict of interest. Unfortunately, this is not always the case and the following represent some of the dilemmas that can occur in museums.

ETHICS IN ACTION

With the exception of the Smithsonian, the people, situations, and museums in the following cases are fictional. The hypothetical situations are composites of real and imaginary situations and reflect actual issues faced by museums. Any resemblance to your museum is purely coincidental.

Collection

Mary Smith was a watercolorist of some renown across the region in which she lived and worked. She was married and had three children. When she died at the age of eighty-five, she gave all of the paintings still in her possession to her husband. When he died several years later, he stipulated in his will that all of Mary's work, some several hundred watercolors, should be given to the local art museum. The museum was delighted to have her watercolors in their collection and displayed them frequently, both in exhibitions that focused solely upon Mary Smith's art work as well as in other shows about landscapes of the region. Forty years later, Mary Smith's youngest daughter Jane, now well on in years, asked the museum if she might have several of her mother's paintings that had great sentimental value to her, for they would provide much comfort to her in her own waning years. It turns out that Jane also has a collection of her mother's early work, examples of which are not already in the museum's collection, and, in conversation, she told the museum that she wants to give it to them when she passes away. Jane has no heirs and a sizeable fortune. She has been a benefactor of the museum for many years.

Would it be unethical for the museum to give to Jane the paintings she requested? How might Jane's promise of her collection have an impact upon the museum's decision? Should this be a factor in making the decision? Can the museum's responsibilities as the long-term guardian of Mary's paintings left to the museum by her husband be traded for her promise of a donation of other works of art? Does the fact that Mary's daughter is a benefactor of the museum have an impact on the decision regarding the collections?

Small Craft

A historical museum in a region noted for its maritime heritage was offered a collection of historic small craft. The museum had a few major maritime vessels—ships and working boats—that had figured in the region's history. The vessels are part of the museum's "working collection," and the museum's collection policy states that the institution agrees to maintain the vessels in its collection in working condition. Because the collection policy requires that the museum accept the financial responsibility of maintaining the collection, the policy also states that acquisitions valued at more than $5000.00 must be approved by the museum's collections committee.

The small craft offered to the museum were classics of their kind but had no special relationship to the history of the area. Each is valued at slightly less than $5,000.00. The museum's director, feeling that these boats would attract devotees of the maritime world to the museum, entered into negotiations with the collection's owner and accepted the small craft for the museum's working collection. At about the same time, the director had a series of conversations with the owner of a local restaurant who wanted to lend a maritime atmosphere to his establishment and sought the museum director's advice. Suddenly, the museum director had a brainstorm—he could loan the small craft to the restaurateur who could hang them in his restaurant. The museum director would thus solve the problem of storage for the small craft and the nearby restaurant would immediately take on the maritime theme that its owner was looking for. The restaurant owner was so pleased with this solution that he offered to pay for a brochure that would describe each boat and identify them as part of the collections of the history museum. The museum director sought out a carpenter to drill holes into the boats so that they could be suspended from the ceiling of the restaurant.

What are the ethical issues that this situation poses for the museum? Did the museum's director have the authority to acquire the vessels on behalf of the museum? Would the museum's responsibility for the small craft be met under the circumstances arranged by the museum director with the restaurant owner? Will the restaurant provide the appropriate setting and "storage" for these objects? How might the public's perception of the museum's stewardship of its collections be affected?

Donations

Fred Smith, a local historical society board member, met his friend Joe Parker for lunch. Joe, who is a sometime donor to the historical society because of his friendship with Fred, reported that he had recently cleaned out his attic and told Fred that he found something he thought Fred would like for the historical society's collection. After lunch Joe went to his car and took out an old wooden plane, a woodworking tool he remembers seeing his grandfather use. He handed it to Fred, saying proudly, "I know it would be perfect for the historical society!" Not wanting to offend Joe, Fred thanked Joe and took the object. Fred suspected that the historical society might have a few other similar planes but he figured that having one more wouldn't hurt, especially because donating it to the society seemed to mean so much to Joe. The next time Fred visited the historical society, he left the plane on a table in the administrative offices with a post-it on it, saying, "For the collections. Fred." When the museum's director found the plane on the table, he put it in nearby clothes closet for safekeeping, knowing that the historical society's collection already contained at least a dozen wooden planes, dating from approximately the same period. All were in better condition.

A few weeks later, an electrical fire in the clothes closet destroyed most of its contents, including the wooden plane. Only the post-it, which blew off the object before the fire, was found in a corner of the closet. But no one remembered to what the post-it had been attached. When the museum director approached Fred to ask him about the post-it note, he discovered that Fred and Joe had had a recent conversation about the plane. Apparently Joe had recently told Fred that in going through some of his grandfather's papers, he discovered that the wooden plane had been given to his great-great-grandfather by a member of the state's oldest families. As a result of discovering this information, Joe now wanted his son, who was a woodworking enthusiast, to have the plane and he asked Fred if he might have the plane back.

What are the ethical issues that this scenario raises? How would these issues be affected if the plane had been accessioned into the collection, or, if the museum director had investigated the wooden plane when it was first dropped off at the museum?

Volunteer Generosity

Jane Jackson has been volunteering for the Grand Nineteenth Century Art Museum for twenty years. She has been a faithful and generous member of the museum's volunteer corps, recruiting many of her friends to serve as volunteers, and single-handedly making service as a volunteer a sought-after position in the area. She has enjoyed her experience immensely and is exceedingly grateful to the museum for having had the opportunity of working with it for so long. Jane has a small painting that she claims she received as a gift from grandmother when she was a child, sometime in the late 1930s. She wants to donate the painting, which she says (as told by her grandmother) dates back to the late 1880s, to the museum. Before sending the deed of gift to Jane, the registrar examines the painting and asks the curator to do some research on it. In so doing, the curator discovers that the painter was born in the early twentieth century and that the painting was from the early 1930s, well after the period covered in the Grand Museum's scope of collections. The museum, not wanting to offend its long-time volunteer and risk alienating her as well as her friends, accepts the painting for its collection, justifying its decision to do so on the basis that the painting "won't take up much room."

Has the museum acted unethically in acquiring the painting? Would your answer be different if you knew that Jane had offered to establish a small endowment, the income from which would be used for the painting's care? Does the museum have an ethical duty to tell Jane Jackson the truth about the date of her painting?

Contemporary Collecting

There is a new director at the La Grange Historical Society, a museum dedicated to documenting and interpreting the history of the La Grange Valley. Over the last fifty years, the Valley has become a vacation resort area. While some of its original families remain, a large number of immigrants have moved to the area to work in its numerous resorts and spas. Over time, some have started their own businesses and others have taken over some of the local enterprises. As a result the makeup of the population of the Valley has changed from its early years and the years of the founding of the historical society. In her first few months at the society, the new director reviews the society's collections and discovers that the most recent object in the collection dates from the mid-twentieth century, just before the area's population has begun to diversify ethnically. She speculates that the fact that the society's collections do not represent the current population will present a challenge both for audience development efforts and for providing future generations with a record of the dramatic changes to life in the region during the mid- to late-twentieth century. Emboldened by attending a workshop on contemporary collecting at a professional meeting, the director makes a proposal to the governing board of the La Grange Historical Society that the institution should embark upon a major collecting initiative that would encompass both later twentieth- and early twenty-first-century artifacts from the region. She envisions this as an opportunity to engage all of the society's local constituents in an effort to build a record of life in the area over the past fifty years. She presents this to the board as an audience-building effort and a way to re-invigorate an organization perceived to serve only its founders, largely an elite Anglo-Saxon group. While understanding the director's arguments, the board is reluctant to approve the proposal. They are concerned that the historical society's collections storage might be inadequate to serve what might result from a full-scale contemporary collecting effort conducted without parameters. They also express reservations about taking on objects that have not "stood the test of time," feeling that some of them, especially those from more recent immigrant groups, might not be of interest to future generations. One of the board members, who supports the director's vision for the museum, dismisses these arguments, pointing out that if "excess" objects are accessioned they can always be sold at a later time. After a long discussion, the board rejects the director's proposal.

Does the governing board have an ethical duty to acquire community-related objects for their collections? In considering the issues related to the capacity of the museum to sustain a collecting effort, have they acted responsibly by rejecting the new director's proposal? How might the proposal have been altered to meet the stated concerns of the governing board? Would your answer be different if the argument of the board member supporting the director swayed the board into accepting the proposed contemporary collecting effort?

"American Idol" at the Smithsonian

Contemporary collecting raises many questions for museums. Will the objects collected—whether they be artworks or historical artifacts—be significant to a museum's educational mission in the future? This question becomes especially acute when objects of contemporary popular culture are considered for a museum's collections. Often if not always mass-produced, such objects may gain significance through their use in a particular context. Consideration of that context becomes key to the acquisition decision-making process as in this example from the Smithsonian's Center for Folklife and Cultural Heritage. Fox News Corp announced that a desk used by the judges on the "American Idol" television program had been acquired by the Smithsonian. A celebrity guest on the program declared that this desk would soon be displayed next to the Star-Spangled Banner. Fox's purpose in making this announcement was to promote a recently completed film (*Night at the Museum: Battle of the Smithsonian*) and lend prestige to the "American Idol" television program. The desk had been previously rejected for acquisition by the National Museum of American History, which houses the Star-Spangled Banner. That museum had no interest in the artifact and was careful to avoid being seen as implicitly endorsing products when accessioning objects. The Smithsonian's Folklife Center considered the desk symbolic of the American tradition of amateur competition. According to the label interpreting the desk on display in the Smithsonian Castle, far from the iconic flag mentioned on the TV show, "Amateur talent competitions have been a feature of American culture since the late 1700s, when fiddle and dance competitions gave musicians a chance to test their virtuosity," not to mention radio and television amateur hours.[8]

Is the acquisition of the desk an implicit endorsement of a commercial enterprise? If so, does the acquisition create an ethical problem for the Smithsonian? How would your answer be affected if the "American Idol" desk were displayed next to the Star-Spangled Banner? If your answer to the first two questions is yes, is it always unethical for a museum to acquire and display objects associated with commercial purposes?

Conservator-Collector

A conservator working at a decorative art museum specializing in nine-teenth-century furniture owned a collection of wedding chests. He already had this collection when he was hired by the museum and stopped collecting to comply with the museum's personnel policy, which discourages staff from collecting types of items also collected by the museum. When the curator of the museum told him that the museum was about to deaccession one of its nineteenth-century wedding chests because it duplicates another in the collection, however, the conservator told the curator that he would be interested in buying the chest from the museum. Acting on behalf of the museum, the curator sold the conservator the chest before offering it to anyone else. Was the sale of the wedding chest to the conservator unethical?

Shortly after the sale, the conservator, whose interest in wedding chests was rekindled by his purchase from the museum, visited a local antique dealer who frequently sold items to the museum. The dealer also had a nacre-inlaid wedding chest for sale and the conservator immediately realized it, too, would make an excellent addition to his collection. After the conservator and the dealer discussed the merits of the wedding chest, the dealer told him that if he were interested in buying the chest, the dealer would give him a very special price because he works for the museum which is such a good client. Does this offer pose an ethical dilemma for the museum?

Antiques Road Show

To capitalize on the popularity of the television program *Antiques Road Show*, a local art museum proposed to its board that it create a new income-producing activity—an antique fair. They approached a local antique dealer and proposed that they sell his objects at the fair, asking that he donate a percentage of the sales to the museum. He agreed and the museum organized a weekend-long event from which it hoped to generate new revenue both from proceeds from the fair as well as increased sales in its café and gift shop. Swept away by his enthusiasm for the event, the director of programs for the museum proposed an added attraction—people could be encouraged to bring their own antiques to the fair and curators from the museum could appraise the objects for them.

Would the museum be unethical were it to follow through on these plans to 1) develop this antiques fair and 2) appraise objects? Explain the rationale for your answers.

A Special Request from a Donor

The Volontier Historical Society has a fine collection of widget-making machines, popular in the region from the eighteenth through the early twentieth century. The society displays a representative selection of these objects; however, the bulk of this fragile and unusual collection remains in storage. Because it is renowned for this collection, the society regularly hosts international widget scholars who study these rare objects. Mr. Big Pockets, an influential person in the Volontier community and a benefactor of the museum, plans to host an antiquarian group at his home for a special dinner in the near future. He would like to demonstrate how the widget-making machines work and has asked the historical society if he might borrow one of them for the evening. He points out that his generosity has allowed the society to restore and exhibit their famous widget-making machinery in the museum and implies that granting this favor is the least the society can do. He also argues that this will be an educational program and will feature objects that otherwise are hidden away in storage.

Would it be unethical for the historical society to loan the widget-making machine to Mr. Big Pockets for the evening? Would your answer be different if Mr. Big Pockets were hosting his event in the galleries of the historical society itself? If Mr. Big Pockets were a trustee of the society? Are there any circumstances that would eliminate any such ethical problems? Explain.

Mineral Fairs

Annual mineral and fossil fairs are awaited enthusiastically by dealers, private collectors, and enthusiasts alike; but they are often shunned by museums because some of the items on sale may have been illegally removed from their place of origin. Paleontologists from the New Hope Natural History Museum have heard about an upcoming fair that is advertising fossils from the Liaoning region of China, a place known for its rich paleontological material as well as for illicit excavations. (Archaeologists do not carry out these excavations and, as a result, the objects have not been properly documented as to their origin and context.) The paleontologists have taken it upon themselves to "rescue" some of the illicitly excavated fossils, arguing that although the items may lack context, with their scholarly expertise, they can provide more information about the objects than most private collectors. By buying them for the museum, the paleontologists will ensure that the objects will not be hidden away in a private cabinet of curiosities, will stay out of the market, and remain in the public trust where they can be appreciated and studied. The paleontologists approach the Director of Science to seek permission to attend the next fair on behalf of the museum and, should they discover items worthy of the museum's collections, purchase a limited number of them.

Would it be unethical for representatives of the museum to attend the Mineral and Fossil Fair? Would it be unethical for them to purchase fossils they believe to have been illicitly excavated? Would their purchase of items from the fair be appropriate for the museum or simply encourage further trade in illicitly excavated minerals and fossils? If the presence of the museum paleontologists adds credibility to the fair, does that itself present an ethical problem for the museum?

Donating Coins

A state historical museum has a respected coin collection and a private collector has offered to donate an assortment of coins to the society. The coins represent a lifetime of collecting and originated in many countries around the world. There is no question of the coins' value. Moreover, the collector is anxious to find a home for the whole collection for he is moving to another part of the world in three weeks and does not want to move the collection to his new home. The museum's curator of coins quickly reviews the collection and finds some items to be very rare; however, while many of the coins are examples of mints issued by the state and would enhance the museum's collection, others are from distant countries and have no relationship to the museum's mission. In addition, the documentation of the foreign coins is incomplete, creating a need for research to ensure that the collector has legal title to all of the coins. The museum has two weeks in which to make a decision about the collection, insufficient time in which to conduct the necessary research concerning the collection's provenance.

While extolling the quality of the locally minted coins and assuring the collector that this historical museum would be the most appropriate home for this part of the collection, the curator expresses reservations about the responsibility entailed in accepting the part of the collection that does not relate to the state. The coin collector responds by saying that the museum must take all of the collection and that the body of coins should not be broken up in any way or sold at any time. He concludes by saying that if the state historical museum does not want his collection, he will offer some items for sale and place the rest at another institution elsewhere.

Would it be unethical for the museum to accept the donation of the coins knowing that a sizeable portion of the collection does not relate to its mission and does not have satisfactory and reliable documentation?

Consider another scenario involving a similar coin collection and the same state historical society. In this instance, however, the collector recently passed away and willed the entire collection to the museum with the stipulation that it not be broken up or sold. Would it be unethical for the museum to accept the donation knowing that all of the collection was not relevant to its mission? Would it be unethical for the museum to deaccession the non-U.S. coins after the will is probated?

Loans to Private Institutions or Events

The GoReady Corporation is a generous supporter of the Frik Frack Art Museum's educational programs and is proud of the difference they have helped the museum make in serving the school children of the region. GoReady highlights the children's programs they have sponsored in some of their advertising, feeling that their association with the Museum enhances their profile in the business community.

GoReady is planning a large dinner for their best clients from around the world, and they have rented a local event space in a former private estate for a private dinner for several hundred people. They have approached the museum to request a loan of ten of the museum's French Impressionist paintings, intending to hang them in the rooms of the estate where they plan to host a cocktail party and dinner. They have offered to pay the museum a generous sum for the loan of the paintings.

Would it be unethical for the museum to agree to the loan? What are the factors that the museum should consider in deliberating about this decision? If Go Ready provided insurance for the paintings, paid for security guards for the rooms in which they would be displayed, and provided the transportation from the museum to the local event space, how might that affect your decision as to whether the loan might be ethical?

Collecting for Whom?

The contemporary art curator for a the Big City Museum of Art has worked for years to build the museum's contemporary collection and in the process has developed close relationships with both dealers and collectors of contemporary art. The dealers know his interests and are quick to alert him to opportunities for the museum to enhance its already outstanding collection. The collectors often chat with him about paintings they are considering and value his opinions and advice. One collector, in particular, has a strong contemporary collection and has hinted that she might eventually donate it to the Big City Museum. The curator, hoping that increased attention to the collector by the museum would sway her to make a firm commitment to donating the collection, makes a proposal to the museum's exhibition committee to mount a special exhibition drawing solely upon her collection. He suggests that the museum also publish a catalogue for the exhibition. The costs involved would come from the museum's special exhibitions fund.

Would it be unethical for the exhibition committee to approve the exhibition? Would your answer be different if the collector offered to cover the costs of the exhibition, the publication of the catalogue or both? What if the collector had made a commitment in writing to donate the collection to the museum in ten years?

FINAL THOUGHTS

A museum's collections and exhibitions are at the core of its raison d'etre and safeguarding the objects in its care is one of a museum's primary functions. The responsibility for this care rests not solely with the collections-related staff but with the institution itself. Transparency about the maintenance and security of its holdings can help a museum acquire and sustain a good reputation. Nonetheless, the management of collections should not be seen as an end in itself but rather as the means by which a museum ensures that its collections are secure and made available for study and research both in the present day and for future generations.

NOTES

1. Terence Besterman, "Museum Ethics," in *Companion to Museum Studies*, ed. Sharon Macdonald (Oxford: Blackwell Publishing, 2006), 438.

2. Since not all museums are collecting institutions, I refer to exhibitions here to include in this discussion organizations like science and children's museums as well as art museums without collections. In their definition of *museum*, both the American Alliance of Museums and the International Council of Museums acknowledge that museums include both collecting and noncollecting institutions.

3. Rebecca Buck, "Ethics for Registrars and Collections Managers," in *MRM5: Museum Registration Methods, 5th Edition*, ed. Rebecca A. Buck and Jean Allman Gilmore (Washington, DC: American Alliance of Museums, 2010), 394.

4. American Alliance of Museums, "Code of Ethics for Museums," American Alliance of Museums website, amended 2000, http://www.aam-us.org/resources/ethics-standards-and-best-practices/code-of-ethics. Please note that issues related to deaccessioning, conservation, and cultural property will be treated in later chapters.

5. International Council of Museums, "ICOM Code of Ethics for Museums," International Council of Museums website, revised 2004, http://icom.museum/the-vision/code-of-ethics/.

6. The section of the ICOM Code of Ethics that focuses upon the removal of objects from collections will be discussed in chapter 6.

7. American Alliance of Museums Curators Committee (CurCom), "A Code of Ethics for Curators," American Association of Museums website, 2009, http://www.aam-us.org/docs/continuum/curcomethics.pdf?sfvrsn=0.

8. Exhibition label quoted in Philip Kennicott, "Passing Judgment: What Does it Mean When Smithsonian Shows 'American Idol' Desk?" *Washington Post*, Sunday, August 30, 2009, http://www.washingtonpost.com/wp-dyn/content/article/2009/08/27/AR2009082704411.html.

ADDITIONAL RESOURCES

American Alliance of Museums Curators Committee (CurCom). "A Code of Ethics for Curators." American Association of Museums website. 2009. http://www.aam-us.org/docs/continuum/curcomethics.pdf?sfvrsn=0.

Buck, Rebecca A. and Jean Allman Gilmore, eds. *MRM5: Museum Registration Methods*, 5th ed. Washington, DC: American Alliance of Museums, 2010.

Donnelly-Smith, Laura. "Blessings and Curses of Doorstep Donations." *Museum*. May/June 2011. http://aam-us.org/resources/publications/museum-magazine/archive/doorstep-donations.

Malaro, Marie and Ildiko Pogány DeAngelis. *A Legal Primer on Managing Museum Collections*. 3rd ed. Washington, DC: Smithsonian Books, 2012.

Matassa, Freda. "Creating Your Acquisition Policy." *ICOM News*, vol. 67, no. 1–2 (2014), 8–9.

Registrars Committee of the American Alliance of Museums. "A Code of Ethics for Registrars, 1984." In *RC-AAM History: History of the Registrars Committee 25 Years*. Edited by Rebecca Buck. Registrars Committee of the American Alliance of Museums website. 2002. http://www.rcaam.org/about/about-rc-aam/rc-aam-history/.

Chapter 5

The Ethics of Caring for and Conserving Collections

When a museum takes an object into its permanent collections, it accessions the object and thereby makes a commitment to care for and conserve that object so that it can be used for research, exhibition, and education. Accessioning, the formal process of accepting an object into a museum's permanent collections and recording it as such, should be a "thoughtful process"[1] that takes into account the responsibilities that caring for the object will entail: providing appropriate storage with a stable environment that will not contribute to the object's deterioration; ensuring that objects are displayed and handled safely; documenting the object's history as well as its use and treatment while in the museum's collections; and conserving the object should that become necessary. All such considerations should be outlined in a museum's collection management policy. And while the responsibilities of caring for collections can, at times, become ends in and of themselves, it is critical that museums always carry out these tasks with the benefit of the public in mind.

Over the course of the twentieth century, museums developed an approach to object care often referred to as *preventive conservation* or *preventive care*. Rather than focusing upon the conservation treatment of individual objects, museums shifted their attention to the overall care of collections, reasoning that if museums could provide better care for all of their collections, the need for conservation intervention would be obviated in many if not most cases. This more holistic approach includes providing the suitable environmental conditions for the objects' storage and display; using appropriate handling procedures when an object is examined or moved; guarding against the intrusion of pests or pest prevention and control; having appropriate emergency procedures in place; and providing ongoing monitoring and documentation of the storage conditions.[2] When museums employ preventive care, they create an environment that minimizes the deterioration of their collections by controlling the heat, humidity, light, contaminants, and pests to which the objects are exposed, thereby limiting if not preventing the deterioration of collections. They also regularly monitor the collections and, optimally, conduct a conservation assessment that identifies priorities for existing conservation treatment.

When the resources are available, preventive care has become the professional standard in museums. And even when it is not possible for a museum to install state-of-the-art environmental controls for its collections, discussions of preventive care have created an awareness of the importance of maintaining a stable, protected environment. The American Alliance of Museums' Code of Ethics for Museums calls for museums to ensure "that collections in its custody are lawfully held, protected, secure, unencumbered, cared for and preserved; collections in its custody are accounted for and documented; [and] access to the collections and related information is permitted and regulated."[3]

Similarly the American Association of State and Local History Statement of Professional Standards and Ethics mandates that "association members shall give priority to the care and management of the historical resources within their care and always shall act to preserve their physical and intellectual integrity." Additionally, this document notes, "It is important to document the physical condition of historical resources, including past treatment of objects, and to take appropriate steps to mitigate potential hazards to people and property."[4]

The International Council of Museums' Code of Ethics for Museums explicitly endorses preventive care as well as conservation:

2.23 Preventive Conservation
Preventive conservation is an important element of museum policy and collection care. It is an essential responsibility of members of the museum profession to create and maintain a protective environment for the collections in their care, whether in store, on display, or in transit.

2.24 Collection Conservation and Restoration
The museum should carefully monitor the condition of collections to determine when an object or specimen may require conservation-restoration work and the services of a qualified conservator-restorer. The principal goal should be the stabilisation of the object or specimen. All conservation procedures should be documented and as reversible as possible, and all alterations should be clearly distinguishable from the original object or specimen.

2.25 Welfare of Live Animals
A museum that maintains living animals should assume full responsibility for their health and well-being. It should prepare and implement a safety code for

the protection of its personnel and visitors, as well as of the animals, that has been approved by an expert in the veterinary field. Genetic modification should be clearly identifiable.[5]

In its discussion of ethical guidelines, the American Alliance of Museums also makes reference to "field-wide" codes of ethics, including those of the American Institute for Conservation of Historic and Artistic Works (AIC). The AIC Code of Ethics details the responsibilities of conservation professionals vis a vis the preservation of cultural property, broadly defined as, "material which has significance that may be artistic, historical, scientific, religious, or social, and . . . is an invaluable and irreplaceable legacy that must be preserved for future generations."[6] And while addressed specifically to the conservation professional, the AIC Code outlines principles of conduct that have a direct impact upon museums considering the conservation of objects in their collections.

I. The conservation professional shall strive to attain the highest possible standards in all aspects of conservation, including, but not limited to, preventive conservation, examination, documentation, treatment, research, and education.

II. All actions of the conservation professional must be governed by an informed respect for the cultural property, its unique character and significance, and the people or person who created it.

III. While recognizing the right of society to make appropriate and respectful use of cultural property, the conservation professional shall serve as an advocate for the preservation of cultural property.

IV. The conservation professional shall practice within the limits of personal competence and education as well as within the limits of the available facilities.

V. While circumstances may limit the resources allocated to a particular situation, the quality of work that the conservation professional performs shall not be compromised.

VI. The conservation professional must strive to select methods and materials that, to the best of current knowledge, do not adversely affect cultural property or its future examination, scientific investigation, treatment, or function.

VII. The conservation professional shall document examination, scientific investigation, and treatment by creating permanent records and reports.

VIII. The conservation professional shall recognize a responsibility for preventive conservation by endeavoring to limit damage or deterioration to cultural property, providing guidelines for continuing use and care, recommending appropriate environmental conditions for storage and exhibition, and encouraging proper procedures for handling, packing, and transport.[7]

In adding an item to its collection, whether it is inanimate or living, a museum implicitly commits to caring for and preserving that item for the benefit of present and future museum visitors and researchers. Assuming that a museum's storage facilities provide a stable environment for its collections, there is an expectation that the collections will also remain stable and deterioration will be restricted. Regular inspections and conservation assessments of the collection should be conducted to identify those objects that are in need of special care.

Certain kinds of objects, however, are accepted into a collection with the understanding that it is probable that conservation treatment will be needed. Wooden boats, for example, are best preserved by being used, yet their use causes them to deteriorate, and preserving them may involve replacing the original wood. It would be irresponsible for a museum to acquire such an object without an understanding of its obligation for the boat's ongoing preservation. Similarly recently excavated archaeological collections must be conserved in order to arrest any deterioration that may naturally result from moving an object from one environment (in this case, underground or under water) to another. A museum's decision to acquire collections that include such objects should take these needs into account.

Sometimes objects are acquired with the understanding that conservation treatment would be desirable and that treatment may reveal important information about the object. For example in 1988, the Los Angeles County Museum of Art acquired what appeared to be a stylish 1840s dress with a matching mantle that one of their curators believed to be fashioned from a late seventeenth-century ensemble. Research conducted in the early 1990s revealed the curator's view to be accurate, and a subsequent decision was made to reconstruct the earlier garment.[8] While a commitment to engage in the reconstruction may not have been made when the garments were acquired, the museum knew that they had the resources and ability to conduct the appropriate research and provide conservation treatment.

The use of ephemeral materials in contemporary and installation art often complicates the acquisition decision-making process, for such materials often deteriorate or are not made to last. For example, in considering a work of art from a contemporary artist made from Styrofoam, the Hirshhorn Museum decided not to acquire the object. The materials were already deteriorating, and the museum reasoned that because the artist was still at the beginning of his career, there would be ample opportunity at a later time to acquire other works by him which might present fewer conservation issues.[9]

The San Francisco Museum of Modern Art (SFMOMA), on the other hand, decided to acquire *Tallus Mater (Madre Tallo/Stem Mother)*, a sculpture by Ana Mendieta made of ficus roots glued together with Elmer's Glue, in spite of the preservation challenges it posed. SFMOMA's director of collections and conservation Jill Sterrett pointed out that sometimes there are criteria other than the condition of the work that need to be taken into consideration when acquiring an object. Of *Tallus Mater*, she said, "Its memory, its place in our history, its place in our culture were regarded to be really so important that we should make it our business to bring it in . . . and to do the research necessary to take care of it."[10]

Historical museums face similar challenges, particularly when they engage in collecting contemporary objects and ephemera. And all museums are increasingly faced with making long-term commitments to ensure that collections of photographs and computer records as well as audio and video materials can continue to be used as the technology for accessing them changes. Once objects are accessioned, museums are often torn between concerns related to the preservation of their collections and the need for items in their collections to be made available to the public for exhibition and research. Resolving ethical challenges implicit in these situations are complex. Nonetheless balancing preservation needs with collections availability should be a central concern of all institutions that maintain collections for public benefit and, in most cases, transparency in decision-making both internally and with regard to the general public can help bring about an understanding of how a museum carries out its business in a responsible manner.

ETHICS IN ACTION

With the exception of Dan Flavin, William Turnbull, and the Tate, the people and institutions in the following cases are fictional. The hypothetical situations combine real and imaginary circumstances and reflect actual issues faced by museums. Any resemblance to a real museum is purely coincidental.

Loans

The XYZ Art Museum has a small but stellar collection of paintings by Frederik Fipps, a nineteenth-century local artist of some renown. Joseph Van Nutt, an industrialist and member of one of the region's leading families, donated most of the collection to the museum in the early twentieth century. The Fipps paintings are exhibited regularly at the art museum. Over the years conservators have treated the paintings according to the latest conservation practices, and recently the conservators completed a project that cleaned all of the paintings and removed some of the built-up sediment that darkened them. The Van Nutt House Museum was established after the last of the local Van Nutts passed away. The house has extensive decorative arts and costume collections, but few of the family's paintings were left on its walls. For the

Van Nutt Museum's fiftieth anniversary celebration, the Van Nutt Museum has asked the XYZ Museum if it could borrow some of the Fipps paintings as the museum attempts to restore the house to reflect the years in which Joseph Van Nutt lived there. The Van Nutt Museum has no environmental controls.

Would it be unethical for the XYZ Museum to lend the Fipps paintings to the Van Nutt under these circumstances? If XYZ lends the paintings to the Van Nutt, does XYZ still have any ethical responsibility for their care and maintenance during the loan period? Can XYZ be absolved from such responsibility by requiring that the Van Nutt insure the paintings during the loan period? Or are there other requirements that XYZ museum might impose upon a possible loan of the paintings? How would the benefit of exposing the paintings to a different audience be a factor in your decision? How might this ethical dilemma be resolved?

Jeb's Farm, House, and Museum

Jeb's Farm is a colonial era museum located in Jebtown, now an urban area in the American South. The farmhouse was constructed in the late eighteenth century, immediately following the American Revolution. Very little is known about the construction of the farmhouse and the family that first lived there. In the early twentieth century when the neighborhood around the farmhouse was changing dramatically and the house and its surrounding land were threatened by urban development, members of the family restored the house to what their research revealed would have been its earliest appearance and donated it to the city of Jebtown to be maintained as a postrevolutionary war farmhouse. The family carefully documented the building's restoration, gathered objects from family members and friends to form a core collection for the house, and, in the style of the day, created elaborate Colonial Revival style English gardens on the surrounding two acres. At about the same time, a group of amateur archaeologists reconstructed a replica of a Civil War soldiers' winter hut in the garden. While archaeological evidence suggests that there may have been similar huts in the vicinity, none were known to be on the farm property. It is believed that the archaeologists salvaged a small amount of building material from surviving shelters located in surrounding communities and used it as the foundation for the farmhouse hut. The hut became a popular venue for Boy Scout programs; however, it is no longer used and is suffering from disrepair.

The city of Jebtown is in the midst of a fiscal crisis. It has limited resources for its historic houses, and the board of Jeb's Farm has been charged by the city with making a number of decisions concerning how to reduce the farm's operating budget. The board is divided, however, in how to move forward. One part of the board is interested mainly in the history of the house and believes that the hut and gardens are not integral to their story. These "house historians" argue that since the hut was not on the property when the house was constructed in the late eighteenth century, it could be dismantled and the gardens replaced with natural plantings that do not need as much care as the current classic English Garden. The result would be a much-reduced budget for hut and grounds maintenance. The house historians would focus their efforts on the interpretation of the house. Others on the board, those interested in the hut and gardens, feel that, although the hut is admittedly a more recent addition to the property, the structure has historical significance. It speaks to the history of the Civil War and also tells the story of the work of amateur archaeologists in saving remnants of the past that would otherwise have been wiped out by the spread of the early suburbs and continued growth of the city. Further, the hut is now close to one hundred years old. The hut and garden supporters make a similar argument about the gardens, which they view as a document of the impact of the Colonial Revival.

If the house historians were to prevail, would it be unethical for the museum to dismantle the hut? What are the factors that the museum might consider in making a decision?

If the hut and garden group prevails, they would bring in conservators to restore the hut so that it could be used as part of the property's history and would find volunteer gardeners to maintain the current garden configuration. The hut has, however, been repaired by volunteers several times during its history. Its roof had several leaks and one of its walls began to sink into the ground and list. A local carpenter patched the roof and rigged up a support structure inside the hut to help prop up the walls, but these repairs are also showing wear. Restoring the hut might be less expensive if the past repairs were removed. If the museum decides to keep the hut, would it be unethical for it to remove evidence of the previous repairs? Or are the earlier restoration efforts now part of the hut's history and therefore should remain to be interpreted as such?

Taxidermy

The Spoontown Natural History Museum has a large taxidermy collection with specimens ranging from large animals to smaller mammals and birds, all from the Spoontown region. The taxidermy bird collection is especially complete and even contains many duplicates. The Museum is experiencing financial problems. Although it can conserve and maintain some of its collections, it cannot reasonably continue to maintain all of them. The bird collection has been identified as an area where considerable savings might be realized if only some of the specimens were conserved. One of the museum's board members had the idea that the duplicate birds might be deaccessioned from the museum's permanent collection and made into a handling collection especially for school groups. He developed a plan for this effort, which included lending the duplicate birds to local schools. Just as the Museum's collections committee was about to meet to discuss the plan, a consulting conservator's inspection of some of the taxidermy collections revealed that several of the stuffed birds had been treated with arsenic, a common practice for preserving skins.

Would it be unethical for the museum to create a handling collection of birds?

What are the factors that the collections committee should consider when discussing the board member's plan?

Contemporary Art

Modern and contemporary art presents many challenges for museums that collect it. Many contemporary works were not made to last; some were made from new and untested materials, while others contain unstable material or items that have become obsolete. The minimalist artist Dan Flavin, for example, created artworks from commercially available fluorescent light bulbs. When the bulbs burned out, conservators were faced with deciding whether changing the bulbs would destroy the original work of art. During Flavin's lifetime, he insisted upon providing the replacement bulbs but also commented that his work was not so much about the bulbs as about the quality of light they emitted.[11]

In the case of *Transparent Tubes*, a polymethyl methacrylate sculpture by William Turnbull at the Tate Gallery, again the museum turned to the artist when the original acrylic began to yellow and deteriorate. Turnbull explained that the transparency of the tubes was key and did not object to replacing the aging tubes with new ones.[12] It has become routine for conservators to work with artists during their lifetimes to understand an artist's intentions and to gain insight into whether the original appearance of the artwork or the original materials are most important to the artist.[13] This information can then inform future conservation decisions. But how should one proceed when this information is lacking? What is the museum's ethical responsibility in the case of a work of art that is expected to deteriorate? What is the museum's responsibility when a work of art deteriorates beyond the point of being exhibitable or usable for research? Would it be unethical for the museum to make a replica of the work for display?

Creating a Record of the Events of September 11, 2001

After September 11, 2001, many historical museums made efforts to document the events of that day in their collections. Some of the objects collected came from spontaneous memorials at viewpoints and gathering places, along highways and in train stations, in churches, and around the World Trade Center site itself. Photocopied flyers, newspaper articles and photos, notes written with Magic Markers were pasted on plywood and sometimes poster board outside of buildings throughout the New York metropolitan region. Collecting the objects protected them from further deterioration or damage due to the weather or to vandalism, but their ephemeral nature immediately presented conservation challenges. A small regional historical museum in a suburban community near New York City hired a new curator in 2003. He discovered that the museum had collected a number of 9/11-related artifacts from local memorials. He examined the collection and concluded that the collection had little to do with the mission of the museum. He felt that the materials had little artistic merit, no historical significance, and, above all, would be prohibitively expensive to conserve. He recommended that the museum throw out the collection.

Would it be unethical for the museum to allow the curator to throw out this collection of objects? Would your answer be different if you knew that the collection had not yet been accessioned? What other options might the museum pursue? Would it be unethical for a museum to collect a body of objects and delay the decision to accession them to an indefinite point in the future?

Cleaning

Cleaning is a much-debated process, for it is not reversible and can change the appearance and sometimes the nature of an object. In some circumstances, accumulated dust or dirt can be considered part of the object's history or identity. Brooks and Eastop note that "soiling may be considered as an unwanted agent of deterioration that should be removed, or the same soiling could be considered a source of valuable information."[14] They go on to state that "all decisions need to be supported by documentation explicitly recording the rationales as well as what was done. Why a treatment was implemented—or was not implemented—should be as important as what the treatment actually was."[15] Consider the following case.

Frank Friend collected mechanical toy soldiers from the time he was a boy until a few years before he passed away. His collection was one of the largest of its kind in the world and contained many rare mechanical objects. One of the distinctions of the collection is that all of the soldiers are wearing uniforms made out of cloth. During his lifetime, Mr. Friend took great pleasure in sitting in his study—the home of his collection as well as that of a library of books about mechanical soldiers—activating the troops and watching them move while he smoked his favorite cigars. After Mr. Friend's death, the James Museum acquired the collection of toys and books as well as some of the study's furnishings from Mr. Friend's estate and began to make plans to create a small permanent installation of the collection. One of the curators lobbied to create a replica of Mr. Friend's study as a centerpiece for the exhibition, arguing that it could serve as a platform from which to not only explore the toy soldiers and their history but also examine one collector's devotion to his avocation. After the museum's conservator surveyed the collection, she recommended that all of the objects be cleaned for they were covered with a layer of nicotine that was not only discoloring but also very slowly weakening the fabric in the uniforms of the soldiers. The curator, on the other hand, felt that the only way to really recreate the authentic atmosphere of Mr. Friend's study would be to keep the objects in the condition they were in when the museum acquired them, nicotine and all. She argued that only with the nicotine on the objects would they look and smell the "right way," epitomizing the life of some collectors and the collecting practices of the early twentieth century.

Would it be unethical for the museum to follow the recommendation of the curator and not clean the mechanical toys? Discuss the ethical ramifications of a decision to clean or not to clean the mechanical soldiers as well as other options the museum might chose to pursue.

Ancient Sculpture

A small regional art museum created from the collection of a local industrialist contains a few examples of Roman and Greek antiquities. These objects were placed in storage for many years and all but forgotten. The museum's board hired a new, energetic director who created a plan to refocus the museum's activities on its permanent collections, creating a long-range plan for collections care as well as a series of exhibitions and programs. The collections were surveyed, the museum's inventory updated, and a conservation assessment was made in order to establish priorities for future care. The director decided that her first exhibition would explore the tastes and interests of the local community in the early twentieth century when the industrialist who established the museum built his collection. The Roman and Greek antiquities would be the focal point of one of the galleries because they were key objects in the industrialist's holdings and also would be less familiar to the museum's visitors than many of the other more frequently exhibited objects and paintings. After reading the conservation assessment, however, she discovered that it was likely that at least one of the sculptures had undergone a major reconstruction in the eighteenth century when it was common for classical sculpture to be "restored." Fragments that were acquired with the statue were attached to it, cracks filled in and covered over, and missing elements were fabricated so that the statue would appear as it might have been when it was first created. Unlike current conservation practice, which favors using reversible treatment whenever possible, the changes made in the eighteenth century may not be reversible.

Would it be unethical for the museum to display the classical sculpture without revealing the conservation treatments that it has undergone? Alternately, would it be preferable to have a conservator attempt to reverse the eighteenth-century reconstruction to reveal the true shape and form of the object without later interventions?

Living Animals in Museums

In addition to zoos, aquaria and botanical gardens, natural history museums, science museums and science centers, living history museums, regional museums, and children's museums all might choose to maintain living populations. These populations must be cared for within the regulations established by the Animal Welfare Act.[16] If a museum accepts the responsibility of caring for living things—whether they serve as scientific specimens, are used for educational purposes or both—it should create a separate policy that demonstrates how the museum will adhere to the applicable laws and regulations as well as provide for the animals' welfare. As with inanimate objects, museums must legitimately acquire their living populations[17] in accordance with an acquisition policy. In addition, the museum's collection policy should demonstrate its commitment to the welfare of the animals in their care, specifying how the museum will maintain them in good health, protect them against physical endangerment, and both monitor and document their health and care.[18] "Further requirements must be met if the animals should happen to represent an endangered species."[19] But ethical problems can arise under circumstances that are not fully covered by law, regulation, or simple common sense. Consider the following hypothetical case.

The PDQ City museum presents exhibitions on the history, natural history, and art of its region. In its natural history section, the museum maintains a "discovery collection," an assemblage of live animals that are representative of those that live in the region and that are used frequently in programs for children. The population includes mice, squirrels, rabbits, turtles, armadillos, and gophers. All are on display in the museum's discovery rooms, housed in fully protected cases that replicate the mammals' natural environments. For many years it was the custom for education department staff members to take the animals out during programs for school children as well as during weekend programs for families. At the conclusion of a program, children were allowed to touch the animals. Over the years, these programs became some of the most, if not the most, popular activities for visitors to the PDQ museum;

they were especially favored among families who brought their children to the museum to celebrate special occasions like birthdays with the animals.

Recently, the PDQ City museum underwent a major expansion project and, as a result, annual attendance increased from 35,000 to close to 90,000. The format of the programs that the museum offers for both school children and families remains the same as before the renovation but many more children can now take part in the programs. Educators remove the animals from the environments in which they live for the programs so that the children can observe them close up and after the programs conclude, children can briefly handle the animals. Suddenly, however, the animal caretaker and visitors alike have noticed a change in the behavior of the nocturnal animals. Some pace frenetically for long periods of time, while others huddle and behave with uncharacteristic passivity. Moreover, their appetites have noticeably declined.

A meeting is called to discuss these developments in the animals' behavior. The educators who attend the meeting are concerned that any attempt to restrict or eliminate the programs with the animals would likely cause plummeting attendance. Parents who are benefactors to the museum want the programs to continue because they appreciate the fact that their children cannot engage in similar activities at any other museum in the region. The museum's director notes that other museums with similar populations in adjacent states with even more visitation than the PDQ continue their programs with living animals without experiencing these negative effects. But the veterinarian consulted by the animals' caretaker confirms that the animals are suffering from stress due to the increased numbers of visitors to the museum.

Would it be unethical for the museum to continue the programs that allow children to handle animals? Or would it be unethical for the museum to eliminate the programs entirely, thus depriving their audiences of the unique experiences of a hands-on approach to its living populations? Has the museum taken sufficient steps to determine the cause of the problem so that a decision can be made about what could and should be done to protect the animals while still enabling the museum's audiences to experience close encounters with animals? Short of eliminating the programs, are there other solutions that the museum might adopt?

A Community's Collection

The Evermore Ethnographic Museum has a historic collection of what-nots, small beaded woven objects created by the Wantnot, a group indigenous to the region in which the museum is located. The beaded patterns on the what-nots tell secret family stories that can only be understood by the families that created them. What-nots are used as part of coming-of-age and marriage ceremonies by the Wantnot. Young girls learn to make what-nots and, once they are married, are expected to weave them for their new family. The women update their what-nots as their families grow and they become essentially a family history interwoven with family secrets. The practice of making what-nots has great significance among the Wantnot; they attribute marital longevity and fertility to the use of proper weaving techniques. Furthermore, what-nots transmit family histories from one generation to another. Although what-not-making was widespread during the nineteenth and early twentieth centuries, it waned in the latter part of the twentieth century. At the beginning of the twenty-first century, however, the Wantnot realized that in order to ensure that their traditional history remains alive, they must revive what-not making. Working with Wantnot elders, the Wantnot Council developed a plan to do encourage what-not weaving that involved consulting the what-not collection of the Evermore Ethnographic Museum. Although small, the Evermore's collection is the most extensive owned by a museum and it is considered by both what-not collectors and the Wantnot to be finest in existence. Representatives of the Wantnot Council along with several Wantnot elders visited the museum director and explained their plan. They would like to use some of the what-nots from the Evermore collection in their revival efforts. They explained to the director that while the what-nots are important and contain significant historical information, it is actually the process of what-not making that is key to the Wantnot culture's survival. The treatment of the twine, the method of weaving, the placement of beads, the songs that are sung, and myths that are recounted are all integral to the process and are, in fact, more important than the artifacts themselves. Thus, the Wantnot Council requested a loan of five what-nots from Evermore's collections and, in order to teach what-not making, explained that they would take the what-nots apart and put them back together again.

On the one hand, would it be unethical for the museum to permit the Wantnot Council to borrow the what-nots knowing that the what-nots would be disassembled and reassembled while they were on loan? On the other hand, would it be unethical for the museum to deny the Wantnot request? What considerations should the museum take into account in making its decision?

FINAL THOUGHTS

The appropriateness of the conservation treatment to be used on an object must be decided on a case-by-case basis, guided by the expertise of a conservator with the necessary expertise. An art historian's perspective on what is suitable might differ from that of an historian, an ethnographer, or a member of a community in which an object originated. Further, trends in conservation and in museum display change. Varnishing used to protect paintings from dirt in one generation can be a conservation problem for the next. Grime that builds up on an object might weaken its integrity but it might also provide important information about the object's history. A museum's responsibility is to maintain its collections and to ensure that they are properly documented. The full history of an object, including decisions made about the object's location, exhibition, storage, cleaning, and conservation, provides a record that can be informative for researchers, museums staff, and the public. Such histories also demonstrate that a museum has fulfilled its responsibility to preserving and maintaining its collections and thus fulfilling its mission and its obligations to the public.

NOTES

1. Marie C. Malaro and Ilkido Pogány DeAngelis, *A Legal Primer on Managing Museum Collections*, 3rd ed. (Washington, DC: Smithsonian Books, 2012), 59–61.

2. Stephen L. Williams, "Preventative Conservation: The Evolution of a Museum Ethic," in *Museum Ethics*, ed. Gary Edson (New York: Routledge, 1997), 198–206; Rebecca A. Buck and Jean Allman Gilmore, eds, *MRM5: Museum Registration Methods, Fifth Edition* (Washington, DC: The AAM Press, 2010).

3. American Alliance of Museums, "Code of Ethics for Museums," American Alliance of Museums website, amended 2000, http://www.aam-us.org/resources/ethics-standards-and-best-practices/code-of-ethics.

4. American Association for State and Local History, "Publication: AALH Statement of Professional Standards and Ethics," American Association for State and Local History website, updated June 2012, http://resource.aaslh.org/view/aaslh-statement-of-professional-standards-and-ethics/.

5. International Council of Museums, "ICOM Code of Ethics for Museums," International Council of Museums website, revised 2004, http://icom.museum/the-vision/code-of-ethics/.

6. American Institute for Conservation of Historic and Artistic Works, "Code of Ethics and Guidelines for Practice," American Institute for Conservation of Historic and Artistic Works website, revised August 1994, http://www.conservation-us.org/about-us/core-documents/code-of-ethics#.U81kl1ZcUso.

7. Ibid.

8. Dina Eastop, "Conservation Practice as Enacted Ethics," in *The Routledge Companion to Museum Ethics: Redefining Ethics for the Twenty-First-Century Museum*, ed. Janet Marstine (New York: Routledge, 2011), 431–33.

9. Getty Conservation Institute, "Ethical Dilemmas in the Conservation of Modern and Contemporary Art," an event organized by the Getty Conservation Institute on April 29, 2009, https://www.getty.edu/conservation/publications_resources/videos/public_lecture_videos_audio/ethical_dilemmas.html.

10. Ibid.

11. Ibid.

12. Dina Eastop, "Conservation practices as enacted ethics," 437–39.

13. Some museums that collect works from living artists—the Whitney Museum of American Art, the Museum of Modern Art, the San Francisco Museum of Contemporary Art, to name just a few—have documentation programs to interview artists about their materials, techniques, and intent for the conservation of their works.

14. Mary M. Brooks and Dinah Eastop, "Matter Out of Place: Paradigms for Analyzing Textile Cleaning," *Journal of the American Institute for Conservation* 45 (2006): 176.

15. Ibid., 178.

16. See the United States Department of Agriculture's website on the Animal Welfare Act for an up-to-date description of the provisions of this law, accessed September 29, 2014, http://awic.nal.usda.gov/government-and-professional-resources/federal-laws/animal-welfare-act.

17. Paul N. Perrot, "Museum Ethics and Collecting Principles," in *Museum Ethics*, ed. Gary Edson (New York: Routledge, 1997), 191.

18. Wuichet and Norton point out that concern for the welfare of captive animals should be the foundation upon which all other directives for their care—conservation, education, science, and recreation—are based. John Wuichet and Bryan Norton, "Differing Conceptions of Animal Welfare," in *Ethics on the Ark: Zoos, Animal Welfare, and Wildlife Conservation*, ed. Bryan G. Norton, Michael Hutchins, Elizabeth Stevens, and Terry L. Maple (Washington, DC: Smithsonian Books, 1995), 278.

19. Ibid.

ADDITIONAL RESOURCES

American Institute for Conservation of Historic and Artistic Works. "About Us, Code of Ethics and Guidelines for Practice." American Institute for Conservation of Historic and Artistic Works website. Revised August 1994. http://www.conservation-us.org/about-us/core-documents/code-of-ethics#.U8ASu1ZcUso.

American Institute for Conservation of Historic and Artistic Works. "Commentaries to the Guidelines for Practice." American Institute for Conservation of Historic and Artistic Works website. Accessed July 11, 2014. http://www.conservation-us.org/about-us/core-documents/guidelines-for-practice#.U8ATd1ZcUso.

Hatchfield, Pamela, ed. *Ethics and Critical Thinking in Conservation.* Washington, DC: American Institute for Conservation of Historic & Artistic Works, 2013.

International Council of Museums—Committee for Conservation (ICOM-CC). "The Conservator-Restorer: A Definition of the Profession." Revised August 1984. International Council of Museums website. http://www.icom-cc.org/47/#.U80r9lZcUsp.

Journal of the American Institute for Conservation, vol. 45, no. 3 (Fall/Winter 2006). Maney Publishing. Special Issue on Cleaning.

Matero, Frank. "Ethics and Policy in Conservation." *The Getty Conservation Institute Newsletter*, vol. 15, no. 1 (Spring 2000). http://www.getty.edu/conservation/publications_resources/newsletters/15_1/feature1_2.html.

Norton, Bryan G., Michael Hutchins, Elizabeth Stevens, and Terry L. Maple, eds. *Ethics in the Ark: Zoos, Animal Welfare and Wildlife Conservation.* Washington, DC: Smithsonian Books, 1995.

Oddy, Andrew, ed. *Restoration: Is it Acceptable?* Occasional Paper 99, British Museum Occasional Papers. London: The British Museum, 1994.

Richmond, Alison and Alison Bracker, eds. *Conservation: Principles, Dilemmas and Uncomfortable Truths.* New York: Elsevier published in Association with the Victoria and Albert Museum London, 2009.

Stanley-Price, Nicholas, M. Kirby Talley, Jr., and Alessandra Melucco Vaccaro, eds. *Readings in Conservation: Historical and Philosophical Issues in the Conservation of Cultural Heritage.* Los Angeles: The Getty Conservation Institute, 1996.

Chapter 6

Ethical Dilemmas of Deaccessioning

Deaccessioning or removing items from museum collections is an accepted part of collection management in U.S. museums. The word *deaccession* refers to a two-part process—first, legally removing an item from a museum's collection, a procedure for which there are clear and detailed guidelines,[1] and second, disposing of the object. Although there are detailed procedures for disposition, this part of the deaccessioning process has become a flashpoint for controversy and is the source of most ethical dilemmas.

It is of primary importance that all museums address the deaccessioning and disposal processes in their collections management policy, particularly the circumstances under which they might deaccession an item. For example, the Collections Management Policy of the Metropolitan Museum of Art lists the following reasons for deaccessioning a work:

1. The object is not relevant to the mission of the Museum or has little value in the Museum's collection.
2. The object is redundant or is a duplicate and is not necessary for research or study purposes.
3. The object is of lesser quality than other objects of the same type in the collection or about to be acquired.
4. The object lacks sufficient aesthetic merit or art historical importance to warrant retention.
5. The Museum is ordered to return an object to its original and rightful owner by a court of law; the Museum determines that another entity is the rightful owner of the object; or the Museum determines that the return of the object is in the best interest of the Museum.
6. The Museum is unable to preserve the object in a responsible manner.
7. The object is unduly difficult or impossible to care for or store properly.[2]

Collection management policies should also detail the procedures to be followed in deaccessioning and disposal, especially policies regarding the purchase of deaccessioned items by museum trustees, staff, and volunteers, and acceptable uses of funds realized from deaccessioning. These policies should not only outline the procedures a museum would follow if it decides to deaccession an item, they also protect a museum against unnecessary accusations of impropriety. Nonetheless ethical dilemmas arise.

One important ethical question revolves around whether a museum's collections should be considered its financial assets. In 1990 the Financial Accounting Standards Board (FASB) proposed Financial Accounting Standards that would have required museums to capitalize their collections. As Stephen K. Urice notes, "Under the proposal, a museum could not receive an unqualified audit of its financial statements unless the museum appraised its collections and included that number as an asset on the museum's balance sheet."[3] Urice recounts, AAM mounted a campaign against such a requirement arguing, among other things, that "the inherent nature of museum collections . . . [is as] property held to accomplish education and charitable missions, not as assets available to support museums' capital or operating expenses."[4]

As a result, the FASB Statement of Financial Accounting Standards No. 116 encourages but does not require museums to capitalize their collections. FASB states that "Contributions of works of art, historical treasures, and similar assets" need not be recognized as revenues and capitalized if the donated items are added to collections held "for public exhibition, education, or research in furtherance of public service rather than financial gain."[5] In addition, the standards require that these collections "are protected, kept unencumbered, cared for, and preserved" and "are subject to an organizational policy that requires that proceeds from the sales of collection items . . . be used to acquire other items for collections."[6]

These regulations are echoed in the various professional codes of ethics. The American Alliance of Museums' Code states that a museum's collections must be "lawfully held, protected, secure, unencumbered, cared for and preserved."[7] It further stipulates that

- acquisition, disposal, and loan activities are conducted in a manner that respects the protection and preservation of natural and cultural resources and discourages illicit trade in such materials
- acquisition, disposal, and loan activities conform to its mission and public trust responsibilities
- disposal of collections through sale, trade or research activities is solely for the advancement of the museum's mission. Proceeds from the sale of nonliving collections are to be used consistent with the established standards of the museum's discipline, but in no event shall they be used for anything other than acquisition or direct care of collections.[8]

The code does not define "direct care of collections," but it has been generally accepted that this term does not include a museum's general operating expenses. In practice, American museums use funds for a range of collections-related purposes including conservation treatment, restoration, storage materials and/or equipment, security equipment, fire/smoke alarm systems, fire suppression systems, pest control, climate control, off-site storage costs, collections management systems, the construction of new collections storage areas, and the salaries of collections management, registrarial, and curatorial staff.

In 2014, the American Alliance of Museums appointed a Task Force to provide further guidance to the field on how to interpret "direct care of collections." The white paper resulting from the Task Force's work underscores the fact that museum collections are cultural, not financial assets. It encourages museums to separate the deaccessioning and disposal processes so as to avoid even the appearance that collections are being sold for financial gain, and it defines *direct care* as "an investment that enhances the life, usefulness and quality of a museum's collection." The white paper also formulates a series of questions to help guide museums in making decisions about how to use funds realized from the sale of deaccessioned objects.[9]

The American Association of State and Local History in its statement on Standards and Ethics similarly prohibits an organization from viewing its historical resources as financial assets and declares that they "shall not be capitalized."[10] The statement further specifies that "collections shall not be deaccessioned or disposed of in order to provide financial support for institutional operations, facilities maintenance or any reason other than preservation or acquisition of collections, as defined by institutional policy."[11] AASLH has also issued an "Ethics Position Paper on the Capitalization of Collections" that details the Association's position against capitalizing collections and provides guidelines for "interpreting, adopting, and implementing AASLH's position."[12]

The International Council of Museums' "Code of Ethics for Museums" goes into more details about the ethical issues related to the disposal of items from a museum's collection:

2.12 Legal or Other Powers of Disposal
Where the museum has legal powers permitting disposals, or has acquired objects subject to conditions of disposal, the legal or other requirements and procedures must be complied with fully. Where the original acquisition was subject to mandatory or other restrictions these conditions must be observed, unless it can be shown clearly that adherence to such restrictions is impossible or substantially detrimental to the institution and, if appropriate, relief may be sought through legal procedures.

2.13 Deaccessioning from Museum Collections
The removal of an object or specimen from a museum collection must only be undertaken with a full understanding of the significance of the item, its character (whether renewable or non-renewable), legal standing, and any loss of public trust that might result from such action.

2.14 Responsibility for Deaccessioning
The decision to deaccession should be the responsibility of the governing body acting in conjunction with the director of the museum and the curator of the collection concerned. Special arrangements may apply to working collections.

2.15 Disposal of Objects Removed from the Collections
Each museum should have a policy defining authorised methods for permanently removing an object from the collections through donation, transfer, exchange, sale, repatriation, or destruction, and that allows the transfer of unrestricted title to any receiving agency. Complete records must be kept of all deaccessioning decisions, the objects involved, and the disposal of the object. There will be a strong presumption that a deaccessioned item should first be offered to another museum.

2.16 Income from Disposal of Collections
Museum collections are held in public trust and may not be treated as a realizable asset. Money or compensation received from the deaccessioning and disposal of objects and specimens from a museum collection should be used solely for the benefit of the collection and usually for acquisitions to that same collection.

2.17 Purchase of Deaccessioned Collections
Museum personnel, the governing body, or their families or close associates, should not be permitted to purchase objects that have been deaccessioned from a collection for which they are responsible.

The Association of Art Museum Directors (AAMD) issued a "Policy on Deaccessioning"[13] that details the processes to be used by art museums when they are considering deaccessioning and also includes in its "A Code of Ethics for Art Museum Directors," a prohibition against deaccessioning that states, "In accordance with the AAMD's policy on deaccessioning and disposal, the director must not dispose of accessioned works of art in order to provide funds for purposes other than acquisitions of works of art for the collection."[14] Similarly, the College Art Association, the national organization of art historians, issued a "Statement Concerning the Deaccession of Works of Art," that states, "Deaccessions may be made *only* for the purposes of future acquisitions."[15]

Even if museums do not consider their collections' financial assets, most ethical dilemmas relating to the disposal of collections result from their perceived financial value. Some museums facing difficult financial circumstances can be tempted to use their collections as collateral for loans or other financial instruments, while others may find that deaccessioning could provide a source of income that will help them survive the threat of dissolution. Certainly the latter was the case with the Delaware Art Museum whose board of trustees decided to sell as many as four works from its collection of 12,500 to repay its debt after the museum lost its credit guarantee from its bank. The debt was incurred as a result of a $32 million expansion project in 2005. In order to finance the project, the museum took out $24.8 million in tax-exempt bonds.[16] The loan was guaranteed by the museum's bank but after the 2008 recession, the bank tightened its lending regulations, the museum's endowment decreased in value, and the museum projected a decrease in contributions from corporate and individual donors. Even after the museum reduced its number of employees, it could not meet the bank's lending requirements. The museum asked their major donors to guarantee the loan, looked into other refinancing options, considered merging with another cultural institution, and discussed restructuring the museum—all to no avail. So the board of the museum voted to deaccession up to four works of art to raise $30 million, which would pay off their current debt of $19.8 million and replenish the museum's endowment.[17] Sanctions from AAMD and the loss of accreditation from AAM did not deter the museum from their decision. Ultimately, one must ask whether a museum is being unethical in selling works from its collection when the alternative is closing the institution. Assuming that the four works to be sold become part of private collections, is it better for these to be lost to the public than to lose the remaining 12,500 artworks among which is the largest collection of British pre-Raphaelite art outside of the United Kingdom? There are no easy answers to these questions and it is perhaps no wonder that ethical dilemmas related to deaccessioning arouse passionate discussion and debate.

ETHICS IN ACTION

In the following hypothetical situations, all people and museums are fictional. The circumstances combine both the real and imagined with ethical dilemmas that occur in museums. Any resemblance to a real situation is purely coincidental.

Selling the "Family Jewels"

The PDQ Museum of Art is well known regionally for its large collection of art deco objects, including a fine collection of posters, jewelry, and decorative arts. Mrs. Bling, the wife of a board member, just donated 50 objects to the collection, all examples of art deco jewelry made in the United States in the 1920s and 1930s. All of the pieces in Mrs. Bling's donation jewelry are in fine condition and some are one-of-a-kind items that were later mass-produced. After accessioning the pieces, the curator of decorative arts decides to conduct one of her periodic reviews of the art deco collection. When she does that, she discovers that some of the other jewelry items held by the museum are very similar to those donated by Mrs. Bling but are in no way of equal quality. Some may even be copies of the originals donated by Mrs. Bling. The curator judges these pieces redundant and proposes that they be deaccessioned. She follows the PDQ deaccessioning procedures and the Collections Committee presents the proposed deaccession to the PDQ governing board for their approval. After the board approves the deaccession, the curator prepares to offer the work to a local art dealer who specializes in jewelry. As she is doing this, however, a volunteer from the registration department approaches her and inquires about several of the pieces. His wife, it turns out, is a collector of antique jewelry and he knows she would be interested in purchasing at least one if not more of the items in question.

Would it be unethical for the museum to sell the items to the volunteer's wife? Why? Would your answer be different if the curator were to turn down the volunteer's request but instead give him advance notice of the name of the dealer who would broker the sale? Would it be different if the jewelry were to be sold by a prominent national or international auction house rather than a local dealer?

Reviving History

Attendance at the 160-year-old Chambersville Historical Society is dwindling, and as a result, the organization's fundraising efforts are also in decline. Foundations talk about the importance of building new audiences and the society's individual donors' interest in history seems to be on the wane. The governing board has decided that the institution needs to project a more vital and energetic profile to its potential audience and that the way to do that is to display more of its collection of 33,000 objects. Space in the current building is limited, however, so a feasibility study is conducted to determine the best way to proceed. The board hires a group of consultants who specialize in "helping cultural institutions reach their full potential—raising new revenue, building new audiences, and creating success." The consultants recommend that the historical society revamp its image by hiring a famous architect to design an all-glass addition to the current building that will convey a transparent, open, and welcoming image to the community; they estimate that the project will cost approximately $9 million, which they feel is a realistic amount for the board to raise; and they project dramatically increased attendance as a result of these changes.

With half the funds raised, the historical society begins construction on the new addition, which everyone agrees will be spectacular. Fund raising continues apace, but construction costs exceed estimates by $3 million. In order to finish the building project on time and on schedule, the board must figure out how to find the financial resources they need. One board member offers to approach the state government for a contribution of $2 million to the building campaign; but even if this appeal is successful, it is unlikely that funds will be available for at least one year. Another board member agrees to put more pressure on local corporations to increase their contributions, and a third suggests approaching the local bank for a loan of $3 million. He reassures the rest of the board members by pointing out that this is likely to be a relatively short-term need. When the board approaches the local bank, however, they are told that a loan of $3 million must be secured with a pledge of the society's collections as collateral.

Would it be unethical for the historical society to move forward with borrowing the funds they need in order to complete their building project? What are other options that it might pursue that would satisfy the bank without using the collections as collateral?

Extra Buses

The Midwest Transport Museum has a collection of carriages, buses, and trains that tell the story of transportation on wheels in the mid-west from the time of the region's settlement through to the present. The collection includes a number of large vehicles as well as smaller objects, toys, and ephemera related to the vehicles. Vehicle storage space is tight and the museums is considering an expansion; but before embarking upon such a large project, they decide to assess all of the collections to determine their condition as well as their present and future conservation and storage needs. In the course of the assessment, the newly hired registrar confirms what she has been told by the curatorial staff—that the museum owns a number of large vehicles that have not been maintained on a regular basis and, as a result, cannot be exhibited. The registrar discovers that most of these vehicles are buses and that they are virtually duplicates of other buses in the collection that are in better, exhibitable condition.

The registrar is a newcomer to the area. In her enthusiasm for uncovering all that the region has to offer, she finds out that there are a number of transportation buffs in nearby towns. These enthusiasts satisfy their passion for all things on wheels by collecting, repairing, and driving old vehicles. They are especially proud of their annual bus rodeo where they compete, driving and showing off their latest acquisitions and sharing stories of the solutions they have found for repairing buses that need parts that are no longer manufactured. They also occasionally take the buses to rodeos in other parts of the country, showing them off to groups far and wide. After meeting some of the transportation buffs and talking with them about their hobby, the registrar begins to devise a way to deal with the museum's bus surfeit.

At the next Collections Committee meeting, the registrar proposes that the museum deaccession its redundant buses, thereby freeing up much-needed conservation resources and storage space. Furthermore, she recommends that the museum donate the seven buses to the local volunteer enthusiasts, believing that with their interest and enthusiasm, the buses would take on a new life as part of the local community. Another member of the committee, an educator who sees the buses on the meeting's agenda, raises another possibility. She tells the committee that she has just learned that the town's private school is looking for a new fleet of buses. The school's in-house mechanics have the capacity to repair the museum's buses and make them operable so that they could be used to transport the school's students. The educator adds, "And, I talked with one of the teachers at the school and she thinks that the school would be willing to pay for our buses!"

Would it be unethical for the museum to deaccession the buses and dispose of them to the local volunteer enthusiasts, as the registrar suggests? Would your answer be different if the museum decides to sell them to the private school? Why? What should the museum consider in making this decision?

Leaking Roof

The Pottersville Museum of History, Art, and Science has long been the only museum in its county. The museum has weathered many changes since it was founded in the late nineteenth century. The remaining members of its founding family not only left the county but also the state for a warmer climate. Their friends and many of the other museum supporters did the same. The local industries whose leaders were the second wave of supporters for the History Museum have all moved away or gone out of business. Board membership has declined, but the stalwart few who remain are dedicated to ensuring that the museum remain relevant to the local population and provide the kinds of high quality exhibitions and programs for which it has acquired renown. Fund raising is always a challenge and after the latest economic downturn, the board is feeling exhausted. The director delivers the news that the roof is falling in. In response, a board member suggests that the museum sell several of its collection of tall case clocks. He notes that, unlike others in the collection, these clocks were not made in Pottersville, although they were acquired from families who lived in the region. He noted, "They're just sitting in storage; we never exhibit them. Why, I saw that a similar tall case clock sold recently at Sotheby's for close to $200,000. If we sold two of them, we could pay for the roof and no one would ever miss the clocks."

Would it be unethical for the museum to sell the clocks? Would your answer be different if you did not know that the board wanted to use the proceeds from the sale of the clocks to repair the roof?

A Hotbed of Contemporary Art

The Elktown Museum of Art has been a fixture in the cultural life of the city of Elktown for close to seventy-five years. Housed in a former municipal office building constructed in the early twentieth century, its collections include hundreds of European paintings by academically trained artists, and its mission is to preserve and interpret nineteenth-century academic art. Today, the museum manages to hold its own, largely serving school groups from Elktown and some of the surrounding suburbs, but does not have a strong following in the local community. Lovers of European painting visit a larger museum, about 90 minutes away, which has a collection with more scope and is one of the finest regional art museums in the country. Elktown's museum is open for limited hours—from Tuesday through Friday from 10:00 a.m. until 5:00 p.m. and on Saturday from 10:00 a.m. until 1:00 p.m.— and does not conduct much public programming because of the limited funds and lack of community interest. The staff is made up largely of volunteers with a paid part-time staff of four. The museum's building, which is close to one hundred years old, is beginning to show signs of age.

Jeff Splash, an investment banker who has lived in Elktown all of his life, has indulged in his passion for contemporary art by amassing a significant collection. He has no heirs and wants to contribute his artworks to the town where he was born and has lived most of his life, but he does not want his collection housed in the somewhat dilapidated building of the art museum. Further, he doesn't believe that nineteenth-century academic art and contemporary pieces like those by Koons, Warhol, and Pashke "go together." He lays down the gauntlet and tells the museum that either the "old things" must go, or he will give his collection to another museum in a neighboring town. Further, he demands that the museum upgrade its galleries and collections storage areas before the donation becomes official, so that all climate control systems are state of the art to protect his collections. The local community is thrilled with the prospect of revitalizing the museum and finds Jeff Splash's offer one that they believe will accomplish that goal. In fact if the collection is to be donated to the art museum, many people in the local community envision the town becoming a magnet for tourism and a hotbed of contemporary art.

Assuming that all of the nineteenth-century paintings have no restrictions on them that would prohibit their deaccessioning, would it be unethical for the museum to deaccession them in order to secure the funds to upgrade its facility and acquire Jeff Splash's contemporary art collection? What role would the community's support for acquiring the Splash collection play in your decision? Should the museum comply with Splash's demands?

After the registrar investigates the collections records, he discovers that three of the finest paintings have restrictions upon them that would require a *cy pres* proceeding[18] in a local court. This process would delay the ability of the museum to answer Mr. Splash within the sixty-day period he has imposed upon the museum to respond to his offer. Further research shows that the value of each of the art works with restrictions is between $300,000 and $500,000. The rest of the paintings would probably not yield much more than a total of $500,000 at auction. The renovation is projected to cost between $1.5 and $2 million. Would your answer to the above questions be different given these facts?

FINAL THOUGHTS

Museums hold their collections to benefit the public. While these accumulated objects might have significant value if they were offered for sale in the marketplace, the fact that they have been donated to or acquired by a museum means that their monetary value is of lesser importance than their value as part of our artistic, cultural, and/or natural heritage. Part of a museum's responsibility in caring for its collections is ensuring that these objects remain in the public domain. Nonetheless, when a museum discovers through a collections assessment, that objects or works of art under its care are either not consistent with its mission or not feasible to maintain, deaccession and disposal may well be considered.

Many museum collections contain hundreds of objects, donated or collected over time, which have little relevance to the museum's mission and which have scarcely seen the light of an exhibition gallery or been the subject of a research request. They remain in storage, taking up space and institutional resources. For these museums, deaccessioning should be a tool to better collections management. A case in point is described by Terri Anderson in "Too Museum of a Good Thing: Lessons from Deaccessioning at National Historic Trust Sites."[19] The Woodrow Wilson House in Washington, DC, discovered 234 doilies in its collections that were unrelated to those donated by Mrs. Wilson in the original 1961 bequest. Documentation for these doilies was scant and the original doily collection donated by Mrs. Wilson was sufficient for doily-related programming or interpretation.[20] In deaccessioning and disposing of the 234 doilies, the Woodrow Wilson House was able to free up storage space and relieve themselves of the expenses of storing these items that were not central to their mission.

The determination to deaccession and dispose of items should be guided by the museum's collections management policy or an independent deaccessioning policy. As Malaro points out, deaccessioning should be as deliberate and careful as the decision-making process for acquisition, if not more so.[21] In addition, the process of deciding whether to deaccession an object should be made separately from the determination of the means of its disposal. In no event should the potential monetary value of an object or work of art be considered as part of the decision to deaccession.[22]

When a museum wishes to dispose of a deaccessioned item of value, it should first offer the item to other museums, either for sale or in exchange for a comparable piece, thus ensuring that the object remains in the public domain. In some cases, simply transferring a work or an entire collection to another museum might be appropriate. Consider the collaboration between the Brooklyn Museum of Art and the Metropolitan Museum—a model of its kind.[23] Finding that it did not have the resources to maintain its costume collection, the Brooklyn Museum brokered an agreement with the Metropolitan Museum, which had the capacity to both care for and exhibit the collection. Under the agreement, the Brooklyn Museum continues to have access to the collection for research and exhibitions, and each time the Met displays one of the costumes from this collection, it is credited as part of the Brooklyn Museum Costume Collection.

Only when all possible avenues for transfer or sale to another public institution are exhausted should a museum have the option of selling the object in question. Public sale is preferred over private, and transparency of the sale process is important to maintaining the museum's integrity. Disclosure of the fact that the museum is selling objects or artworks from its collection should be made in the sales catalog as well as the purposes to which funds received from the sale will be put. Keeping records of deaccessioned objects and their disposal is an important aspect of the process. Both should be documented in the museum's collection management records. And finally, use of the proceeds from the object or artwork's sale should support the mission of the museum and ultimately redound to the benefit of the public.

NOTES

1. For a discussion of the deaccessioning and disposal processes, see Rebecca Buck and Jean Gilmore, eds., *Museum Registration Methods 5th edition* (Washington, DC: American Association of Museums Press, 2010); Marie Malaro and Ildiko

Pogany DeAngelis discuss the legal and ethical issues in Malaro and DeAngelis, *Legal Primer on Managing Museum Collections*, 248–72.

2. Metropolitan Museum of Art, "Collections Management Policy," last revised June 10, 2014, http://www.metmuseum.org/about-the-museum/collections-management-policy#care.

The Association of Art Museum Directors (AAMD) provides a similar list of criteria for deaccessioning and disposal in "AAMD Policy on Deaccessioning," 2010, Association of Art Museum Directors website, https://aamd.org/standards-and-practices.

3. Stephen K. Urice, "Deaccessioning: A Few Observations," American Law Institute—American Bar Association Continuing Legal Education, *Legal Issues in Museum Administration,* SR005 ALI-ABA 207 (2010).

4. Ibid.

5. Financial Accounting Standards Board, "Summary of Statement No. 116: Accounting for Contributions Received and Contributions Made," 1993, Financial Accounting Standards Board website, http://www.fasb.org/jsp/FASB/Pronouncement_C/SummaryPage&cid=900000010226.

6. Financial Accounting Standards Board, Statement No. 116: Accounting for Contributions Received and Contributions Made," FAS116-4, 1993. Financial Accounting Standards Board website, http://www.fasb.org/jsp/FASB/Document_C/DocumentPage?cid=1218220128831&acceptedDisclaimer=true.

7. American Alliance of Museums, "Code of Ethics for Museums," American Alliance of Museums website, amended 2000, http://www.aam-us.org/resources/ethics-standards-and-best-practices/code-of-ethics.

8. Ibid.

9. American Alliance of Museums, "Direct Care of Collections: Ethics, Guidelines and Recommendations," to be issued in 2016.

10. American Association for State and Local History, "Publication: AALH Statement of Professional Standards and Ethics," American Association for State and Local History website, updated June 2012, http://resource.aaslh.org/view/aaslh-statement-of-professional-standards-and-ethics/.

11. Ibid.

12. American Association for State and Local History, "Technical Leaflet: Ethics Position Paper: The Capitalization of Collections," American Association of State and Local History website, Fall 2003, http://resource.aaslh.org/view/ethics-position-paper-the-capitalization-of-collections/.

13. Association of Art Museum Directors, "AAMD Policy on Deaccessioning," Association of Art Museum Directors website, 2010, https://aamd.org/standards-and-practices.

14. Association of Art Museum Directors, "A Code of Ethics for Art Museum Directors," in "Professional Practices in Art Museums," 2011, 17–18, https://aamd.org/sites/default/files/document/2011ProfessionalPracitiesinArtMuseums.pdf.

15. College Art Association, "Statement Concerning the Deaccession of Works of Art," revised October 27, 2013, College Art Association website, http://www.collegeart.org/guidelines/sales.

16. Margie Fishman, "Museum to Sell Art to Pay Debt," *The News Journal*, March 27, 2014, http://www.delawareonline.com/story/entertainment/arts/2014/03/26/delaware-art-museum-sell-four-works/6913117/.

17. Ibid.

18. "*cy pres*: the doctrine in the law of charities whereby when it becomes impossible, impracticable, or illegal to carry out the particular purpose of the donor a scheme will be framed by a court to carry out the general intention by applying the gift to charitable purposes that are closely related or similar to the original purposes." From Stephen E. Weil, "Deaccession Practices in American Museums," in *Rethinking the Museum and Other Meditations* (Washington, DC: Smithsonian Institution Press, 1990), 117, fn. 7.

19. Terri Anderson, "Too Museum of a Good Thing: Lessons from Deaccessioning at National Trust Historic Sites," in *Museums and the Disposals Debate*, ed. Peter Davies (Edinburgh: MuseumsEtc, 2011), 230–53.

20. Ibid., 231.

21. Malaro and DeAngelis, *A Legal Primer on Managing Museum Collections*, Chapter Five.

22. Ibid.

23. Metropolitan Museum of Art, "The Brooklyn Museum Costume Collection," by Kevin Stayton, Chief Curator, Brooklyn Museum, Metropolitan Museum of Art Website, accessed October 24, 2014, http://www.metmuseum.org/research/curatorial-research/the-costume-institute/american-woman-symposium/collection-sharing/brooklyn-museum-costume-collection. This article provides an excellent overview of the history of the Brooklyn Museum's costume collection and the collaboration developed with the Metropolitan Museum of Art.

ADDITIONAL RESOURCES

Davies, Peter, ed. *Museums and the Disposals Debate.* Edinburgh: MuseumsEtc, 2011.

Weil, Stephen E., ed. *A Deaccession Reader.* Washington, DC: American Association of Museums, 1997.

Chapter 7

Ethical Problems Related to Fundraising and Other Income-Producing Activities

Museums raise money for their operations in a number of ways—they raise money from individuals, foundations, and corporations, and they earn income from providing services and programs, admissions, shop and restaurant sales, and the like. Because museums operate for the public benefit, all of the ways that they generate money can be openly scrutinized, and it is important for them to be as open as possible about their financial dealings to avoid the appearance of impropriety.

The need to raise funds has become a fact of life for museums in the United States. Even museums supported by government funding must seek private support for special projects, and museums with generous endowments find that they rarely generate enough income to satisfy their financial needs. Thus, museums, like most other arts organizations, usually find it necessary to seek support from individuals, foundations, and corporations in order to mount exhibitions, develop special programs, and maintain and expand their facilities. This situation challenges museums to deal with incidental aspects of fundraising that may involve ethical problems. For example, some donors may attempt to influence the content of a project they support; others may expect special recognition or personal services in return for their contribution. As wealth becomes concentrated in the hands of fewer individuals and businesses, the sources from which to seek philanthropic dollars will decrease. Consequently, donors may subject museums to increased pressure to control the museum's use of the funds they donate, creating potential conflicts of interest or the appearance of such conflicts.[1] More and more, museums will be confronted with situations in which their integrity as independent educational institutions working to benefit the public will be tested and they will need to be vigilant to ensure that they retain their reputations as reliable, responsible entities.

Of course, museums have always been subject to pressure from donors whether the donors give objects or contribute financial support. But with the increasing concentration of wealth and the rise of different kinds of support from businesses as well as social entrepreneurs, giving to museums has changed and more challenges to the integrity of a museum's exhibitions and programs are arising. For example, in recent years corporate support has evolved from relatively straightforward philanthropic contributions, usually made through a corporation's foundation or other entity created to demonstrate its social responsibility, to corporate sponsorships that are "not giving to benefit society but . . . contracting for marketing opportunities"[2] and are developed through the business's marketing or advertising arm. As a senior vice president for public relations of a major U.S. corporation that supports the arts wrote, "Sponsorships are much more focused on marketing and sales. When someone comes to us with a request to sponsor an event, we're looking for heavy exposure of our logo. We want to build our brand. We want to enhance our market position. We are seeking to help build earnings. Often, we want to use sponsorships for customer entertainment, so the sponsorship has to be relevant and attractive to our customers."[3] Malaro and DeAngelis warn, "The dangers for museums in this change of emphasis are substantial."[4] Beyond the obvious problem of sponsors determining what exhibitions are mounted, there is a more insidious issue. "More often the pressure comes from within the museum itself, where curators know that if their exhibitions hope to see the light of day, their ideas must appeal to sponsors and to audiences that sponsors hope to reach. In effect, the choice of exhibitions is governed by the marketplace."[5]

In a similar vein, according to Merryman, Elsen, and Urice, "A museum often has to make difficult choices about where to draw the line between propriety and cupidity, generating revenue and selling out, accepting a helping hand and opening itself up to undue influence."[6] And they add, "Some of the concessions now being made to business sponsors by museums . . . are debatable rather than clearly unacceptable," citing the instance of the "Corcoran Gallery of Art in Washington permitting Ford to put a car on display outside an exhibition the company sponsored." In the case of "New York's Metropolitan Museum giving itself over to wedding receptions in return for a donation of $550,000 . . . public mockery forced it to beat an embarrassed retreat."[7]

Marlaro and DeAngelis are further concerned with the impact that the increase in corporate sponsorships might have on the "spirit of philanthropy. Museums . . . depend heavily on donations of objects, money, and time from the general public. Why do museums afford corporate sponsors special treatment? Should individual donors or lenders now expect some quid pro quo?"[8]

Professional organizations provide guidance to museums by issuing standards related directly to fundraising activities as well as addressing the larger issue of undue donor influence in their codes of ethics. The American Alliance of Museum's Code of Ethics for Museums addresses fundraising under the section on governance, declaring that the museum's "governing authority ensures that . . . the museum's collections and programs and its physical, human and financial resources are protected, maintained and developed in support of the museum's mission" and "governance promotes the public good rather than individual financial gain."[9]

AAM supports the Association of Fundraising Professionals Code of Ethical Principles and Standards as a source for detailed guidance concerning the solicitation and use of philanthropic funds[10] and provides further direction in its "Standards Regarding Developing and Managing Business and Individual Donor Support."[11] This document urges museums to maintain consistency in their fundraising practices by developing policies regarding individual and business support. First and foremost, a museum's policy should "address the obligation of members of the staff or governing authority to disclose any interest in the [funding] relationship under consideration" so that the museum might avoid a conflict of interest or even the appearance of one.[12]

A museum's policies should address the issue of who in the museum (including governing board members and staff) has the authority to communicate with donors, making or changing agreements with them, and the policies should define how much information (financial, tax and legal) the museum will share with its supporters. These policies should also define the types of support that would be acceptable to the museum as well as the process that it will follow to determine if support from a certain donor or business is appropriate.[13] This might include, for example, a children's museum stating explicitly in its fundraising policy that it will not accept support from industries that promote or produce alcohol, handguns, and cigarettes or a conservation society or zoo ruling out support from businesses that use animals for research.

In addition, AAM recommends that a museum should develop standards for donor recognition based upon the level of support it receives; "should ensure that a relationship of trust is established and maintained with its donors by respecting the private nature of information about the donor and the donation" while balancing its "obligation to maintain public accountability"; define "whether and under what circumstances it will accept anonymous gifts"; determine how it will handle uncollectable pledges, should the need arise; and require record keeping regarding donations "in accordance with applicable law and record-retention policies." The AAM Standards also note, "A museum should respond to all public and media inquiries about its support from businesses and individual donors, including allegation of unethical behavior, with a prompt, full and frank discussion of the issue, the institution's action and the rationale for such actions a museum must be prepared for inquiries from the media and the public concerning its fundraising."[14]

Further, the standards identify areas where problems might arise when a museum accepts support from a business. They encourage museums to clarify how it will allow its name and logo to be used by a business supporter as well as how the museum-business relationship may be promoted by the business concern. They note that vendors should not be required to contribute to the museum and urge museums to be cautious about entering into an exclusive relationship with a business entity—that is, one that will restrict its ability to raise funds from similar businesses.[15]

Finally a conflict of interest or the appearance of a conflict can arise when a funder of an exhibition loans an object or objects to the exhibition. AAM addresses this situation in its "Standards Regarding Exhibiting Borrowed Objects" by stating that museums should "make public the source of funding [for an exhibition] when the lender is also a funder of the exhibition. If a museum receives a request for anonymity, the museum should avoid such anonymity where it would conceal a conflict of interest (real or perceived) or raise other ethical issues."[16]

The standards concerning borrowed objects also discuss the importance of museums having a policy concerning the possibility of earning revenue from the sale of objects borrowed for an exhibition. According to AAM such a policy should prohibit "the museum from accepting any commission or fee from the sale of objects borrowed for exhibition."[17] In other words, if a museum borrows a painting from a private collector and that painting is sold as a result of the exhibition or shortly thereafter, it is improper for the museum to receive a fee from the sale.

In fact, some museums like the Metropolitan Museum of Art include provisions in their codes of ethics. The Met states that "while loans of works of art by a Trustee to the Museum can be of great benefit to the Museum, it should be recognized that exhibition of a work of art at the Museum can enhance its value. A Trustee should not lend any work of art to the Museum or maintain it on loan if he or she is actively planning to sell it."[18]

In its "Professional Practices in Art Museums," the Association of Art Museum Directors (AAMD) states that

- Particular care must be taken to assure that fundraising is conducted in a manner consistent with professional standards. The museum should avoid any fund-raising practices that could damage the community's trust or its respect for the institution. The concept of public benefit rather than private benefit to individuals or taxable entities should apply while recognizing that a variety of stake-holders may incidentally benefit from fundraising activities.
- Sources of financial support should be publicly disclosed whenever possible. Requests for anonymity should be respected, except where doing so would conceal a real or perceived conflict of interest. The museum must retain artistic control at all times; sources of financial support must not be allowed to compromise or unduly influence the integrity of any program.[19]

AAMD's policies on "Managing the Relationship between Art Museums and Corporate Sponsors"[20] warn that as American businesses increasingly view art museums "as venues for sponsorship both to serve the public interest and to address corporate relations and marketing goals," this support "presents challenges to ensure that the museum's artistic integrity and educational mission is not compromised by external commercial interests."[21]

AAMD lists a series of questions that each of its museums should answer before accepting corporate sponsorship or support, including the following:

- Are the corporation's reputation, values, products and services consistent with the museum's and its community's standards of quality and integrity?
- Is the corporation's approach to sponsorship responsible and respectful of the museum's mission and program?
- Are the corporation's motives in supporting the arts transparent and acceptable to the museum? Is there a real or perceived conflict of interest in accepting this support?
- Are the requests for recognition beyond what the museum would normally offer to donors?
- Does the corporation seek input and/or influence on the content of the sponsored program?
- Is the corporation's sponsorship—in terms of public perception and the image and practice of the museum—ultimately a benefit that supports the museum's fulfillment of its mission?[22]

These questions are useful in navigating the potential ethical issues that corporate sponsorship might present to all museums.

AAMD's "Revenue Generation: An Investment in the Public Service of Art Museums" provides comparable guidance concerning revenue generation.[23]

The American Association for State and Local History (AASLH) addresses possible ethical issues related to fundraising and earned income in their "Statement of Professional Standards and Ethics." Regarding fundraising, it notes, "Historical organizations and their representatives must protect the integrity of their institutions from both the reality and the appearance of undue influence by donors, sponsors and other sources of financial support."[24] Guidance for revenue-producing activities is more detailed:

Activities that involve the marketing and sale of products, programs, services, and facilities are acceptable ways to produce support revenues and increase public awareness of, and participation in, historical activities.

A. No such activities shall be undertaken that violate or compromise the integrity of an institution's mission, the ability of an institution or individual to meet professional standards or an institution's not-for-profit status.
B. Control of products (e.g., exhibitions, publications, collections, programs) shall neither be delegated nor abrogated to outside parties in order to obtain financial support.

C. Historical organizations shall review the potential cultural sensitivity of materials considered for commercial use with representatives of the appropriate affiliated communities.

Like AAM, the International Council of Museums (ICOM) addresses fundraising and financial support in the section of their Code of Ethics section on governance stating the following:

1.9 Funding
The governing body should ensure that there are sufficient funds to carry out and develop the activities of the museum. All funds must be accounted for in a professional manner.

1.10 Income-generating Policy
The governing body should have a written policy regarding sources of income that it may generate through its activities or accept from outside sources. Regardless of funding source, museums should maintain control of the content and integrity of their programmes, exhibitions and activities. Income-generating activities should not compromise the standards of the institution or its public.

Additionally in the section of the ICOM Code on the communities served by a museum and those represented in its collection, the Code states, "When seeking funds for activities involving contemporary communities, their interests should not be compromised."[25]

All of the professional organizations focus upon the concern that museums should ensure that fundraising does not undermine their purpose—income-generating activities should instead support the institution's mission and promote activities for the public benefit. These codes of ethics also underscore the necessity of avoiding any conflict of interest with funding sources or any perception of such a conflict, whether individual or corporate. Transparency is key. While these mandates may seem straightforward, exceptions abound. Moreover, the public has become increasingly sensitive to issues surrounding sources of nonprofit funding, opening museums to public scrutiny not just for the content of their exhibitions but also for the sources of support that make these programs possible.

For example, groups concerned with climate change and global warming have recently questioned the appropriateness of oil industrialist David H. Koch's involvement with several major museums. One of the country's wealthiest individuals, Koch is also a generous philanthropist, supporting the arts, education, and medical research. He is known to be skeptical about man-made or anthropogenic climate change and politically conservative on some issues.[26] Koch is an Emeritus Trustee of the Metropolitan

Museum of Art, on the Board of Trustees of the American Museum of Natural History and the Advisory Board of the Smithsonian's National Museum of Natural History. While his influence at the Met, where he served as a trustee and donated $65 million to fund a renovation of the plaza in front of the museum, may not have swayed the Met Board in their decisions about the content of programs or exhibitions, his funding of the plaza makeover led some individuals to criticize the Met's willingness to accept his support because they did not agree with his political and environmental views.[27] In addition, many artists and environmentally concerned groups have wondered if his support of the two natural history museums has led the museums to soft pedal information about the negative impact of oil companies' practices on climate change in their current exhibitions.[28]

Other objections regarding the sources of museums' funding are more general in nature. In London protestors singled out exhibitions at the Tate Modern and the National Gallery because both museums refused to reveal details of their financial relationships with BP (British Petroleum), the company considered responsible for a massive oil spill in 2010.[29] And artists participating in the São Paulo Biennial called upon the show's organizers to return money they received from Israel because of its actions in Gaza. The artists argued, "It is clear that the sources of cultural funding have an increasingly dramatic impact on the supposedly 'independent' curatorial and artistic narrative of an event."[30] The protests against Israeli support led the organizers to remove the Israeli Embassy logo from their banners and promotional materials.

At a time of heightened public scrutiny of nonprofits with increasingly rapid communication over the Internet and social media, it is clear that museums need to be attentive to these controversies, even when they appear to unnecessarily politicize the matter at hand. The above-cited examples raise numerous questions worthy of consideration, if only to better prepare a museum for dealing with a controversy over corporate or business support arise. One can ask whether a museum should be concerned about the business reputation of its sponsors. If a museum accepts support from a sponsor with a reputation for acting unethically, will that reputation redound upon the museum? Should a corporation's practices influence a museum's decision about whether to accept the corporation's support? Would it be unethical to accept a donation from a corporation for an exhibition on a topic in which the corporation has involvement or interest, even if the corporation doesn't demand control over the exhibition? Would it be unethical for the museum management or staff to alter their perspective on an exhibition just because a representative of a corporation is on the board, whether or not he has provided support for the exhibition and not influenced its content? The following cases, both hypothetical and real, explore other instances of possible ethical difficulty surrounding fundraising to increase a museum's revenues. Not all raise distinct ethical issues but they do indicate some of the gray areas that emerge when sensitivities about financial support are heightened.

ETHICS IN ACTION

With the exception of Camille O. and William H. Cosby, Jr. and the Smithsonian's National Museum of African Art, all of the names of people and institutions in the following cases are fictional. The hypothetical situations are composites of real and fictional circumstances and reflect actual issues faced by museums. Any resemblance to an identifiable museum is purely coincidental.

Mr. Bad Guy

Joe Gangster has a formidable reputation for unlawful and unethical activity in business. Nothing stands in his way when he wants to make a business deal. Although never convicted of a crime, he has been arrested many times and is suspected of being the leader of the mafia in an oil-rich nation. Although much of his business is abroad, his primary residence is in a mid-Western American city where he lives in a lavish mansion in the "best" neighborhood. He is getting older and has begun to think about wanting to leave a positive mark upon his home city. He has always been a member of the Science and Industry Museum (SIM, for short), contributing modest gifts each year and occasionally attending exhibition openings when he is in town. He has just heard that SIM is planning a major capital campaign—the museum wants to expand its facility and create a major center for "Science and the Future." Joe admires the work that SIM does and is convinced that, if the museum had the money to involve the world's best futurologists and use cutting-edge technology, the new center could position SIM in the forefront of science museums both nationally and internationally. He wants to help make this happen and approaches the museum about being a major donor to help ensure that the Hall of Science and the Future is built and is successful. Would it be unethical for the museum to accept money from him, given his notorious background? Would your answer be different if you knew that Joe would only support the museum's expansion project if the Hall of Science and the Future were named after him?

Borrowing Objects

The Smithsonian's National Museum of African Art mounted an exhibition on the occasion of its fiftieth anniversary that reflected upon its beginnings when it was a neighborhood museum that displayed both African and African American artwork. This exhibition, *"Conversations: African and African American Artworks in Dialogue,"* juxtaposed African works from the museum's collections with African American artworks from the collection of Camille O. and William H. Cosby, Jr. Although known to be significant, the Cosbys' collection had not been exhibited publically prior to the mounting of "Conversations."[31]

Coincident with the exhibition's opening, fifteen women made allegations of sexual abuse against Mr. Cosby. Questions were raised about the appropriateness of a national museum displaying works from his collection given these circumstances and, as a result, the museum made the following statement:[32]

The National Museum of African Art's mission is to inspire conversations about the beauty, power and diversity of African arts and cultures. We began planning for the *Conversations* exhibition two years ago to help showcase the history of American art created by persons of African descent. It brings the public's attention to artists whose works have long been omitted from the study of American art history. We are aware of the controversy surrounding Bill Cosby, who, along with his wife Camille, owns many of the works in the *Conversations* exhibition. Exhibiting this important collection does not imply any position on the serious allegations that have been made against Mr. Cosby. The exhibition is centrally about the artworks and the artists who created them.[33]

Is this an adequate response? Should the museum return the Cosby collection because of the accusations made about Mr. Cosby's alleged abusive behavior?

It turns out that Mrs. Cosby serves on the museum's advisory board. Knowing this fact, would you consider the Cosbys' loan of the paintings to the exhibition a real or apparent conflict of interest? Would your answer be different if you knew what Mrs. Cosby's role was in the decision-making process concerning the "Conversations" exhibition? Would your answer be different if you knew that Mrs. Cosby had also given the museum a substantial grant to support the exhibition's development? What policies or procedures might the museum have in place to address the issues that this situation presents?

Finally, questions were raised among the public about whether a museum should display works from private collections without having an understanding that the works will be donated to the museum at a later date.[34] Indeed, some museums have a practice that requires that the private collections they display be promised to them to avoid even the appearance of possible personal benefit to the lender, for the exhibition in a museum of any work validates that work by confirming its attribution, raising its profile, and also possibly enhancing its value in the marketplace. The collection of the National

Museum of African Art focuses upon African rather than African American art, so it would be unlikely that the Cosby collection would be an appropriate addition to their holdings. Does this fact alter your opinion of whether it was ethically proper or improper for the museum to show the Cosby's collection?

Money and Mission

The Flashy Museum of Art, dedicated to cultivating a love for beauty through art, is having financial problems. Income is down due to the fact that many of the supporters of the museum are giving money to new cultural organizations that have recently opened in the region. The museum is making plans to reduce the number of temporary exhibits it produces, cut back the hours during which it is open to the public, and lay off a number of staff members including several in the education department to help reduce costs for the coming fiscal year. Suddenly the chair of the museum's governing authority calls a special executive committee meeting and announces to the committee that he thinks he has found a solution to the museum's current problems. A friend of his has just told him that the Science for All Foundation is willing to give the museum a large grant to expand its educational program offerings for schoolchildren from kindergarten through the twelfth grade. The chair reports that when he pointed out to his friend that the Flashy Museum is dedicated to art and not to science, the friend responded, "Oh, don't worry about it. Other art museums have been funded to do the same kinds of projects. We don't have a problem with that." The chair explains to the executive committee that the grant would provide ample support to retain the museum's current staff, make the layoffs unnecessary, cover the cost of any scientific equipment required for the programs, and underwrite transportation to the museum for students in schools throughout the whole region. But the support would have to be used to underwrite science programs. The chair emphasizes how this grant would solve the museum's financial difficulties for the next five years. The director concedes that the Flashy staff is highly creative and even might be able to come up with a way of using some of the museum's art collections for science programming, but she quickly calculates that the science education project would have to be the focus for most of the museum's educators, leaving only one educator free to continue all of the current school and family programs that relate directly to the museum's mission of "cultivating a love for beauty through art."

Would it be unethical for the Flashy Museum of Art to accept this grant and devote the majority of its resources to providing science education? Would it be acceptable if the science programs supported by the grant made 50 percent of the art on display relevant to science?

Not all of the executive committee members could be present at their meeting and the chair suggests that the committee reconvene in a week when Mr. Fred Flashy, Jr., the one remaining heir of the museum's founder, can take part in the discussion about whether to pursue funding from Science for All. When the committee reconvenes, Mr. Flashy, Jr. reveals that he recently uncovered a letter from his father that explained his motivation behind founding the museum. The letter goes into great detail about Fred Flashy's disdain for the science classes he had to take in school and his belief that it was his exposure to the performing and visual arts that led to his success not only in school but also in his business career. As a result he founded the museum to keep the arts before the public eye and ensure their prominence in the region. Does this additional information change your view about whether the Flashy should move forward with Science for All funding?

Storage

The local natural history museum has been cultivating a major donor, Mr. Big Bucks for a number of years. Each year Mr. Bucks has increased his contribution to the museum. The museum hopes that he will eventually make a substantial bequest to the museum and the donor has, in fact, hinted at this possibility to the museum's director several times. The museum has just completed the construction of a new collection storage facility and for the first time is able to house all of its scientific specimens as well as its global art and material culture collections in safe, climate-controlled spaces. There is even ample space to house additions to the collection for the foreseeable future. Mr. Bucks noticed this fact during a recent tour of the new space. It turns out that he collects watercolors and has a large collection of paintings. The storage facility that he is currently using to house his collection, however, is slated to close and he will have to relocate his collection. Several weeks after his tour of the new storage, Mr. Bucks telephones the museum director and asks if he might use the storage space for his collections while he looks for new space. He expects to be able to find the space in a year or two and since the museum has so much extra space, he reasons that it is unlikely that storing his collection will create a shortage of storage space for the museum's own artifacts and specimens. He asks the museum's director when someone on the staff can pick up his collection to transport it to the museum.

Would it be unethical for the museum to store Mr. Bucks' collection? Would your answer be different if you knew that Mr. Bucks would pay a fee to the museum to store his collection?

During the negotiations about the storage of Mr. Bucks' collection, the registrar reveals that he has discovered that the storage is not appropriate for watercolors. Would it be unethical for the museum to refrain from giving this information to Mr. Bucks?

Corporate Sponsorships

The Ralph Museum collects and interprets the arts of its region and considers inspiring creativity a key part of its mission. The Ralph has successfully recruited some of the region's wealthiest people to its board and over the years these board members have been very generous to the museum. As a result the Ralph is considered one of the preeminent museums in its region. Its dedicated development staff keeps meticulous fundraising and donor records. These records include extensive information about the museum's donors and their personal interests.

In recent years, the museum has begun to cultivate corporate donors, especially from those businesses that seek to make an impact in the region. Ready Widgets is an innovative software developer that moved into the region five years ago. It is cultivating a positive corporate image and wants to enhance its reputation among the area's most prominent citizens. Ready Widgets is very proud of its business acumen and creativity. Its board believes that a relationship with the Ralph would bolster the company's image as well as provide access to a desirable client base. To cultivate a relationship with the senior staff at Ready Widgets, the Ralph's development officers and CEO present data documenting the types of people who come to the Ralph, what brings them there, and why. Ready Widgets finds this data compelling and is ready to negotiate a corporate partnership involving a Gallery of Innovation as well as annual fellowships for prominent contemporary artists. These artists would spend part of the year at the Ralph, lending their visibility and cachet to the museum and, at the same time enhancing Ready Widget's image as a supporter of innovation in the arts. The negotiations are going well, but Ready Widgets has asked for more and more information from the Ralph about its major individual donors, particularly their contributions to the museum as well as their personal interests. Although pleased to present data about the museum's visitors and its overall donor profile, the development office is reluctant to reveal the information that Ready Widgets is now requesting, which has been collected over many years and is considered confidential. The CEO is inclined to give the information to Ready Widgets because she wants to close the deal and sees Ready Widgets' support and visibility as more important to the museum than "a few personal details" about the museum's major donors. She calls the chair of the museum's governing body to talk over the situation. The chair responds by saying that if the Ralph is willing to give out the type of information that Ready Widgets wants, he can get even more support than what Ready Widgets is promising from the

Doodad Corporation, a competing business in the area that has been wanting a relationship with the museum for years. The board chair goes on to say that Doodad would raise the ante even further, providing significantly greater support than Ready Widgets, if the museum allows Doodad to put a kiosk advertising its products in the museum's atrium and becomes the museum's exclusive sponsor for technology-related products.

Would it be unethical for the Ralph to provide the information requested by Ready Widgets? Would it be unethical for the Ralph to break off their negotiations with Ready Widgets to start discussions with Doodad, which offers more money in exchange for the same information and a kiosk in the atrium?

Annual Gala

Every year the Old Line Ladies Auxiliary organizes a gala dinner for the Old Line Historical Society. Their success at running the event is legendary in the region—the event not only raises much-needed money for the historical society but also has become extraordinarily popular. The Ladies Auxiliary makes all of the arrangements and hires all of the vendors for the event on behalf of the society, including hiring the graphic designer who creates the invitation, the event planner who decorates the room, the florist who provides the flowers, the lighting designer who adds a special mood to the evening, and the caterer who creates a memorable dinner. The caterer who the ladies relied upon for many years recently retired, so this year the ladies are in the market for a new caterer. They interview several, taste their culinary creations, and then ask for budget estimates from each. When they meet to make their decision about hiring the caterer, Ms. Kickback, the head of the Ladies Auxiliary, reveals that she is a friend of Ms. Bakewell, one of the caterers in the competition. Ms. Kickback reports that Ms. Bakewell told her she is very excited about the possibility of catering Old Line's annual affair. Further, Ms. Bakewell understands that Old Line is always in a precarious financial situation and needs to raise as much money from the annual gala as possible. As a result, Ms. Bakewell told Ms. Kickback that if she were selected as caterer, she would contribute half of her proceeds from catering the event to the museum. Ms. Kickback enthusiastically supports Ms. Bakewell's proposal for the event and tells the committee that she will vote for Ms. Bakewell and hopes that everyone else will as well.

Would it be unethical for the museum to hire Ms. Bakewell to cater their annual gala? Would your answer be different if you knew that Ms. Bakewell's estimate for the cost of the event were significantly greater than that of the other caterers? Would it make a difference if you knew that her product was far superior to the others?

Restricted Funds

The Looney Tunes Museum of Music received a substantial bequest in the 1990s that was restricted to the support of an annual lecture and performance. This year the museum's budget is especially tight. Several staff positions have been eliminated and, as a result, Jim, the curator who usually arranges the annual lecture, has been occupied with other tasks. He did not have the time to organize a meeting of the lecture selection committee early enough in the year, so that plans for the lecture and performance could be made. Given the general state of the museum's finances, Jim suggests that instead of holding the lecture this year, the funds can be used to send him and the director to the annual musical museums association meeting where they might hear about the latest trends in the field, network with professionals, and maybe even come up with ideas about people who might be candidates for the endowed lectureship in future years.

Would it be unethical for the museum to use the restricted funds to send Jim and the director to the annual meeting? When the director presents the proposed use of the funds to the museum's board, one of the board members suggests that, instead of using the money for travel, the museum can use the restricted funds to ease cash flow. He proposes that the museum borrow money from the restricted fund to pay salaries until the museum receives its annual grant from the state music association. Once the state money comes in, he says, the borrowed funds can be returned to the restricted lecture fund for use in future years. Another board member, feeling that this use of the restricted funds will be unethical, suggests that the museum can just use the funds for operating expenses. After all, money is very tight and the donor who gave the museum the support in the 1990s would not want to see the museum suffer when they have his money in the bank. Would it be unethical for the museum to follow either of these board members' suggestions?

Pop-Up Books

The Jefferson Paul Children's Museum has been cultivating Ms. Money for many years. She is a generous donor to other cultural organizations in the region but not to the children's museum and the museum has hopes that they might eventually benefit from some of her largesse. Ms. Money is aware of the museum's interest in her but has not yet heard about a project that it is doing that she would be interested in supporting. During a recent local book fair, however, Ms. Money learned that there is a big market for illustrated pop-up children's books in region and so she decides that she would like to help the museum take advantage of this burgeoning market by engaging several local artists to create children's books and sell them at the museum.

If the books are popular, she reasons, they could create a nice revenue stream for the museum. She writes a check and sends it to the museum with a letter explaining her desire to underwrite the creation of a series of pop-up books. The museum's director, who was previously unaware of Ms. Money's intentions, receives the check one day in the mail. She is pleased to have finally attracted Ms. Money's attention, but she also immediately notices that the funds that Ms. Money has provided will only cover part of the hard production costs for the book, nor will the funding cover any of the costs of staff or consultants' time—the museum has no publication staff; so staff would either have to be diverted from other projects or the museum would have to hire outside consultants to help realize this project. The director also remembers the piles of unsold books published by the museum ten years ago when the museum had a publication department and which are now languishing in the museum's basement storage area waiting for buyers.

Are there any ethical issues here? Would your answer be different if Ms. Money were to stipulate as a condition of the grant that her artist son must design the books? Would it matter if he were not the only designer in the project? Would it matter if her son were willing to donate his fees for creating the pop-up books to the museum, thus freeing up more project money to be used for staff or consultants who might have to work on the project?

Naming Opportunities

The Arthur Aquarium has a large campus. Located adjacent to the State University it is a major center for marine biology as well as an important public gathering place. Ten years ago, John Taylor Douglass, founder of a small local business that became a multinational corporate enterprise, gave the aquarium $20 million for the renovation of its main public building. In return, the aquarium named the main building for Douglass promising to use his name on the building, tickets, brochures, newsletters, and advertisements in perpetuity. In addition to its renown as a research center, the aquarium established itself as an important center for innovation in early education and became a model for children's programming not just in aquaria but also in museums across the country. At the same time, the John Taylor Douglass Hall became synonymous with Arthur Aquarium. Recently it was revealed that Douglass is a pederast—he was convicted of child molesting and was sentenced to a prison term of thirty years.

Would it be unethical for the aquarium to remove Douglass's name from the building? Would the museum be acting unethically if it removed his name without his consent, which the museum assumed would not be given? Would it be unethical for the museum to do nothing in this situation? Would your answers be different if Mr. Douglass's name were on an exhibition or program space inside the aquarium rather than on one of the organization's main public buildings?

Anonymous Donation

Marshall Arms College has long been a prestigious liberal arts college, but financial struggles in recent years have threatened its elite status. Money is tight for all college departments and administrative offices, not least of all for its Armory Museum. Nonetheless the museum maintains its reputation for excellence, particularly because of its collection of medieval arms and armor. The president continually challenges everyone at the college—administrators and faculty members alike—to find new avenues of support and has even gone so far as to suggest that faculty salary increases and bonuses may be linked to successful fundraising. The director of the Armory, Dr. May Wheen, a respected art historian specializing in medieval art, has noticed that a visitor, who she knows to be a former student of the college, frequents the arms and armor galleries. This visitor, Jake Studly, spends several hours at a time closely studying the objects on display. He is always alone and is easily identifiable by his rather eccentric dress. Studly also frequently stops by Dr. Wheen's office to discuss his latest observations and to thank her for maintaining such an excellent collection. Although he seldom has anything new to add to Dr. Wheen's already extensive knowledge of the collection, she listens to him patiently and encourages his interest, often suggesting books and articles that he might read if he wishes.

One day, Mr. Studly's visit to the museum director's office takes a different turn. He tells Dr. Wheen that he is considering a possible multimillion dollar donation to the museum. He is interested in helping ensure that the Armory can continue to maintain and expand its arms and armor collection. He wants to make a donation to the museum's acquisitions fund sizable enough to allow the museum to compete at art auctions with larger, more well-endowed museums. He stresses, however, that while he wishes the principal of the gift to be used for acquisitions, he would place no restrictions on the use of the interest that accrues to the fund and, in fact, he would not restrict the use of the principal for the medieval collections. His only condition is that the museum send him periodic reports on its collecting activities. He wants no publicity regarding the donation, preferring to remain anonymous.

Dr. Wheen is overjoyed with the prospect of this donation and immediately calls the college president, "Remember Jake Studly, that rather odd honor student at the college in the late 90s, who was a real loner but who used to hang around the Armory and we thought might be stalking one of the curators? It turns out that he just loves our collection. Remember I told you that he still hangs out here and comes to talk to me regularly? Well, it seems that he has become a really successful investment banker and today when he stopped by to chat, he went on and on about how much he owes the college for exposing him to history and helping him develop his passion for medieval art. He wants to ensure that students continue to have the same kind of college experience that he had and feels that by giving our collections fund a huge boost he will, in fact, accomplish that. He will give us ten million dollars immediately for the acquisitions fund and he doesn't care how we use the interest as long as the principal is devoted maintaining the excellence of the collection!"

The president agrees that this is, indeed, a wonderful development and notes that, if carefully invested, the principal could yield sufficient income to offset a portion of the museum's annual operating costs. He discusses with Dr. Wheen the procedures for accepting such a large gift. The Armory subsequently becomes the beneficiary of Mr. Studly's largesse. Dr. Wheen, at the same time, is privately hoping that she might see an increase in her salary as a result of successfully cultivating a new donor to the Armory.

Some time passes and several rare medieval items come up for auction. The Armory makes plans to bid on the items. One morning the president receives a phone call from a friend who is a journalist and who is working on a story about the indictment of several investment bankers for insider trading. The journalist wants to let the president know that two of the bankers about to be indicted are alums of Marshall Arts College and Jake Studly is one of the two. Distressed by the news, the president immediately calls Dr. Wheen and suggests that it would be prudent to return Mr. Studly's gift. Dr. Wheen, seeing her salary increase fly out the window, immediately begins to argue the opposite case: "Just think what we will be losing—a chance to continue the college's tradition of having one of the finest arms and armor collections in the nation. And, after all he hasn't been convicted yet. Maybe he really didn't do anything wrong. If we return the money we'll be judging him before the courts do."

What factors should the president and Dr. Wheen take into account in determining their next steps? Would it be unethical for the museum to retain the donation? Are there any ethical problems involved in returning the donation?

A few weeks later another journalist, Frieda Frontline, calls Dr. Wheen. The Attorney General's investigation into Mr. Studly's financial practices has revealed that he wrote a large check to the museum. Ms. Frontline tells Dr. Wheen that a community action group is about to have a press conference exposing the details. She begins to probe further into Studly's relationship with the museum. Should Dr. Wheen speak to Ms. Frontline without contacting the president of the college? If she talks with the president and he tells her to go ahead with the call, what advice would you give her about responding to the journalist's allegations? What ethical problems could you foresee arising from such a conversation?

The day after Dr. Wheen's conversation with Ms. Frontline, Robert Blather, the host of Marshallville Today, a regional TV talk show, contacts Dr. Wheen to ask her to be his guest on the show. The Armory just reinstalled its permanent arms and armor collection and both the museum and the college were hoping to attract wide attention to the exhibition to bolster the reputation of the college and assist in fundraising. Dr. Wheen calls the president to tell him the good news. He is enthusiastic about the media coverage that her TV appearance could generate and urges her to go ahead with the interview. To prepare for the interview, May Wheen starts to watch Marshallville Today regularly and realizes that the program has become popular because of Robert Blather's tendency to bring up controversial issues and use them to ask embarrassing questions. Suddenly, she realizes that the invitation could be a thinly veiled pretext to involve the museum in Studly's alleged improper conduct. Would you advise Dr. Wheen to appear on the program? If you would, how would you advise her to prepare for it? If during the program Robert Blather raises questions about Jake Studly's relationship with the museum, how would you advise her to respond?

FINAL THOUGHTS

Fundraising has long been a necessary part of a museum's activities, and concerns about undue influence on programmatic decisions from people who donate money and objects to a museum are also longstanding. But the climate is changing. Fundraising has become a central activity for museums and the public scrutiny of this activity has increased. The Sarbanes-Oxley Act of 2002, which was directed at improving governance, management, and accounting standards for public companies in the United States as a result of scandals involving corporations and accounting firms, has also had a major impact upon nonprofit organizations.[35] The importance of transparency and accountability in handling an institution's finances has been underscored and public expectations of responsible stewardship of resources—finances as well as collections—have risen. At the same time, social media have become prominent, allowing for a rapid exchange of facts, falsehoods, and attendant opinions. Often there is a fine line between impropriety and the appearance of impropriety; yet there are just as many cases where a public outcry occurs over issues that are not unethical but which nonetheless stimulate significant controversy.

The hypothetical cases in this chapter present a mix of instances—some cases involve ethical issues, while others focus upon matters of personal or public opinion or outrage. Guidelines from professional organizations can help identify points relating to fundraising about which there may be public concern but, no matter how comprehensive or thorough they may be, they will not cover every instance. Museums must tread cautiously, ensuring that their programmatic decisions are guided by sound curatorial advice based on the expertise that the public has come to expect of a museum's staff, not the interests of members of a museum's governing body or its donors. For some museums, governance committees have taken on a more active role not just in overseeing the governance of the organization but also in ensuring that the museum's activities stand up to public scrutiny. This may be an essential step in protecting the museum's integrity and reputation and in making sure that public benefit rather than individual or corporate interests prevail.

NOTES

1. Sally Yerkovich, "Is There a Future for Museum Ethics?" Paper presented at "Museums, Politics, and Power," a joint conference of the International Council of Museums-US, ICOM-Russia, and ICOM-Germany, September 2014.

2. Marie C. Malaro and Ildiko Pogány DeAngelis, *A Legal Primer on Managing Museum Collections*, 3rd ed. (Washington, DC: Smithsonian, 2012), 315.

3. Marilyn Laurie, "Corporate Funding for the Arts," in *The Arts in the World Economy: Public Policy and Private Philanthropy for a Global Cultural Community*, eds. Olin Robison, Robert Freeman, and Charles A. Riley II (Hanover, NH: University Press of New England, 1994), 69–70.

4. Malaro and DeAngelis, *A Legal Primer on Managing Museum Collections*, 315.

5. Ibid.

6. John Henry Merryman, Albert E. Elsen, and Stephen K. Urice, *Law, Ethics and the Visual Arts*, 5th ed. (The Netherlands: Kluwer Law International, 2007), 1226.

7. Ibid.

8. Malaro and DeAngelis, *A Legal Primer on Managing Museum Collections*, 315.

9. American Alliance of Museums, "Code of Ethics for Museums," American Alliance of Museums website, amended 2000, http://www.aam-us.org/resources/ethics-standards-and-best-practices/code-of-ethics.

10. Association of Fundraising Professionals, "Code of Ethical Principles and Standards," amended October 2014, Association of Fundraising Professionals website, http://www.afpnet.org/files/ContentDocuments/CodeOfEthicsLong.pdf.

11. American Alliance for Museums, "Standards Regarding Developing and Managing Business and Individual Donor Support," American Alliance of Museums website, accessed November 14, 2014, http://www.aam-us.org/resources/ethics-standards-and-best-practices/financial-stability.

12. Ibid.

13. Ibid.

14. Ibid.

15. Ibid.

16. American Alliance of Museums, Standards Regarding Exhibiting Borrowed Objects," American Alliance of Museums website, accessed November 14, 2014, http://www.aam-us.org/resources/ethics-standards-and-best-practices/education-and-interpretation.

17. Ibid.

18. Metropolitan Museum of Art, "Ethical Guidelines for Trustees, Officers and Key Employees The Metropolitan Museum of Art As Approved by the Board of Trustees on May 13, 2014," 4.

19. Association of Art Museum Directors, "Professional Practices in Art Museums," Association of Art Museum Directors website, 2011, https://aamd.org/sites/default/files/document/2011ProfessionalPracitiesinArtMuseums.pdf.

20. Association of Art Museum Directors, "Managing the Relationship Between Art Museums and Corporate Sponsors," 2007, Association of Art Museum Directors website, https://aamd.org/sites/default/files/document/Corporate%20Sponsors_clean%2006-2007.pdf.

21. Ibid.

22. Ibid.

23. Association of Art Museum Directors, "Revenue Generation: An Investment in the Public Service of Art Museums," 2007, Association of Art Museum Directors website, https://aamd.org/standards-and-practices.

24. American Association for State and Local History, "Publication: AALH Statement of Professional Standards and Ethics," American Association for State and Local History website, updated June 2012, http://resource.aaslh.org/view/aaslh-statement-of-professional-standards-and-ethics/.

25. International Council of Museums, "ICOM Code of Ethics for Museums," International Council of Museums website, revised 2004, http://icom.museum/the-vision/code-of-ethics/.

26. Wikipedia, "David H. Koch," accessed December 10, 2014, http://en.wikipedia.org/wiki/David_H._Koch.

27. Thomas P. Campbell, "Opening of the Met's New David H. Koch Plaza," September 10, 2014, Metropolitan Museum of Art website, http://www.metmuseum.org/about-the-museum/now-at-the-met/2014/opening-of-the-mets-new-david-h-koch-plaza.

28. Mary Emily O'Hara, "Should Oil Barons Like David Koch Be Funding Our Museums?" VICE, September 12, 2014, http://www.vice.com/read/should-oil-barons-like-david-koch-be-funding-our-museums-912.

29. Rachel Spence, "Who Funds the Arts and Why We Should Care," *Financial Times*, September 19, 2014, http://www.ft.com/intl/cms/s/2/4313691c-3513-11e4-aa47-00144feabdc0.html.

30. Mostafa Heddaya, "São Paulo Biennial Curators Join Artists in Repudiating Israeli Sponsorship," Hyperallergic, August 28, 2014, http://hyperallergic.com/146308/sao-paulo-biennial-curators-join-artists-in-repudiating-israeli-sponsorship/.

31. Smithsonian National Museum of African Art, "*Conversations: African and African American Artworks in Dialogue* from the Collections of the Smithsonian National Museum of African Art and Camille O. and William H. Cosby Jr.,"

Smithsonian National Museum of African Art, accessed November 24, 2014, http://conversations.africa.si.edu.

32. Philip Kennicott, "An Art Loan from Bill Cosby Draws the Smithsonian into a National Debate," *The Washington Post*, November 20, 2014, http://www.washingtonpost.com/lifestyle/style/an-art-loan-from-bill-cosby-draws-the-smithsonian-into-a-national-debate/2014/11/20/bde2794a-70e5-11e4-ad12-3734c461eab6_story.html.

33. National Museum of African Art website, accessed December 8, 2014, http://africa.si.edu.

34. Ibid.

35. The Sarbanes-Oxley Act 2002, Sarbanes-Oxley Act 2002 website, http://www.soxlaw.com/index.htm.

ADDITIONAL RESOURCES

Association of Fundraising Professionals. "Guidelines, Codes, Standards: Code of Ethical Standards." Association of Fundraising Professional website. Amended October 2014. http://www.afpnet.org/files/ContentDocuments/CodeOfEthicsLong.pdf.

King, Elaine A. and Gail Levin, eds. *Ethics and the Visual Arts*. New York: Allworth Press, 2006.

Malaro, Marie C. and Ildiko Pogány DeAngelis. *A Legal Primer on Managing Museum Collections*. 3rd ed. Washington: Smithsonian, 2012. On restricted gifts, pages 150–65.

Chapter 8

Controversy and Censorship

As educational and research institutions, museums place value upon the integrity of the information that they present and, indeed, the public relies upon museums to be authoritative sources for authentic and reliable information in their programs and exhibitions. The Codes of Ethics of the American Alliance of Museums, International Council of Museums, and American Association of State and Local History focus upon the importance of well-founded scholarship and the integrity of the information that museums present. AAM's Code states:

> Museums serve society by advancing an understanding and appreciation of the natural and cultural common wealth through exhibitions, research, scholarship, publications and educational activities. These programs further the museum's mission and are responsible to the concerns, interests and needs of society.
>   Thus, the museum ensures that:
>
> • programs support its mission and public trust responsibilities
> • programs are founded on scholarship and marked by intellectual integrity
> • programs are accessible and encourage participation of the widest possible audience consistent with its mission and resources
> • programs respect pluralistic values, traditions and concerns[1]

Similarly, ICOM's Code of Ethics, 4.2 on the Interpretation of Exhibitions states:

> Museums should ensure that the information they present in displays and exhibitions is well-founded, accurate and gives appropriate consideration to represented groups or beliefs.[2]

The American Association for State and Local History (AASLH) includes a section on "Intellectual Freedom" in their Statement of Professional Standards and Ethics, which asserts, "Historical scholarship and interpretation depend upon free and open exploration and interpretation of the human experience."[3]

Censorship, the deletion or suppression of material considered objectionable, is not addressed directly by these codes. But when the integrity of an exhibition or program is breached—either before the exhibition or program occurs and potentially controversial or offensive material is omitted from a show or a program is called off, or a controversial object or objects are removed after an exhibition is installed—censorship occurs. Controversies arise when sensibilities are offended by an exhibition's content or interpretation as well when there are differences in interpretation or questions of accuracy. While the former situation is more common than the latter, museums must face the possibility of confronting either case. In her book, *Censorship and the Arts: Law, Controversy, Debate, Facts*, Brenda Cossman distinguishes between censorship that occurs when a controversy is made public and aired extensively in the media and censorship by curators/directors, funders, political officials, and community members, which can occur "behind closed doors," often in anticipation of a controversy and in an attempt to minimize possible contention.[4] First, we will consider two cases, one of which speaks to the issue of sensibility and the other of which questions the accuracy of the interpretation provided in an exhibition. Both cases were aired publicly, although the results differ in each case. Then a third case illustrates an instance when the potential for self-censorship arises during an exhibition's development.

ETHICS IN ACTION

Hide/Seek: Difference and Desire in American Portraiture

The case of *Hide/Seek: Difference and Desire in American Portraiture* at the Smithsonian Institution's National Portrait Gallery in 2010 is one in which a public controversy led to the removal of a video in the exhibition. The removal, while quieting the original complaints, incited accusations of an ethical breach, and stirred a wider public outcry and debate.

Hide/Seek was the first major survey to examine the influence of sexual difference upon modern American portraiture. It traced how art reflects society's evolving attitudes toward sexuality, desire, and romantic attachment, and through looking at both the history of the portrayal of gays and lesbians in American art and the artistic expressions of gay and lesbian artists through portraiture, the exhibition, as its title suggests, also explored the power of the portrait to reveal and conceal.

The exhibition included 105 works of art—101 images along with four videos. One month after it opened, the Cybercast News Service (CNS) published an article under the headline, "Smithsonian Christmas-Season Exhibit Features Ant-Covered Jesus, Naked Brothers Kissing, Genitalia, and Ellen DeGeneres Grabbing her Breasts." Although quoting the show's curators extensively, and thus pretending to present a balanced approach, the news article, in fact, focused attention on some of what could be considered the exhibition's more sensational works, and "A Fire in My Belly," a video by David Wojnarowicz video, in particular. It described the video as showing "among other images, ants crawling over the image of Jesus on a crucifix, two halves of a loaf of bread being sewn together, the bloody mouth of a man being sewn shut, a hand dropping coins, a man undressing, a man's genitals, a bowl of blood, and mummified humans." The article went on to comment on the fact that family programs are being held in the exhibition galleries, thus openly exposing children to the works in question, and quoted a tax policy specialist who suggested that, because the Smithsonian is funded with taxpayers' dollars, "taxpayers should decide what is presented" there.[5]

Response was immediate. U.S. Congressional representatives issued statements (some in words echoing the CNS article) decrying the show and also calling for a review of the Smithsonian's funding. In one instance, Eric Cantor, soon to become Majority Leader of the U.S. House of Representatives, said, "This is an outrageous use of tax payer money and an obvious attempt to offend Christians during the Christmas season. When a museum receives taxpayer money, the taxpayers have a right to expect that the museum will uphold common standards of decency. The museum should pull the exhibit and be prepared for serious questions come budget time."[6] Other Congressmen joined Cantor, threatening to cut the budget of not just the Portrait Gallery but of all of the Institution's twenty-six research centers and museums. The head of the Smithsonian acted quickly. Within twenty-four hours, he told the Director of the National Portrait Gallery to remove "A Fire in My Belly" from the show, and it was removed. This act quieted the Congressional debate over the Portrait Gallery show but introduced a different controversy about its appropriateness. Accusations of censorship by the Smithsonian arose.

The decision to remove "A Fire in My Belly" from the exhibition was widely called into question in the larger cultural community as was the speed with which the decision was made and the process that was followed in reaching the decision. The Smithsonian's board of regents appointed an advisory panel to review the future of Smithsonian exhibition planning policies and practices. The panel affirmed the Smithsonian's role as a cultural space that has the responsibility to present "thoughtful exhibitions and programming with themes or content that may at times be considered controversial or sensitive." It supported "curatorial freedom of expression, expertise, and authority," noting that these are "critical to a flourishing museum" and stated that "in the absence of actual error, changes to exhibitions should not be made once an exhibition opens, without meaningful consultation with the curator, director, Secretary, and the leadership of the Board of Regents." The panel called for more open communication with Congress and with the public about its exhibitions and, in perhaps their most controversial recommendation, for "public input at pre-decisional exhibition planning phases."[7]

The results of the Smithsonian panel's deliberations did little to quiet the debate in the larger arts community. Some called for the video to be put back into the exhibition. The Andy Warhol Foundation, one of the exhibition's supporters, threatened to deny any future support to the Smithsonian if the work were not restored; individuals who loaned items to *Hide/Seek* sought to rescind the loans. Major newspapers called for the resignation of the head of the Smithsonian. Protests were held across the country and in Europe, many showing the censored video, and versions of the video were made available on many websites including YouTube.[8] After the exhibition closed at the Smithsonian, it was reconstituted and traveled to both The Brooklyn Museum and the Tacoma Art Museum, where it appeared with the Wojnarowicz video and without contention.

It was generally agreed that removing the video from the exhibition after its opening in Washington, DC, was an act of censorship, an action interfering with the intellectual integrity of the exhibition, and, as a result, a violation of museum codes of ethics. Yet, viewing this decision from the perspective of the Secretary of the Smithsonian who at the time of making his decision knew that his institution was due for reauthorization by Congress in the coming months, and that the budgets, not just of the National Portrait Gallery but of all twenty-six of the Smithsonian's museums and research organizations, would be closely examined and possibly reduced significantly, might yield a different judgment. After all, his action seemingly squelched at least the Congressional controversy.

So in retrospect, one can ask whether the removal of the video was justified and, if so, on what grounds? One might also ask if by removing the video from the exhibition, the Smithsonian missed an opportunity to convene a public dialogue about the issues in question and to engage both sides of the question in a productive debate? Would public debate have fairly aired the disparate points of view on the issues involved or inflamed the controversy further?

Would your answers to these questions be different if the organization in question were a small, nonprofit museum? Can common ground be established on an emotionally charged subject?

Phantom Home

Not all controversy results in censorship. Consider the case of *Phantom Home*, an exhibition that opened in 2013 at the Galerie Nationale du Jeu de

Paume in Paris, a museum devoted to photography of the nineteenth through the twenty-first centuries. *Phantom Home* presented six series of photographs by contemporary Palestinian Bedouin photographer Ahlam Shibli, each of which explores the concept of *home*. They include "Self Portrait Palestine, 2000," photographs of places that have meaning in Shibli's life; "Eastern LGBT, International, 2004/2006," images of people from Eastern Europe who left their places of birth because their home societies would not allow them to live according to their sexual preferences; "Dom Dzieka. The house starves when you are away, Pologne, 2008," documenting the living conditions of children for whom foster institutions become home; "Trackers, Palestine/Israel, 2005," photographs of Palestinians of Bedouin descent who fought as volunteers for Israel; "Trauma, Corrèze, France 2008–2009," images of residents of Corrèze who were members of the *Resistance* against the Nazis as well as those who fought in colonial wars in Indochina and Algeria; and "Death, Palestine, 2011–2012" depicting ways in which families and communities memorialize Palestinians who fought in the Second Intifada against Israel from 2000–2005. The curators of the exhibition note:

> *Death*, Ahlam Shibli's latest photographic series . . . shows how Palestinian society preserves the presence of "martyrs"—in the artist's own words. *Death* contains a broad representation of the absent ones through photographs, posters, graves, and graffiti displayed as a form of resistance.
>
> The exhibition includes six of the photographic series produced by Ahlam Shibli during the last decade. Most of the works are accompanied by captions assigning each photograph to a specific time and place in an investigative process that often implies long empirical and conversational contact with the subject in question.[9]

Shibli wrote the exhibition labels as well as most of the text in the small brochure that accompanies the show. The latter introduces each section of the exhibition and details Shibli's approach to her subject matter. On the section "Death" she writes that it "exhibits some of the ways in which the ones who are absent become present again—'represented': Palestinian fighters . . . ; militants . . . ; and the prisoners. . . . The representations designate any person who lost his or her life as a result of the Israeli occupation of Palestine: a martyr." A label for one of the images in the show states, "Photos of the martyr Khalil Marshoud in the family living room being dusted by his sister. On the poster, a gift from the Abu Ali Mustafa Brigades, he is called the General Secretary of the al-Aqsa Martyrs' Brigades of Balata."[10]

After the exhibition opened, Jewish organizations including CRIF, the Conseil Représentatif des Institutions Juives de France, and the Simon Wiesenthal Center in Los Angeles expressed their outrage. They focused particularly upon the photograph series "Death," claiming that the images glorify the Palestinian suicide bombers, and decried the use of the word *martyr* to describe the dead or imprisoned young people. They called for the exhibition to be closed. To bolster their position, they organized public demonstrations in front of the museum.

Support to continue the show and to uphold the museum's right to artistic expression came from the Comité International pour les Musées et Collections d'Art Moderne (International Committee for Museums and Collections of Modern Art—CIMAM—an international committee of ICOM) and the French Ministry of Culture, one of the funders of the Jeu de Paume. The Ministry reinforced the mission of the museum to promote diverse artistic expressions through the medium of photography, and at the same time asked that the museum post additional notices in the exhibition that would emphasize the fact that its text was provided by the artist, not the museum. The Jeu de Paume complied with the Ministry's request and stood firm in not closing the show or altering the exhibition in any manner.[11]

In this case the public controversy, although covered extensively in the media, social media, and on blogs, did not overwhelm the resolve of the Jeu de Paume to allow for unexpurgated artistic expression. Thus, we can ask what differences are there between *Hide/Seek* and *Phantom Home*. When an exhibition is attacked for presenting material that some find offensive, what options does a museum have? Should fear of losing support from major donors play a role in determining a museum's response to negative reactions to its work? How might a museum anticipate and prepare for a controversy? How might they resolve the controversy once it occurs? How might a museum turn a controversy into an asset?

Self-censorship

The fear of inciting public outrage over an exhibition can lead to self-censorship on the part of curators and directors behind closed doors. This usually happens away from public view or goes unnoticed. After a succession of public controversies in Washington, DC, museums in the late 1980s and 1990s—the cancellation of the Mapplethorpe exhibition at the Corcoran Gallery of Art, the dismay expressed over the revisionist interpretation in the National Museum of American Art's *The West as America: Reinterpreting Images of the American Frontier, 1820–1920*, and the cancellation of the original plans for an exhibition about the *Enola Gay* at the National Museum of Air and Space to cite only a few—it was often speculated that a period of self-censorship began to take hold as museums tried to sidestep further public controversy. And now, as some museums begin to shift their focus from collections to audiences and engage their communities in new ways, it has been argued that museums are embracing controversial topics and using them to encourage public dialogue about contemporary issues, thus trying to bring controversy "in house."[12] Nonetheless, external censorship and self-censorship remain concerns for museums.

Consider the case of a history museum that is developing a major exhibition on the history of the interstate highway system, highlighting the first interstate highway in the United States, which happens to cross its home state. The museum plans to treat the entire history of the highway, from the early stages of clearing land and building the road to the contemporary challenges of maintaining and updating the roadway to accommodate continually increasing traffic and providing adequate policing. The museum is collaborating closely with the public authority in charge of public works, drawing upon their vast archives, interviewing their staff and developing with them a series of public programs that will take place during the time that the exhibition is installed in their galleries. While the exhibition is being developed, the media uncovers a major scandal involving the public works authority and high officials in the state, including the current governor. The scandal and the public works authority become one in the public mind, overshadowing the more than fifty years of positive impact the public authority has had upon the state. The curator and the director know that the problem that has been uncovered is real but has probably been overstated in the press. They also know that the public works authority is very sensitive about the negative publicity they have been receiving. They value their partnership with the public authority because many of the authority's board members have significant influence in the state as well as ties to the museum's major supporters. How should the museum treat topics related to the scandal in the exhibition? What is at stake as the museum goes forward with developing the exhibition? Who are the stakeholders? What kind of additional information might the museum gather to help them make their decision? If the museum were to adapt the exhibition content to sidestep the issues related to the current scandal, who would benefit? Who would lose out? Are there strategies that the museum could employ to help mitigate the problems that might arise?

FINAL THOUGHTS

Although creating exhibitions on controversial subjects can be challenging, embracing rather than avoiding controversy without altering exhibition or program content is key. By appropriately framing the issues and encouraging open and responsible discourse, we can enhance the public's perception of museums as places where open and inclusive conversations are held on difficult subjects to promote greater understanding and hopefully diffuse emotions. A museum with its authentic collections, curatorial expertise, and responsibility to maintain and build upon the public trust that it enjoys should welcome the opportunity to take the lead in creating a positive civic discourse. Such an approach would enhance the museum's profile as a safe place for difficult discussions and thereby help reshape the contentious, divided societies in which we now live. Further by respecting "pluralistic values, traditions and concerns"[13] it is very much in concert with the professional codes of ethics.

After the *Hide/Seek* controversy, the National Coalition Against Censorship issued "Museum Best Practices for Managing Controversy" that recommended, among other things, that museums adopt a "Freedom of Speech Commitment," a statement affirming the museum's dedication to artistic and intellectual freedom.[14] In addition, the statement recommends a transparent process of exhibition development that includes community engagement prior to the exhibition's installation and makes suggestions about handling controversy that happens once an exhibition is in place. While the suggestions were created with art museums in mind, they can easily be adapted to other disciplines.

Some history museums, for example, have used the technique of facilitated dialogue to prepare all staff and board members for exhibitions with potentially difficult subject matter. In this process all staff, from maintenance and security personnel to the director, participate in a series of discussions about the proposed exhibition that can uncover concerns, fears, and misunderstandings related to the exhibition's subject matter as well as to the tensions the topics generate in the present-day communities who would be the potential audiences. Separate discussions with the board of trustees allow members to express their concerns and staff to offer suggestions about how they would deal with possible problems as the exhibition develops. These discussions can open lines of communication that might not otherwise exist; they also inform exhibition development by alerting the institution to issues it needs to address to ensure that the exhibition is accepted by political and community leaders as well as the general public.

Nothing can guarantee in advance that an exhibition or program will not stir the emotions of someone and incite a public debate. But by engaging in an open and transparent content development process, museums, their boards, and their staff can be well informed and better prepared to take on controversy when it arises.

NOTES

1. American Alliance of Museums, "Code of Ethics for Museums," American Alliance of Museums website, amended 2000, http://www.aam-us.org/resources/ethics-standards-and-best-practices/code-of-ethics.

2. International Council of Museums, "ICOM Code of Ethics for Museums," International Council of Museums website, revised 2004, http://icom.museum/the-vision/cide-of-ethics/.

3. American Association of State and Local History, "Statement of Professional Standards and Ethics," American Association of State and Local History website, updated June 2012, http://resource.aaslh.org/view/aaslh-statement-of-professional-standards-and-ethics/.

4. Brenda Cossman, *Censorship and the Arts: Law, Controversy, Debate, Facts* (Toronto, Ontario: Ontario Association of Art Galleries, 1995), 27.

5. Penny Starr, "Smithsonian Christmas-Season Exhibit Features Ant-Covered Jesus, Naked Brothers Kissing, Genitalia, and Ellen DeGeneres Grabbing her Breasts," CNS News, Monday, November 29, 2010, http://www.cnsnews.com/news/article/smithsonian-christmas-season-exhibit-fea.

6. Penny Starr, "Boehner and Cantor to Smithsonian: Pull Exhibit Featuring Ant-Covered Jesus or Else," Tuesday, November 30, 2010, http://www.cnsnews.com/news/article/boehner-and-cantor-smithsonian-pull-exhibit-featuring-ant-covered-jesus-or-else.

7. Smithsonian Institution, *Report of the Regents Advisory Panel*, Smithsonian Institution Website, January 31, 2011, http://newsdesk.si.edu/releases/report-regents-advisory-panel-january-31-2011.

8. YouTube, Fire in My Belly by David Wojnarowicz, Diamanda Galas, accessed December 9, 2013, http://www.youtube.com/verify_age?next_url=http%3A//www.youtube.com/watch%3Fv%3D0fC3sUDtR7U.

9. Marta Gili, Carles Guerra, Joao Fernandes, and Isabel Sousa Braga in *Ahlam Shibli Phantom Home [Foyer Fantome], #104*, Galerie Nationale du Jeu de Paume website, accessed December 9, 2013, http://www.jeudepaume.org/index.php?page=article&idArt=1837.

10. Galerie Nationale du Jeu de Paume, *Ahlam Shibli Phantom Home [Foyer Fantome], #104*, Galerie Nationale du Jeu de Paume website, accessed December 9, 2013, http://www.jeudepaume.org/index.php?page=article&idArt=1837.

11. Richard Landes, "Notice at the Jeu de Paume in Response to the Controversy about "Phantom Homes," The Augean Stables, July 21, 2012, www.theaugeanstables.com.

12. See Christopher B. Steiner, "Museum censorship," in *The Routledge Companion to Museum Ethics: Redefining Ethics for the Twenty-First-Century Museum*, ed. Janet Marstine (New York: Routledge, 2011), 393–413, for a discussion of engaging censorship and promoting dialogue.

13. American Alliance of Museums, "Code of Ethics for Museums," American Alliance of Museums website, amended 2000, http://www.aam-us.org/resources/ethics-standards-and-best-practices/code-of-ethics.

14. National Coalition Against Censorship, "Museum Best Practices for Managing Controversy," National Coalition Against Censorship website, issued May 7, 2012, http://ncac.org/resource/museum-best-practices-for-managing-controversy/. The statement also outlines strategies that can be adopted to prepare in advance for programs or exhibitions with potentially difficult subjects as well as those that can be used with the public and the press after an exhibition or program opens.

ADDITIONAL RESOURCES

Dubin, S. C. *Displays of Power: Controversy in the American Museum from the Enola Gay to Sensation.* New York: New York University Press, 1999. A discussion of the recent history of controversies in museums.

ancient art, art works and objects confiscated during World War II, and human remains and objects protected by the Native American Graves Protection and Repatriation Act. Although several statutes govern matters relating to the ownership of objects that fall into each of these areas, they do not resolve all of the issues related to a museum's ownership. In cases where a museum might be the legal owner of an object, ethical questions can arise that suggest that the museum should forfeit that ownership and return the object to its country of origin or to the cultural group from which it originated. When the ownership of an object in a museum's collection is disputed and no relevant law applies to or disposes of such a dispute, is it unethical for the museum to retain the object? Conversely, would a museum be acting ethically if it were to return an object from its collection to someone or some group claiming ownership without eliciting more substantive evidence than hearsay to support its decision to do so?[4] If a museum accepts an object with incomplete provenance from a donor and then later determines that the object was stolen, what is the museum's responsibility to the donor? Finally, would it be ethical for a museum to return an object to a museum that does not have the resources to care for it or to one located in an area where the museum's collections may be endangered by military conflict? Each of these questions raises complex issues that can be answered only on a case-by-case basis.

ARCHAEOLOGICAL OBJECTS AND ANCIENT ART

The codes of ethics and standards for museums established by professional organizations address the responsibility of museums regarding their collections, particularly as they relate to art works or artifacts for which the provenance or provenience may be questioned. According to the American Alliance of Museums' (AAM) "Code of Ethics for Museums," a museum ensures that

- Acquisition, disposal, and loan activities are conducted in a manner that respects the protection and preservation of natural and cultural resources and discourages illicit trade in such materials.
- Acquisition, disposal and loan activities conform to . . . [a museum's] mission and public trust responsibilities. . . .
- The unique and special nature of human remains and funerary and sacred objects is recognized as the basis of all decisions concerning . . . [a museum's] collections
- Competing claims of ownership that may be asserted in connection with objects in its custody should be handled openly, seriously, responsively and with respect for the dignity of all parties involved.[5]

Further, AAM has issued "Standards Regarding Archaeological Material and Ancient Art" that urge museums to establish standards for determining the provenance of archaeological objects and ancient art and to publish these guidelines in their collection management policies.[6] The standards stress the need for thorough provenance research both on objects before they are acquired by a museum as well as on those already in a museum's collections. They also "recommend that museums require documentation that the object was out of its probable country of modern discovery by November 17, 1970, the date on which the UNESCO Convention on the Means of Prohibiting and Preventing the Illicit Import, Export, and Transfer of Ownership of Cultural Property was signed."[7]

Similarly, the Association of Art Museum Directors (AAMD) adopted "2013 Guidelines on the Acquisition of Archaeological Material and Ancient Art" that AAMD describes as "voluntary standards for acquisitions that are stricter than the requirements of applicable law."[8] A comparison of the AAM and AAMD guidelines reveals that both documents encourage thorough provenance research with written documentation. Putting aside the slight differences in wording of the two documents, the greatest difference between the two is that AAM's Standards apply to existing collections as well as to prospective acquisitions while AAMD's Guidelines apply only to the latter.[9] Thus, AAM promotes thorough provenance research on all archaeological artifacts and ancient art currently in a museum's collections, while AAMD is more concerned with provenance research relating to new acquisitions.[10]

ICOM deals with issues relating to cultural property throughout its "Code of Ethics," noting that the notion of stewardship includes rightful ownership, permanence, documentation, accessibility, and responsible disposal. The ICOM Code states that museums should have valid title to all objects in its collections and warns, "Evidence of lawful ownership in a country is not necessarily valid title."[11] This statement refers to the fact that in countries governed by civil law (e.g., France, Switzerland) a person who purchases an object in good faith obtains good title after a specified period of time. According to civil law, the law in the country of the purchaser specifies a time period, and, during that time, a person claiming legal ownership may seek recovery of an object that was stolen from the good faith purchaser.[12] If no one makes a claim on an object purchased in good faith during the specified time period, then, the purchaser obtains good title. In contrast in common law countries (e.g., the United States, England) someone "who purchases property from a thief, no matter how innocently, acquires no title to the property."[13]

Like the AAM and AAMD codes, ICOM is concerned that museums conduct a due diligence investigation and establish the full history both for the objects it acquires and also for those that it borrows for exhibitions. "Museums should avoid displaying or otherwise using material of questionable origin or lacking provenance. They should be aware that such displays or usage can be seen to condone and contribute to the illicit trade in cultural property."[14] Further the Code addresses how museums should work in collaboration with the communities they serve as well as with the communities represented in their collections. This includes cooperating with those communities:

> Museums should promote the sharing of knowledge, documentation and collections with museums and cultural organisations in the countries and communities of origin. The possibility of developing partnerships with museums in countries or areas that have lost a significant part of their heritage should be explored.

returning cultural property:

> Museums should be prepared to initiate dialogues for the return of cultural property to a country or people of origin. This should be undertaken in an impartial manner, based on scientific, professional and humanitarian principles as well as applicable local, national and international legislation, in preference to action at a governmental or political level.

and the restitution of illegally exported objects:

> When a country or people of origin seeks the restitution of an object or specimen that can be demonstrated to have been exported or otherwise transferred in violation of the principles of international and national conventions, and shown to be part of that country's or people's cultural or natural heritage, the museum concerned should, if legally free to do so, take prompt and responsible steps to cooperate in its return.[15]

The ICOM Code also addresses cultural objects from an occupied country, stating

> Museums should abstain from purchasing or acquiring cultural objects from an occupied territory and respect fully all laws and conventions that regulate the import, export and transfer of cultural or natural materials.

And, finally, ICOM prohibits any activity that might support the illicit trade of artifacts,

> Members of the museum profession should not support the illicit traffic or market in natural or cultural property, directly or indirectly.

In spite of the guidance provided in these codes of ethics and the extensive discussion and debate on the topic of archaeological objects and antiquities, ethical dilemmas remain. The guidance seems straightforward but, in reality, the situations to which it refers are quite complex. Museums acquire artifacts for which provenance is almost, but not completely, established and determine that, in these cases, the research and educational value of the object and the resulting public benefit outweigh the risks that the gaps in provenance might indicate ethical or even legal issues.

The Saint Louis Art Museum's acquisition of the Mummy Mask of Ka-Nefer-Nefer demonstrates some of the issues that arise when an object's ownership history is questioned. On April 3, 1998, the Saint Louis Art Museum (SLAM) purchased the Mummy Mask of the Lady Ka-nefer-nefer from Phoenix Ancient Art, dealers in rare antiquities with galleries in Geneva and New York.[16] Before buying the mask, SLAM investigated its provenance,[17] confirming that it was discovered in 1952 at Saqqara, Egypt, during an excavation led by Mohammed Zakaria Goneim.[18] Goneim found the un-mummified body of Ka-nefer-nefer wrapped in a palm reed mat among a number of burials above the unfinished Step Pyramid of the third Dynasty rule of Sekhemkhet.[19] Dating to the Nineteenth Dynasty (1347–1197 BC), this was the only identified burial among those that Goneim discovered.[20] In spite of its uniqueness, the mask was not displayed with other objects from the same archaeological dig in an exhibition at the Cairo Museum immediately after its discovery.[21] Instead, according to correspondence received by SLAM, it was seen in a gallery in Brussels in 1952.[22] This fact suggests that the mummy mask was exported from Egypt shortly after its discovery.[23]

According to the provenance on the art museum's website, the mask next appeared in the collection of the Kaloterna family in Switzerland in the 1960s. The document files at the Saint Louis Art Museum note, "The name 'Kaloterna' may be a misspelling of the common Croatian name 'Kaliterna.'" Sometime in the 1960s, an anonymous Swiss collector purchased the mummy mask from the Kaloterna family. "The Swiss collector also had an address in Croatia, and it is possible that the collector became acquainted with the Kaloterna (or Kaliterna) family there."[24] Phoenix Ancient Art purchased the mask from the Swiss collector in 1995. To be sure that the mask was not considered stolen property, SLAM contacted the Director of the Museum of Egyptian Antiquities in Cairo, the Art Loss Register, INTERPOL, and the International Foundation for Art Research (IFAR). They could not find the piece listed on any stolen property databases and the Director of the Museum in Cairo "declined to identify the mask as stolen or otherwise improperly held."[25] SLAM also investigated the background of the Phoenix Ancient Art and Hicham Aboutaam, one of its principals, and asked a well-respected scholar to conduct an independent investigation of the mask's provenance. The background check revealed nothing untoward and the scholar concluded that the "mask had in all likelihood left Egypt lawfully under then-applicable Egyptian law."[26] Based upon this research, on March 12, 1998, the Collections

Committee of the Museum's board of trustees approved the purchase of the mask for close to $500,000.[27]

The Egyptian provenance differs from that of the Saint Louis Art Museum. Records in Egypt state that after the mask was excavated in Saqqara in 1952, it was stored in there until 1959 when it was shipped to Cairo, to be conserved in preparation for an exhibition in Tokyo, Japan.[28] "The Mask was 'received by police guards'" in Cairo; however, it did not travel to Japan.[29] It was shipped back to Saqqara in 1962. In 1966 it was sent to a Cairo for conservation in a box numbered "fifty-four."[30] In 1973 the Egyptian Museum in Cairo conducted an inventory of the box's contents and discovered that the Mask was no longer there.[31] The Egyptian Museum's records do not register a "transfer to a private party between 1966, when the Mask was last seen, and 1973."[32]

Beginning in late 2005 and 2006, questions were raised about the mask's provenance on the Museum Security Network, an online Google group that is a channel for distributing "news and information pertaining to cultural property protection, preservation, conservation, and security."[33] The operator of the network contacted the FBI, INTERPOL, and SLAM concerning the mask's provenance.[34] Dr. Zahi Hawass, Secretary General of the Supreme Council of Antiquities for the Ministry of Culture, Cairo, Egypt, subsequently contacted SLAM stating that the mask had been stolen and requested its return. In response, the Saint Louis Art Museum asked Hawass for documentation that the mask had been stolen. The museum did not receive information that satisfied them and refused the requests to return the mummy mask.[35]

In January 2011, representatives of the U.S. government approached SLAM about the mask, threatening to seize it. Shortly thereafter, SLAM filed a complaint for declaratory judgment against the United States, stating that the statute of limitations had expired so that the relevant laws could not be enforced and, furthermore, that the government did not have dispositive proof that the mummy mask of Ka-Nefer-Nefer is Egypt's property.[36] In March of 2011, the United States "filed an *in rem* forfeiture claim,[37] . . . asserting that there was probable cause to believe that at some time between 1966 and 1973, the mask had been stolen from Egypt and later introduced unlawfully into the U.S."[38] The district court dismissed the U.S. government's claim stating that its claim had failed to allege sufficient factual and legal bases. The United States then moved to file an amended complaint, but the district court refused to give it the required permission to do so. In June of 2014, the United States Court of Appeals for the Eighth Circuit affirmed the lower court's decision on procedural grounds, that the United States had missed a filing deadline. In its decision, the Court of Appeals stated that the United States had failed to provide sufficient information to support its claim that the mask had been "introduced into the United States contrary to law."[39] In a concurring opinion, however, Judge Murphy warned, "Courts are bound to recognize that the illicit sale of antiquities poses a continuing threat to the preservation of the world's international cultural heritage. Museums and other participants in the international market for art and antiquities need to exercise caution and care in their dealings in order to protect this heritage and to understand that the United States might ultimately be able to recover such purchases."[40]

The case of the Mummy Mask of Ka-Nefer-Nefer illustrates many of the ambiguities than can arise even when a museum performs due diligence and constructs as complete a provenance for an object as possible. Although the court cases about the mummy mask have concluded, opinions are divided about how to resolve this and other cases involving ancient artifacts. Some archaeologists claim that it is unethical for a museum to continue to build a collection of archaeological objects and ancient art from other places and cultures. They argue that a museum, simply by acquiring archaeological artifacts, calls attention to their value and, thus, contributes to the "commercial demand for antiquities."[41] Consequently, a museum may be considered to indirectly or implicitly encourage illegal excavation and illicit trade in similar things.[42] Presumably such archaeologists could not only find that the Saint Louis Art Museum's continued possession of the Mummy Mask of Ka-Nefer-Nefer would be unethical, but they might make similar judgments about other museums' collections of archaeological artifacts and ancient art. Directors of many encyclopedic or universal museums—those that collect and display artifacts from diverse cultures and time periods—dismiss the archaeologists' arguments and see no ethical issue here. They deny that their collecting has an impact upon the market for illicit antiquities and further question the right of sovereign nations to protect whatever "they consider to be *their* cultural property" when the object in question may be traced to an ancient civilization and culture that is not necessarily related to the modern nation.[43] They also suggest that encyclopedic museums are "cosmopolitan institutions dedicated to the proposition that, by gathering and presenting representative examples of the world's diverse artistic cultures 'under one roof,' work to dissipate ignorance and superstition about the world and promote tolerance of difference itself."[44] They argue that the educational value of encyclopedic museums far outweighs any inducement they might provide to the market in illicit antiquities.

Given these opposing viewpoints, it is not surprising that the debate continues. UNESCO adopted the Convention on the Means of Prohibiting and Preventing the Illicit Import, Export and Transfer of Ownership of Cultural Property in 1970. This agreement, ratified by 128 countries, recognizes "that the illicit import, export and transfer of ownership of cultural property is one of the main causes of the impoverishment of the cultural heritage of the countries of origin of such property and that international co-operation constitutes one of the most efficient means of protecting each country's cultural property against all the dangers resulting there from." It calls for parties to the Convention to "undertake to oppose such practices with the means at their disposal, and particularly by removing their causes, putting a stop to current practices, and by helping to make the necessary reparations."[45] The Convention thereby discourages museums and collectors from acquiring objects that left their countries of origin after 1970. The United States Senate gave its unanimous advice and consent to ratification of the Convention in 1972 and the United States became a party in 1983, following enactment of implementing legislation. Since that time, repatriation has become an acceptable practice. Nonetheless, the unrest in Iraq and Syria and the attendant destruction of objects of their cultural heritage have bolstered the stand of some experts who believe that Western museums should keep even disputed antiquities to save them from harm.[46]

ART CONFISCATED DURING WORLD WAR II

World War II caused enormous destruction not only of human life but also to cultural heritage. Two types of restitution claims have ensued: one relating to the spoils of war taken from Germany to Russia at the end of the war and another relating to the return of art and objects of cultural heritage appropriated by the Nazis.[47] The latter is of primary concern here, for it has the greatest impact upon American museums. Although the acts of confiscation occurred more than seventy-five years ago, attention has been refocused upon them more recently and claims for restitution are ongoing. The theft of art and cultural objects between the years of 1933 and 1945 was called to popular attention in the mid-1990s by publications such as *The Rape of Europa*, *The Lost Museum* and *Beautiful Loot*,[48] and more recently by films such as *The Rape of Europa, Monuments Men*, and *The Woman in Gold*. In addition, after the dissolution of the Soviet Union and the declassification of archives after fifty years, new information about wartime activities related to art and cultural objects became available. These activities have had an impact upon U.S. museums that acquired art during the last fifty to seventy-five years, for during that time some of the works of art looted by the Nazis have found their way into the art market and American collections.[49]

In the late 1990s several notable legal cases were highlighted in the media—for example, the restitution of Egon Schiele's "Portrait of Wally" as well as of Matisse's "Odalisque." To assist museums in resolving claims relating to art confiscated during the War, the Association of Art Museum Directors (AAMD) issued a "Report of the AAMD Task Force on the Spoliation of Art during the Nazi/World War II Era (1933–1945)." The report acknowledged that "each claim presents a unique situation which must be thoroughly reviewed on a case-by-case basis" and called for careful provenance research on all works that may have been confiscated from their owners during the war; vigilance about acquiring complete provenance for future purchases as well as for gifts, bequests, and loans; disclosure on a museum's website of records about works with gaps in provenance for the years between 1933 and 1945; timely response to claims against a work and an attempt to resolve the claim through mediation; and the creation of a third-party data base to include information about "1. Claims and claimants, 2. Works of art illegally confiscated during the Nazi/World War II era and 3. Works of art later restituted."[50]

This report was updated in 2001 in response to the Presidential Advisory Commission on Holocaust Assets in the United States' report, *Plunder and Restitution*, to include the following statement:

> It should be the goal of member museums to make full disclosure of the results of their ongoing provenance research on those works of art in their collections created before 1946, transferred after 1932 and before 1946, and which were or could have been in continental Europe during that period, giving priority to European paintings and Judaica.[51]

And in 2007, AAMD issued "Art Museums and the Identification and Restitution of Works Stolen by the Nazis" that provides an update on the activity related to the identification and restitution of Nazi-looted art and provenance research and poses ten questions that museum directors should address to "ensure continued transparency in the acquisition and presentation of their collections, to facilitate the identification of works that were stolen by the Nazis and not restituted, and to ensure prompt and sensitive responses to claimants."[52]

- Has the museum identified—or is it in the process of identifying—all objects in its collection that underwent a change in ownership between 1933 and 1945, and that were in continental Europe between those dates?
- Has the museum made it a priority to conduct provenance research on those objects, while balancing this commitment of financial and staff resources with its ongoing educational responsibilities to the community?
- Has the museum made public the results of its provenance research, and is it continuing to do so?
- Is the museum sharing its findings with peer institutions to assist them with their research into comparable works, and is the museum contributing information to centralized databases and related art recovery information resources.
- Given the complicated nature of ownership claims, is the museum balancing a swift and compassionate response to claimants with its responsibility as an

institution to act with care and prudence in protecting the works it holds in trust for the public?

- Is a prospective ownership claim accompanied by definitive proof, or is further research required to confirm the claim, and is the museum able to assist with that research?
- What are the steps a museum should take in establishing whether a claim is legitimate?
- When new research provides conclusive evidence of prior rightful ownership, is the museum taking responsible action even if no formal claim has been made?
- Before purchasing a work or accepting a gift or loan with an incomplete ownership history, has the museum undertaken additional research to determine its Nazi-era provenance status?
- Is the museum updating its provenance research to the best of its ability as new information becomes available?[53]

The International Council of Museums published, "Recommendations Concerning the Return of Works of Art Belonging to Jewish Owners."[54] The Recommendations reference ICOM's Code of Professional Ethics concerning the necessity for museum employees to "act with integrity and in accordance with the most stringent ethical principles," and, similar to the AAMD document, urge museums to identify objects in their collections that may have been acquired before, during, or after World War II.[55]

Drawing upon the AAMD and ICOM documents as well as the "Washington Conference Principles on Nazi-Confiscated Art" (see below), the American Alliance of Museums (AAM) issued "Standards Regarding the Unlawful Appropriation of Objects During the Nazi Era," which contains detailed procedures to help ensure that Nazi-era objects will not be acquired by museums and protect museums against claims being brought against loaned objects in their custody.[56] The Standards also address what research should be conducted to ensure that existing collections contain no objects with Nazi-era provenance; how museums should respond; should they discover that their collection contains unlawfully appropriated objects; and how they should address claims of ownership made in connection with objects in their custody. The AAM Standards underscore the responsibility of museums as stewards of their collections, suggesting, "When faced with the possibility that an object in a museum's custody might have been unlawfully appropriated as part of the abhorrent practices of the Nazi regime, the museum's responsibility to practice ethical stewardship is paramount."[57]

Pursuant to an agreement reached in 2000 with the Association of Art Museum Directors (AAMD) and the Presidential Advisory Commission on Holocaust Assets in the United States (PCHA), AAM framed "Recommended Procedures for Providing Information to the Public about Objects

Transferred in Europe during the Nazi Era."[58] These procedures are based on the premise that online access to information about items in museum collections that might have been unlawfully seized during the Nazi era would facilitate restoration of these objects to their rightful owners. It states that every museum should:

1) Identify all objects in its collection that were created before 1946 and that it acquired after 1932, that underwent a change of ownership between 1932 and 1946, and that were or might reasonably be thought to have been in continental Europe between those dates. . . . In the event that a museum is unable to determine whether an object created before 1946 and acquired after 1932 (a) might have been in continental Europe between 1932 and 1946 and/or (b) underwent a change of ownership during that period, it should still be treated as a covered object;

2) Make currently available object and provenance (history of ownership) information about covered objects accessible online; and

3) Give priority to continuing provenance research on those objects as resources allow.[59]

The Recommended Procedures go on to describe the Nazi-Era Provenance Internet Portal where museums can post information about the "covered objects" in their collections and where members of the public can search for objects that may have been owned by their family. The Portal was designed to facilitate the restitution of objects stolen during World War II.[60]

The urgency of the restitution of cultural heritage lost during World War II has been emphasized through major intergovernmental conferences and resolutions. These include the Washington Conference Principles on Nazi-Confiscated Art (1998), the Declaration of the Vilnius International Forum on Holocaust-Era Looted Cultural Assets (2000), and the Terezin Declaration that resulted from the Holocaust-Era Assets Conference in Prague and Terezin (2009).[61]

But the task remains difficult. As AAMD's "Art Museums and the Identification and Restitution of Works Stolen by the Nazis" advises:

Ownership records are often incomplete, wartime documents may have been destroyed, and standards of record keeping have changed over time. Provenance research requires the expert physical examination of works of art, and the thorough investigation of museum archives, auction and exhibition catalogues, monographic studies, and catalogues of collections, dealer records, photographic archives, and publications of the wartime activities of dealers and collectors. It can require examination of archives in foreign countries, access to documents that may not be publicly accessible, and considerable time, expertise, expense and diligence. New documents . . . become available each year.[62]

Yet, even when issues of ownership are clear, some museums resist returning works of art from their collection. For example, in 2013 Holocaust survivor Leone Meyer sued the University of Oklahoma, claiming that Pissarro's "Shepherdess Bringing in the Sheep" is rightfully hers. She alleged that it was taken from her father during the Nazi occupation of France. In 2000, the painting was bequeathed to the University's Fred Jones Jr. Museum by the person who had owned it since 1956. There is no dispute over the painting's history. After the war, Swiss courts declared that the person who then had possession of the painting was its legitimate owner under the Swiss civil law provision whereby ownership of such property becomes conclusive when the property is in a person's possession for more than five years, regardless of the item's previous ownership history. The University of Oklahoma is opposing Meyer's lawsuit on procedural grounds, saying it "does not want to keep any items it does not legitimately own but also wants to avoid a bad precedent by automatically giving away gifts it receives to anyone who claims them."[63] The University acknowledges that Meyer is the rightful heir to the painting, but still resists returning it.

The case has been widely publicized, with the Oklahoma House of Representatives Member Paul Weselhoft urging the public to avoid the museum until it returns the painting to its rightful owner.[64] And Meyer sued not only the University of Oklahoma but also the American Alliance of Museums (AAM) and the Association of Art Museum Directors (AAMD). She claimed that AAM failed to "hold the Fred Jones Museum to the high standards required" for accreditation, and that AAMD "failed to monitor Fred Jones Museum's lack of compliance with" their guidelines concerning Nazi-looted art.[65] The publicity that was generated by the lawsuits and the public dismay over the University's position illustrates how the tactic of fighting a World War II–era claim could be damaging to an institution's reputation.

Some museums have taken creative approaches to identifying owners of paintings in their collection that the museum acquired after 1946 and were known to be located in Europe between 1933 and 1945. In February 2015 The Stedelijk Museum in Amsterdam took a very public approach to gathering more information about items in their collections for which provenance is uncertain. The museum opened *The Stedelijk Museum in the Second World War*, an exhibition commemorating the seventieth anniversary of Dutch liberation. The exhibition tells the story of the Museum's support of Jewish artists, collectors, and dealers in exile during the 1930s; the construction of a bunker under sand dunes to protect the museum's collections during the war; museum exhibitions and acts of resistance during German occupation; and the Stedelijk's celebrations after the war. It also features the provenance research that identified sixteen works that may not belong to the Stedelijk. These works as well as the research into their past histories were made part of the exhibition in the hope that visitors might recognize names or offer other clues that might help the museum trace the original owners.[66] As time passes and the connections to original owners become even more remote, one would hope that other museums will devise other inventive means by which to help clarify the provenance of World War II–era pieces.

NATIVE AMERICAN GRAVES PROTECTION AND REPATRIATION ACT

The Native American Graves Protection and Repatriation Act (NAGPRA) "describes the rights of Native American lineal descendants, Indian tribes, and Native Hawaiian organizations with respect to the treatment, repatriation, and disposition of Native American human remains, funerary objects, sacred objects, and objects of cultural patrimony."[67] The legislation provides the following definitions of these "cultural items": *human remains* are the "physical remains of a Native American"; *funerary objects*, which may be associated or unassociated with human remains, are those objects that were "placed near individual human remains as part of a death rite or ceremony"; *sacred objects* are those ceremonial objects "needed for the modern-day practice of traditional Native American religions";[68] and *cultural patrimony* refers to an object that has "ongoing historical, traditional, or cultural importance central to the Native American group or culture, itself, rather than property owned by an individual Native."[69]

NAGPRA requires federal agencies and museums receiving federal funding to inventory their holdings of Native American human remains and associated funerary objects and to share these inventories with the appropriate Indian tribe or Native Hawaiian organization. Photocopies of the inventories are also sent to the Secretary of the U.S. Department of the Interior, and the information in them is posted in the Federal Register. Museums receiving federal funding and federal agencies must also create summaries of other applicable cultural items in their collections and share them the appropriate tribes or organizations. The tribes and Native Hawaiian organizations then might contact the museum, make a claim on the human remains and/or objects in question, and reach an agreement with the museum about the disposition of the remains and/or other objects.

When disputes between native groups and museums arise, they may be heard by the NAGPRA Review Committee, an advisory group whose role is to monitor and review the implementation of NAGPRA and to resolve disputes "between Indian tribes, Alaska Native villages and corporations, and Native Hawaiian organizations with museums and Federal agencies."[70] Many differences between native groups and museums, however, are resolved outside of the NAGPRA review process. The Willamette Meteorite is a case in point. The 15.5-ton iron meteorite fell to earth over 10,000 years ago. The "largest . . . ever found in the United States and the sixth largest in the world,"[71] the meteorite, or *Tomanowos* as it was called by the Clackamas Chinook, was culturally significant to the Clackamas who lived in the area (now the state of Oregon) long before Europeans settled there.[72] According to the American Museum of Natural History's exhibition text quoted on their website,

> Tomanowos is a revered spiritual being that has healed and empowered the people of the valley since the beginning of time. The Clackamas believe that Tomanowos came to the valley as a representative of the Sky People and that a union occurred between the sky, earth and water when it rested on the ground and collected rainwater in its basins. The rainwater served as a powerful purifying, cleansing and healing source for the Clackamas and their neighbors. Tribal hunters, seeking power, dipped their arrowheads in the water collected in the meteorite's crevices. These traditions and the spiritual link with Tomanowos are preserved today through the ceremonies and songs of the descendants of the Clackamas.[73]

In the middle of the nineteenth century, the Clackamas Chinook were relocated to the Grand Ronde Reservation and lost touch with Tomanowos, even though their knowledge of the meteorite and its meaning to the tribe were perpetuated. Today, the Clackamas Chinook are part of the Confederated Tribes of Grande Ronde.

In 1902, Ellis Hughes came across the meteorite on land adjacent to his own that was owned by the Oregon Iron and Steel Company in the Willamette Valley, near the present-day city of Portland. Hughes moved the meteorite onto his property and claimed ownership. After several lawsuits the Iron and Steel Company was determined to be the rightful owner of the meteorite. The Company subsequently put it on display as part of the 1905 Lewis and Clark Exposition in Portland, and then sold it to Mrs. William Dodge, who donated it to the American Museum of Natural History. It has been on display at the Museum almost continuously since then and has also served as an important object for scientific research.[74]

In 1999, the Confederated Tribes of the Grand Ronde Community of Oregon made a repatriation request to the NAGPRA Review Committee for the return of the Willamette Meteorite. After negotiations reached a stalemate, the American Museum of Natural History sued the tribe, claiming, "the meteorite, which was found in the Upper Willamette Valley in Oregon, was 'a natural feature of the landscape, rather than a specific ceremonial object,' as described in the law."[75] Both the NAGPRA claim and the lawsuit were circumvented after the Museum and the Tribes reached a historic agreement that allows the museum to retain the object while recognizing the Tribes' relationship with the Meteorite, allowing the Tribe to "re-establish its relationship with the Meteorite with an annual ceremonial visit to the Meteorite."[76]

> The agreement reflects mutual recognition of and respect for the traditions of both the Tribe and the Museum. As part of the agreement, the Tribe agrees to drop its claim for repatriation of the Willamette Meteorite and not to contest the Museum's ownership of it. However, the agreement also stipulates the Meteorite would be conveyed to the Tribe if the Museum failed to publicly display it, except for temporary periods for preservation, safety, construction and reasons beyond the reasonable control of the Museum. Also in keeping with the agreement, the Museum will place a description of the Meteorite's significance to the Clackamas in the Hall of the Universe, alongside a description of the Meteorite's scientific importance.[77]

Since the signing of the agreement, members of the Tribe have made an annual visit to the Natural History Museum to celebrate their relationship with Tomanowos in a private ceremony.[78]

When NAGRPA was enacted in 1990, many museums feared that Native American claims would severely deplete their collections. Instead, compliance with NAGPRA has ushered in new collaborative relationships between museums and Native American groups, enriching both.[79] Whether working through the NAGPRA review process or negotiating privately with Native Americans, Indian tribes and/or Native Hawaiian organizations, museums have repatriated human remains and cultural objects and have entered into caretaking and/or collections and information sharing agreements for objects that have not been repatriated. As a result, museums have become more sensitive to the issues involved in displaying the art and artifacts of other cultures, particularly Native American, and they are more careful when acquiring new objects, including human remains, from Native cultures. A recent survey of forty natural history and anthropology museums reveals that 75 percent of these institutions no longer accept "any materials covered by NAGPRA, whether human remains or artifacts."[80]

Some museums have chosen to become repositories for unidentified human remains, accepting all human remains offered to them, agreeing to care appropriately for them, and devoting the resources necessary to identify and repatriate them as appropriate. These museums consider playing such a role as preferable to leaving the unidentified object in the private domain and, perhaps, the open market. The Maxwell Museum of Anthropology in Albuquerque, New Mexico, for example, "assumes all associated legal, ethical, and financial obligations, including complying with NAGPRA regulations and state laws regarding archaeological human remains."[81] The museum acknowledges responsibility for scientific research as well as repatriation to tribes in their collections policy, which "states that the Maxwell actively consults with any tribe seeking consultation, facilitates repatriation according to NAGPRA, and permits non-destructive research by an qualified researcher on any of the collections it curates."[82] Thus, in agreeing to take on collections of unidentified human remains and archaeological objects, the Maxwell Museum has positioned itself so as to accept ethical responsibility to care for all unidentified human remains that it acquires.

As part of their work with the Maxwell Museum on human remains, Heather Edgar and Anna Rautman conducted a survey of the acquisition policies of forty museums and found that, unlike the Maxwell, most of them do not accept human remains or NAGPRA-related objects. Forty-nine percent of these museums cite ethical considerations as the most important determinant in their decision *not* to become custodians of these materials. Conversely, "28 percent of respondents at museums that *do* take human remains also listed ethics as most important in their policy making."[83] The diversity of views regarding acquiring and maintaining human remains in museum collections demonstrates that there are ethical issues that remain unresolved.

NAGPRA has sensitized museums in the United States to a number of issues. It has made them more immediately aware of their roots in Western European traditions and the fact that not all cultures and societies treat cultural heritage in the same way. It has also highlighted concerns surrounding the display of human remains and sacred objects as well as to those related to the restitution of cultural property.

ETHICS IN ACTION

All people and museums in the following cases are fictional. The hypothetical situations combine real and imaginary circumstances to provide examples of ethical issues that can arise in museums. All resemblances to a real museum are coincidental.

Looted Antiquities

The Roosevelt Museum of Ancient Art has a fine collection of antiquities and is known for its path-breaking exhibitions based upon excavations conducted by its staff of archaeologists. The museum's collection contains many archaeological specimens from museum-sponsored excavations in the late nineteenth and twentieth centuries as well as gifts of antiquities from private collectors of ancient art. Fortunately, the museum has an ample acquisitions fund that it uses to purchase unique and important collections when they become available through auction houses and private dealers. One of the private dealers with whom the museum has done business contacted the chief curator about a unique collection, an assemblage of artifacts reputed to be from a gravesite in Afghanistan that includes an elaborate gold medallion belt, long sword, and iron dagger with a hilt decorated in gold, as well as seals and gold coins. Although without provenience, it has been determined that the assemblage probably dates from the Parthian Empire. These artifacts are extraordinarily beautiful and as a group tell a story of vast riches and enormous power. Although the dealer is not sure how the artifacts made their way to Switzerland where he purchased them, he assures the museum that the assemblage was legally imported into the United States and he can provide all necessary documentation to prove legal ownership. He is interested in selling the artifacts as soon as possible and has told the curator that if the museum does not buy them, he will break up the assemblage and sell the individual artifacts separately, thereby destroying their value as an assembled collection that provides historical and cultural information that might not be discernable from the artifacts individually.

What ethical issues should the museum consider in determining whether to acquire the assemblage? Would it be unethical for the museum to acquire the assemblage even without complete provenience in order to prevent its dispersal? Should a museum acquire an object that, although legally owned by the seller under U.S. law, may have left been obtained overseas in violation of the laws of its country of origin?

Borrowing from Private Collections

The SoandSo Museum has a strictly enforced policy concerning the provenance of objects that it acquires. No works of art are accepted into the museum's collections unless the curators have provided thorough documentation of an object or artwork's history. Recently, the museum was offered an opportunity to be the first venue for an exhibition of ancient art from private collections that will travel to two other sites nationally. The exhibition is especially appealing because it will contain a number of objects that would be on public view for the first time. While the SoandSo does not collect ancient art, many of its paintings and contemporary works were inspired by the ancient world. In addition, objects in the traveling show would resonate well with the works displayed in SoandSo's permanent collection galleries. Hosting the exhibition would be a coup for the SoandSo, elevating its status among the philanthropists and collectors of the region. SoandSo's board members are thrilled with the possibility of hosting this show; they feel it would not only enhance the museum's image but also help expand its pool of potential donors, which is especially advantageous since the museum is about to launch a major capital campaign. Before presenting the exhibition proposal to the Collections and Exhibitions Committee, the curators researched the traveling exhibition only to discover that a number of its objects have no legitimate provenance and may well have been looted.

What ethical considerations might arise as a result of displaying borrowed objects of questionable provenance? Does the SoandSo Museum's policies regarding the provenance of its acquisitions have a bearing on these ethical considerations?

Human Remains

Wilhelm William is moving from his family's mansion in the suburbs to a condominium in the center of town. In the process of disposing of many of his family's possessions, he discovers a human skull that belonged to his father. He remembers hearing stories about the skull when he was a child. Family lore traced the skull to an ancient tribe. The skull used to have a prominent place on the mantelpiece of the mansion's living room alongside a ceramic bowl that was supposedly found with the skull. While Wilhelm admires the bowl and intends to keep it, he always found the skull rather ghoulish. Now he wants to dispose of it but suspects, if the family tales are true, that it may have some scientific or historical value. He offered it to several large museums in the region, none of which were interested in acquiring it. His last hope is the local natural history museum, a small but worthy organization.

During his meeting with the museum's curator, Wilhelm mentions the ceramic bowl and the curator asks if the museum might examine the two objects together, explaining that the bowl may provide evidence concerning the provenience of the skull. Wilhelm agrees to loan both items to the museum. The intern assigned by the curator to do preliminary research concludes that if the skull can be associated with the bowl, the skull may be a major discovery. It may be the only extant human remains of a very ancient culture that heretofore was not known to have a presence in the region. The intern suggests that more research be done to confirm the scientific and historical value of the objects. It may be some time, however, before the museum can raise the necessary resources to conduct research sufficient to reach a viable conclusion. In addition, if the intern's research turns out to be accurate and the human remains can be traced to a federally recognized Native American tribe, the museum may have to repatriate them.

The curator visits Mr. William but does not mention either the potential historical value of the items or the possibility of repatriation. She tells him that the museum is very interested in the skull but that there are a number of operational and financial issues that must be resolved before it can accept it. In addition, because it has provided clues that have helped identify the skull, the museum would like to keep the ceramic bowl until it is able to complete its assessment. Having offered the skull to several other museums already, Mr. Williams is impatient. He would like the museum to return his ceramic bowl and tells the curator that he has decided that if her museum does not accept the skull he will destroy it.

What are the ethical considerations regarding the possible acquisition of the skull by the museum? Does the museum have an ethical obligation to tell Mr. Williams what the research conducted by the museum has revealed? Does the museum have an ethical obligation to accept and preserve the skull in light of Mr. Williams' threat to destroy it if the museum does not choose to acquire it?

A Donor's Wishes

The Fudge Museum of Art at Loco State University has a substantial collection of antiquities, including a fine collection of ancient coins. Recently, the director of the Fudge was contacted by one of the University's major donors about a collection of Roman coins that he wished to donate to the Fudge. The director visited the prospective donor in his home and after a delightful lunch, viewed the collection, which turned out to include some very rare pieces, the likes of which are not known to be in any public collection in this country. The director expressed her enthusiasm over the coins. If they were to be donated to the museum, she reasoned privately, the publicity surrounding this donation would benefit the museum's standing in the numismatic community as well as attract hundreds of new visitors. Thinking it best to plan ahead, she decided to discuss aspects of the acquisition process with the collector. She made him aware of the fact that the coins would have to go before the collections committee; however, since the coins were clearly within the museum's mission and would only strengthen the museum's already outstanding collection of ancient coins, it was unlikely that the committee would raise an objection to the donation unless there were issues of provenance. The director knew the collector to be an enthusiast of ancient Roman history who has published meticulously detailed studies on Roman coins, and, as a result, she expected him to have detailed records about the provenance of his collection. When she raised the issue of the collection's provenance, however, she was surprised to hear him say that since he has clear title to the coins, he did not feel it was necessary to provide provenance information about the donation. After the director left the meeting, she realized that she could not, in good conscience, propose the acquisition to the collections committee because of the lack of complete ownership history.

The collector, too, had second thoughts after his meeting with the director. He felt insulted that the director asked about his collection's provenance and, in so doing, seemed to question the collection's legitimacy. The collector immediately called his close friend, Loco State's president, to complain that the museum director had dared to question his integrity. Knowing that his friend the collector was extremely sensitive and sometimes volatile, the president tried to calm the collector down by assuring him that he would have a word with the director to see if he could rectify the situation.

When the president called the director, she explained that the museum has responsibility for obtaining complete provenance regarding the objects that it acquires. The president dismissed this procedure as an "overly excessive concern with details." He pointed out that the collector is well known in coin collector circles and is such a meticulous researcher that he is certain to have checked the provenance of the items in his collection when he purchased them. He just doesn't feel that he needs to share that information. The president said that he did not want to jeopardize the university's relationship with the collector, who also happens to be a major supporter of the school.

What are the ethical considerations relating to the acquisition of this coin collection? Are there any conflicts of interest in this scenario? If so, are they sufficient to present ethical problems? How might they be resolved?

American Indian Sacred Objects

The Jason Rule Museum of Art is a privately funded museum in a large city. The museum's collections manager identified several objects in the Native American collections that may be considered sacred objects under the Native American Graves Protection and Repatriation Act. She discussed this with her supervisor, the chief curator of the museum, recommending that the museum hire an outside expert to assist in researching the objects. The chief curator consulted with the director and the museum's legal counsel, and they all agreed that the museum should follow the collections manager's recommendation. Consequently, the collections manager hired an expert to examine the objects, prepare a summary of her findings, and assist the museum in contacting the relevant tribes—all of the steps required under NAGPRA. The museum director presented the expert's report to the museums' governing board, recommending that the museum deaccession and repatriate the sacred objects. The board, noting that museum receives no Federal funding and therefore is not legally compelled to comply with NAGPRA, decided against the director's proposal, wishing to keep the collection intact.

What are the ethical considerations regarding the retention or return of the sacred objects in the museum's collection? Describe them and discuss how they might be resolved.

World War II–era Works

Located in a former industrial city in the American Midwest, the Franklin Museum was established as an encyclopedic museum in the early twentieth century. Over the past twenty-five years, it has focused its activities upon highlighting the strengths of its collections—American art as well as the art of Asia and Africa. The Franklin's European paintings, never its strong suit, have become more and more peripheral to the museum's exhibitions and programs. Many have not seen the light of an exhibition gallery in years, if ever. As a result, the museum's registrar is working on a collections survey with an eye to deaccessioning many of its European paintings, most of which were acquired during the last half of the twentieth century. Several years ago, fifteen of the European paintings were determined to have inconclusive provenance and might have changed hands during World War II. Information about these works was placed on the Nazi-Era Provenance Internet Portal, but no inquiries were received. The registrar recently hired a collections assistant to conduct further provenance research on the fifteen paintings. Try as he might, the assistant could not uncover any additional information about the paintings' prewar ownership. The registrar is eager to finish this project, feeling that sufficient resources have already been devoted to it, given other more pressing collection needs. She is ready to recommend to the director that the museum deaccession the paintings with indeterminate provenance.

What are the ethical considerations here? How might these considerations be affected if you knew that, as a rule, the museum sells its paintings through Bartleby's, a well-known auction house with a well-staffed research department conducting provenance research on all of the World War II–era objects and paintings it is consigned?

The director, the museum's collections committee and governing board approve the deaccessioning of the fifteen paintings with the condition that they be sold through an auction house that will do additional provenance research. The Franklin's collection management policy stipulates that the museum must make its decision about deaccessioning independently from decisions about disposal, and requires at least a three-month waiting period between the two determinations. At their next meeting, the Franklin's board reviews the decision to deaccession and approves the consignment of the paintings to Bartleby's.

A few weeks after the museum's registration staff gives the works to Bartleby's, Jefferson Bland, the head of the provenance research department, contacts the museum to say that Bartleby's has completed all possible provenance research. While a complete ownership history still cannot be constructed, Bartleby's is approximately 85 percent certain that the paintings were not looted during the War. Do the museum's ethical considerations change? Is the near certainty regarding the painting's provenance sufficient to avoid an ethical problem?

The Franklin decides to move forward with the sale and at their next European Paintings auction Bartleby's sells all fifteen of the paintings to private collectors. One morning a year later, the director of the Franklin Museum opens the morning newspaper to discover that Bartleby's has been sued by the descendants of a German Jewish family for selling paintings that were forcibly taken from their great-grandfather by the Nazis in the years leading up to World War II. The auction house is accused of falsifying their provenance research in order to sell valuable works of art and disperse collections previously in the hands of museums.

Is a general statement about an accusation such as the one made about Bartleby's sufficient to affect the ethical conduct of the museum? What action should the museum take, if any?

Native American Art

The Edwardina Museum of Anthropology and Art has the largest collection of textiles and pottery from the American Southwest on the East Coast. John Henry, a former member of the Edwardina's governing board and a renowned collector of Native American cultural objects, has offered the museum his collection of Zuni pottery. Mr. Henry is very proud of his collection and believes that it stands not only as a valuable collection for research and exhibition but also as evidence of his ability to build a fine collection. As a former board member or the Edwardina, Mr. Henry understands that he cannot demand that the museum put all of his collection on permanent display, but he is adamant about the collection staying together. He feels so strongly about this that he is willing to pay for the construction of a new collections storage area in which the collection could be stored as a unit. The Edwardina's chief curator is already familiar with the collection and understands that it complements the museum's existing collection, would be a significant research resource, and contains some unique and valuable pieces that the museum would otherwise be unable to obtain. As the chief curator examines the collection more closely, however, she sees that it also contains several ceremonial pieces similar to those that the museum repatriated under the Native American Graves Protection and Repatriation Act.

What ethical considerations should the museum keep in mind as it negotiates with Mr. Henry regarding his proposal?

Collections Access

Consider the following three scenarios:

1. The Art Museum of America has a large collection of materials from a local Indian tribe which include some human remains and ceremonial objects. Complying with NAGPRA, the museum notified the tribe about

these materials and, at the tribe's request, repatriated the human remains and some of the ceremonial objects. The museum and the tribe established a congenial relationship and tribal members often help museum curators with their research on the objects that remain in the museum. One day one of the tribal elders, someone who had not previously visited the museum, asked to see the collections. When he viewed the objects with the chief curator, he discovered that one of them was once used in an ancient, little-known sacred ceremony. Both he and the curator were thrilled with this discovery—the curator because the object sheds new light on the tribe's cultural traditions and the tribal elder because this object may assist the tribe in reviving its ancient tradition. The elder consulted with the tribal council to tell them of his discovery and to determine how to best preserve this object and perpetuate the traditions for which it was used. The tribe decided that it would be best for the object to remain in the museum's care, but they request that the museum never exhibit the object and restrict access to it, allowing only select tribal members to handle it and permitting the tribe to hold an annual private ceremony at the museum using the object.

2. The Freetown History Museum was offered a collection of nineteenth- and twentieth-century clothing from the William Richley family, one of the city's founding families. A long-time supporter of the Museum, the Richleys also offered to construct a new textile storage area to help preserve the items in perpetuity. Because the museum already has a substantial costume collection, the gift is very attractive. Fredonia Richley, the matriarch of the family, placed a restriction on part of the collection, however. She requested that access to the wedding gowns in the collection be restricted to the family and that they be permitted to borrow dresses to wear at future family weddings.

3. The Friendly Family Plum Drying Corporation is known worldwide. The family patented special plum-drying machinery that has made them a master among prune producers. Their prunes are known to be some of the most flavorsome and moist produced anywhere. And the production process is top secret. Each year for the past forty years, the Friendlies have commissioned a contemporary painter to create a work of art about some aspect of plum-drying. As a result over the years, the corporation has amassed an impressive contemporary painting collection. Although it has never been displayed publically, the Friendly Family Plum Drying Corporation's collection is known throughout the region. The collection is rumored to be one of the best, if not the best, collection of its kind in private hands. The Art Museum of America is pleasantly surprised to learn that the corporation is considering donating the collection to the Museum and the director readily agrees to meet with Mr. Friendly, the chairman and CEO. Over the years

Mr. Friendly has been impressed with the Art Museum's painting exhibitions as well as its ability to care for and conserve its paintings. He knows their conservator to be one of the most highly regarded professionals in the region. At his meeting with the museum director, Mr. Friendly lays out his plan. Although Mr. Friendly would like the paintings to become part of the museum's collections, he stresses the top-secret nature of some of them because they depict aspects of the closely guarded plum-drying process. He tells the museum director that he wishes to place a restriction on the donation of these paintings. They would only be displayed at the museum once a year, at an evening event that would coincide with the corporation's annual business meeting. Only Friendly family corporation executives and selected employees would be allowed to attend.

What are the ethical considerations that the museums should take into account in each of these three scenarios? How do they differ? How should the museums handle each of these situations?

FINAL THOUGHTS

The 1970 UNESCO Convention, the enactment of NAGPRA in 1990, and steps taken in the late 1990s to further the restitution of cultural heritage stolen or forcibly sold during World War II have altered museum practice. They have helped museums become more aware of their responsibility regarding acquisitions, particularly with respect to an item's provenience and provenance; their duty to repatriate Native American human remains and ceremonial objects; and their obligation for the restitution of stolen works. They have also heightened awareness concerning issues related to ownership and led to the creation of guidelines and standards for dealing with collections in instances that are not governed by law. With the leadership of AAM, AAMD, and ICOM, professional benchmarks for ethical stewardship have been developed for antiquities and ancient art, Native American human remains and objects of cultural heritage and art confiscated from 1933 until 1946. These have been important steps forward. As a result, museums are creating partnerships and collections-sharing agreements with other museums internationally and have developed beneficial relationships with Native American cultural groups. Such arrangements have also contributed substantially to furthering the understanding of our shared cultural heritage.

The Cleveland Museum, for example, voluntarily returned to Cambodia a tenth-century statue of Hanuman, the Hindu monkey god, after uncovering evidence that it was probably looted during the country's civil war.[84] In addition, the Cleveland Museum entered into an agreement whereby it would carry out future joint projects with the National Museum of Cambodia.[85] This is but one of many instances where museums create relationships across cultural and national boundaries, which have the potential for enriching the work of both museums and their benefit to their respective communities.

The UNESCO Convention, NAGPRA, and standards regarding art stolen during World War II include specific provisions for particular situations, yet they propound principles that could apply more broadly to museum operations. The public reputation of museums would be enhanced if museums adopted higher standards for all acquisitions, not just antiquities and ancient art; if the collaborative practices and partnerships that emerged as a result of NAGPRA were applied to all projects that touch upon the lives and histories of living communities; if all human remains in museum collections were given dignity and respect; and if the increased transparency encouraged by the principles developed for the restitution of Nazi-looted art were to be applied to all collections. In sum, it would be an important step for the profession to create guidelines for ethical stewardship that apply to all objects in their collections, not just on a case-by-case basis. Application of these principles would promote greater public understanding of how our museums work to ensure that the public can benefit to the fullest from their resources both today and into the future.

NOTES

1. Patty Gerstenblith, "Ownership And Protection Of Heritage: Cultural Property Rights For The 21st Century: The Public Interest in the Restitution of Cultural Objects," *Connecticut Journal of International Law* 16 (Spring 2001): 198–99.

2. Ibid., 199 and Paul M. Bator, "An Essay on the International Trade in Art," *Stanford Law Review* 34, no. 2 (January 1982): 301–02, http://www.jstor.org/stable/1228349.

3. Clemency C. Coggins, "United States Cultural Property Legislation: Observations of a Combatant," *International Journal of Cultural Property* 7 (1998): 57.

4. As Schubert points out, in making a decision to return an object or artwork to a previous owner, a museum must balance its fiduciary duties and ultimately act in the best interests of the public. Jessica Schubert, "Prisoners of War: Nazi-Era Looted Art and the Need for Reform in the United States," *Truro Law Review* 30, no. 3 (2010): 675–95.

5. American Alliance of Museums, "Code of Ethics for Museums," amended 2000, American Alliance of Museums website, http://www.aam-us.org/resources/ethics-standards-and-best-practices/code-of-ethics.

6. American Alliance of Museum, "Standards Regarding Archaeological Material and Ancient Art," American Alliance of Museums website, accessed March 6, 2015, http://www.aam-us.org/resources/ethics-standards-and-best-practices/collections-stewardship/archaeological-material-and-ancient-art.

7. Ibid.

8. Association of Art Museum Directors, "Introduction to the Revisions to the 2008 Guidelines on the Acquisition of Archaeological Material and Ancient Art," in "2013 Guidelines on the Acquisition of Archaeological Material and Ancient Art," January 29, 2013, Association of Art Museum Directors website, https://aamd.org/standards-and-practices.

9. Sharon H. Cott and Stephen J. Knerly, Jr., "Comparison of the Report of the AAMD Task Force on the Acquisition of Archaeological Material and Ancient Art (revised 2008) and The American Association of Museum Standards Regarding Archaeological Material and Ancient Art (July 2008)," ALI-ABA Course of Study, Legal Issues in Museum Administration, April 1–3, 2009, Boston, MA.

10. For a detailed description of the development of AAMD's Guidelines and AAM's Standards see also Patty Gerstenblith, "The Meaning of 1970 for the Acquisition of Archaeological Objects," *Journal of Field Archaeology* 38, no. 4 (2013): 262–66.

11. International Council of Museums, "ICOM Code of Ethics for Museums," International Council of Museums website, revised 2004, http://icom.museum/the-vision/code-of-ethics/, 3.

12. Marilyn Phelan, "Legal and Ethical Considerations in the Repatriation of Illegally Exported and Stolen Cultural Property: Is There a Means to Settle the Disputes?" INTERCOM, accessed March 20, 2015, p. 6, http://www.intercom.museum/conferences/2004/phelan.html.

13. Ibid.

14. "ICOM Code of Ethics for Museums," 8.

15. Ibid., 10.

16. Saint Louis Art Museum, "Mummy Mask of the Lady Ka-nefer-nefer," Saint Louis Art Museum website, Ancient Art Collections, 66, accessed February 23, 2015, http://slam.org:8080/emuseum/view/objects/asitem/6827/65/displayDate-esc?t:state:flow=90f5ef23-a8ca-4c38-a593-7dcfc9fc42d2.

17. *Art Museum Subdist. of the Metro. Zoo. Park v United States*, 4:11-cv-00291-HEA at para. 25, E.D. Mo. Complaint for Declaratory Judgment, February 15, 2011.

18. "The Discovery of a New Step Pyramid: A Third Dynasty Find at Sakkara," *Illustrated London News*, 980–81.

19. M. Zakaria Goneim, *The Lost Pyramid* (New York: Reinhart & Company, 1956), 65.

20. M. Zakaria Goneim, *Excavations at Saqqara Horus Sekhem-khet—The Unfinished Step Pyramid at Saqqara*, vol. I (Cairo: Impremerie L'Institute Français D'Archéologie Orientale, 1957), 6.

21. Saint Louis Art Museum, "Mummy Mask of the Lady Ka-nefer-nefer, Provenance," Saint Louis Art Museum website, fn. 1, accessed May 25, 2015, Http://slam.org:8080/emuseum/view/objects/asitem/search@/0?t:state:flow=91905ad7-73f4-4e28-a6e6-108beed30078.

22. Ibid., fn. 2.

23. Ibid., fn. 1.

24. Ibid., fn. 3.

25. The Art Museum Subdistrict of the Metropolitan Zoological Park and Museum District of the City of Saint Louis and the Country of Saint Louis v. The United States of America, 7.

26. Ibid., 6–7.

27. Saint Louis Art Museum, "Mummy Mask of the Lady Ka-nefer-nefer, Provenance," fn. 6

28. *United States v. Mask of Ka-Nefer-Nefer*, No. 12-2578 at 2 (8th Cir. June 12, 2014).

29. Ibid.

30. *Mask of Ka-Nefer-Nefer*, No. 12-2578 at 2-3.

31. Ibid., 2–3.

32. *Mask of Ka-Nefer-Nefer*, No. 12-2578 at 3.

33. "Info and Contact," Museum Security Network, accessed February 27, 2015, http://www.museum-security.org.

34. At about the same time, Malcolm Gay, a local journalist, raised questions about the mask's provenance and cited a website that claims that the mask was looted from the Saqqara storerooms in the late 1980s. Malcolm Gay, "Out of Egypt. From a long-buried pyramid to the Saint Louis Art Museum: The Mysterious voyage of the Ka-Nefer-Nefer mask," *Riverfront Times*, February 15, 2006, http://www.riverfront-times.com/2006-02-15/news/out-of-egypt/full/.

35. Laura Elizabeth Young, "A Framework for Resolution of Claims for Cultural Property," A Master's Project, Presented to the Arts and Administration Program of the University of Oregon in partial fulfillment of the requirements for the degree of Master of Science in Arts Management, Eugene, Oregon, December 2007: 61–63.

36. *Art Museum Subdist.*, 4:11-cv-00291-HEA at para. 2.

37. *In rem* forfeiture is a "proceeding . . . directed against the *res*, or the thing involved in some illegal activity specified by statute," Wex Legal Dictionary, Legal Information Institute, Cornell University Law School website, accessed May 22, 2015, https://www.law.cornell.edu/wex/forfeiture.

38. "St. Louis Art Museum Prevails in Ka Nefer Nefer Mummy Mask Case," Committee for Cultural Policy, June 15, 2014, http://committeeforculturalpolicy.org/st-louis-art-museum-prevails-in-ka-nefer-nefer-mummy-mask-case/.

39. Opinion, op cit., 12.

40. Ibid., 14.

41. Alex W. Barker, "Archaeological Ethics: Museums and Collections," in *Ethical Issues in Archaeology*, eds. Larry J. Zimmerman, Karen D. Vitelli, and Julie Hollowell-Zimmer (New York: AltaMira Press, 2003), 72.

42. Alison Wylie, "On Ethics," in *Ethical Issues in Archaeology*, ed. Larry J. Zimmerman, Karen D. Vitelli, and Julie Hollowell-Zimmer (New York: AltaMira Press, 2003), 10. In "A Proposal for Museum Acquisitions in the Future," archaeologist Clemency Coggins recommends that all trade in antiquities be halted for a period of twenty or thirty years to stem the trade in illicit objects. *International Journal of Cultural Property* 7 (1998): 434–37.

43. James Cuno, *Who Owns Antiquity? Museums and the Battle over Our Ancient Heritage* (Princeton: Princeton University Press, 2008), 146.

44. James Cuno, *Museums Matter: In Praise of the Encyclopedic Museum* (Chicago: The University of Chicago Press, 2011), 8.

45. UNESCO, "Convention on the Means of Prohibiting and Preventing the Illicit Import, Export and Transfer of Ownership of Cultural Property," November 14, 1970, UNESCO website, http://portal.unesco.org/en/ev.php-URL_ID=13039&URL_DO=DO_TOPIC&URL_SECTION=201.html.

46. Tom Mashberg and Graham Bowley, "Islamic State Destruction Renews Debate Over Repatriation of Antiquities," *The New York Times*, March 31, 2015, http://www.nytimes.com/2015/03/31/arts/design/islamic-state-destruction-renews-debate-over-repatriation-of-antiquities.html. A different approach for protecting collections in danger is outlined in "Protocols for Safe Havens for Works of Cultural Significance from Countries in Crisis" issued in September 2015 by the Association of Art Museum Directors. This document enumerates procedures for museums "interested in a united effort to offer safe havens to works in danger of being destroyed or looted as a result of war, terrorism or natural disasters." https://www.aamd.org/document/aamd-protocols-for-save-havens-for-works-of-cultural-significance-from-countries-in-crisis.

47. Anne Laure Bandle and Raphael Contel, "Reparation Art: Finding Common Ground in the Resolution of Disputes on Russian War Spoils and Nazi-Looted Art," in *Art, Cultural Heritage and the Market: Ethical and Legal Issues*, ed. Valentina Vadi and Hildegard E. G. S. Schneider (New York: Springer, 2014), 28–30.

48. Lynn H. Nicholas, *The Rape of Europa: The Fate of Europe's Treasure in the Third Reich and the Second World War* (New York: Vintage Books, 1995); Hector Feliciano, *The Lost Museum: The Nazi Conspiracy to Steal the World's Greatest Works of Art* (New York: Basic Books, 1997); and Konstantin Akinsha and Grigorii Kozlov, *Beautiful Loot: The Soviet Plunder of Europe's Art Treasures* (New York: Random House, 1995).

49. Estimates of the number of works in American collections vary widely. In "Documenting Nazi Plunder of European Art," Greg Bradsher, National Archives and Records Administration's Assistant Chief, Archives II Textual Reference Branch, quotes Philip Saunders, editor of Trace, the stolen art register, as stating, "There are at least 100,000 works of art still missing from the Nazi occupation." Greg Bradsher, "Documenting Nazi Plunder of European Art," *The Record* (Washington, DC: National Archives and Records Administration, November 1997), http://www.archives.gov/research/holocaust/records-and-research/documenting-nazi-plunder-of-european-art.html.

50. Association of Art Museum Directors, "Report of the AAMD Task Force on the Spoliation of Art during the Nazi/World War II Ear (1933–1945)," June 4, 1998, Association of Art Museum Directors website, https://aamd.org/standards-and-practices.

51. Ibid.

52. Association of Art Museum Directors, "Art Museums and the Identification and Restitution of Works Stolen by the Nazis," May 2007, Association of Art Museum Directors website, https://aamd.org/sites/default/files/document/Nazi-looted%20art_clean_06_2007.pdf.

53. Ibid.

54. International Council of Museums, "ICOM Recommendations concerning the Return of Works of Art Belonging to Jewish Owners," January 14, 1999, International Council of Museums website, http://archives.icom.museum/worldwar2.html.

55. Ibid.

56. Personal Communication, Julie Hart, Senior Director, Standards & Excellence Programs, American Alliance of Museums, April 10, 2015.

57. American Alliance of Museums, "Standards Regarding the Unlawful Appropriation of Objects During the Nazi Era," 1998, American Alliance of Museums website, http://www.aam-us.org/resources/ethics-standards-and-best-practices/collections-stewardship/objects-during-the-nazi-era.

58. American Alliance of Museums, "Recommended Procedures for Providing Information to the Public about Objects Transferred in Europe during the Nazi Era," 2001, American Alliance of Museums website, http://www.aam-us.org/docs/default-source/professional-resources/nepip-recommended-procedures.

59. Ibid.

60. Nazi-Era Provenance Internet Portal, accessed July 5, 2015, http://nepip.org/index.cfm?menu_type=.

61. U.S. Department of State, "Washington Conference Principles on Nazi-Confiscated Art," December 3, 1998, United States Department of State website, http://www.state.gov/p/eur/rt/hlcst/122038.htm; Vilnius International Forum on Holocaust-Era Looted Cultural Assets, "Vilnius Forum Declaration," October 5, 2000, Commission for Looted Art in Europe website, http://www.lootedartcommission.com/vilnius-forum; Holocaust-Era Assets Conference, "Terezin Declaration," June 30, 2009, Holocaust-Era Assets Conference website, http://www.holocausteraassets.eu/program/conference-proceedings/.

62. Association of Art Museum Directors, "Art Museums and the Identification and Restitution of Works Stolen by the Nazis," May 2007, Association of Art Museum Directors website, https://aamd.org/standards-and-practices.

63. Associated Press, "NY court revives suit over Nazi stolen art at Oklahoma Univ," newsok.com, March 14, 2015, http://newsok.com/court-revives-lawsuit-of-nazi-stolen-art-displayed-at-university-of-oklahoma/article/feed/811703?custom_click=rss&utm_source=feedburner&utm_medium=feed&utm_campaign=Feed%3A+newsok%2Fhome+(NewsOK.com+RSS+-+Home).

64. Courtney Francisco, "UPDATE: Lawmaker telling patrons to avoid OU until famous art stolen by Nazis is returned," KFOR.com, February 7, 2014, http://kfor.com/2014/01/29/could-could-artwork-that-became-nazi-loot-be-hanging-in-ous-museum/.

65. Rick St. Hilaire, "Two Court Battles Raise Questions of Liability for AAM, AAMD, and Other Cultural Property Organizations," Cultural Heritage Lawyer, February 5, 2015, http://culturalheritagelawyer.blogspot.com/2014/02/two-court-battles-raise-questions-of.html. The claims against AAM and AAMD were subsequently dismissed.

66. Stedelijk Museum, "The Stedelijk Museum in the Second World War," Stedelijk Museum website, accessed April 10, 2015, http://www.stedelijk.nl/en/exhibitions/the-stedelijk-museum-the-second-world-war. Mary M. Lane, "The Dutch Stedelijk Museum Questions Origins of Some of its Art," *The Wall Street Journal*, February 26, 2015, http://www.wsj.com/articles/the-dutch-stedelijk-museum-questions-ownership-of-its-art-1424977203.

67. National Park Service, U.S. Department of the Interior, "Native American Graves Protection and Repatriation Act (NAGPRA): A Quick Guide for Preserving Native American Cultural Resources," 2012, National Park Service website, http://www.nps.gov/history/TRIBES/Documents/NAGPRA.pdf.

68. Ibid.

69. National Park Service, U.S. Department of the Interior, "National NAG-PRA, Native American Graves Protection and Repatriation Act," National Park Service website, accessed July 30, 2015, http://www.nps.gov/nagpra/MANDATES/25USC3001etseq.htm.

70. National Park Service, U.S. Department of the Interior, "National NAGPRA, About the Review Committee," National Park Service website, accessed May 1, 2015, http://www.nps.gov/NAGPRA/REVIEW/.

71. Jeanette Greenfield, *The Return of Cultural Treasures*, 3rd ed. (New York: Cambridge University Press, 2007), 331.

72. Michelle Alaimo, "Meteorite Mission: Tribal members visit Tomanowos in New York City," *Smoke Signals*, July 1, 2014, http://www.grandronde.org/news/smoke-signals/2014/07/01/meteorite-mission-tribal-members-visit-tomanowos-in-new-york-city/#sthash.MfQ1mvjb.dpbs.

73. American Museum of Natural History, "The Willamette Meteorite, Exhibition Text," The American Museum of Natural History website, accessed May 6, 2015, http://www.amnh.org/exhibitions/permanent-exhibitions/rose-center-for-earth-and-space/dorothy-and-lewis-b.-cullman-hall-of-the-universe/planets/planetary-impacts/the-willamette-meteorite.

74. Douglas J. Preston, "The Willamette Meteorite," *Dinosaurs in the Attic: an Excursion into the American Museum of Natural History* (New York: Ballantine Books, 1986), http://www.usgennet.org/alhnorus/ahorclak/MeteorTreasures.html.

75. Benjamin Weiser, "Museum Sues to Keep Meteorite Sought by Indian Group," *The New York Times*, February 29, 2000, http://www.nytimes.com/2000/02/29/nyregion/museum-sues-to-keep-meteorite-sought-by-indian-group.html.

76. American Museum of Natural History, "Willamette Meteorite Agreement," June 22, 2000, America Museum of Natural History website, http://www.amnh.org/exhibitions/permanent-exhibitions/rose-center-for-earth-and-space/dorothy-and-lewis-b.-cullman-hall-of-the-universe/willamette-meteorite-agreement.

77. Ibid.

78. Micelle Alaimo, "Meteorite Mission: Tribal members visit Tomanowos in New York City." Ibid.

79. Martha Graham and Nell Murphy, "NAGPRA at 20: Museum Collections and Reconnections," *Museum Anthropology* 33, no. 2 (2010): 105–24.

80. Heather J. H. Edgar and Anna L. M. Rautman, "Contemporary Museum Policies and the Ethics of Accepting Human Remains," *Curator: The Museum Journal* 57, no. 2 (April 2014): 244.

81. Ibid.

82. Ibid.

83. Ibid.

84. Steven Litt, "Cleveland Museum of Art returns Hanuman sculpture to Cambodia, saying new evidence indicates it was probably looted," *The Plain Dealer*, May 11, 2015, http://www.cleveland.com/arts/index.ssf/2015/05/cleveland_museum_of_art_return.html.

85. Ibid.

ADDITIONAL RESOURCES

Gerstenblith, Patty, ed. "Special Issue: Ethical Considerations and Cultural Property." *International Journal of Cultural Property*, vol. 7, no. 1 (1998).

Malaro, Marie C. and Ildiko Pogány DeAngelis. "Objects Improperly Removed from Their Countries of Origin." In *A Legal Primer on Managing Museum Collections*, 3rd ed. Washington, DC: Smithsonian Books, 2012, 83–135.

Trope, Jack F. and Walter R. Echo-Hawk. "The Native American Graves Protection and Repatriation Act: Background and Legislative History." *Arizona State Law Journal*, vol. 24 (1992), 35–73.

Vadi, Valentina and Hildegard E. G. S. Schneider, eds. *Art, Cultural Heritage and the Market: Ethical and Legal Issues*. New York: Springer, 2014.

Chapter 10

Museum Visitors

Ethical Issues Concerning Diversity and Access

As institutions "grounded in the tradition of public service,"[1] museums balance their role as preservers of cultural heritage with their need to have meaning for the public, providing an opportunity for visitors to see and learn from the collections that they hold in trust. The policy report *Excellence and Equity*, published by the American Alliance of Museums in 1992, acknowledged museums' burgeoning efforts to reach broad and inclusive audiences and make an institution-wide commitment to education, "sharing knowledge with the public."[2] Since then, museums have sought to define their missions in terms of social responsibility, engaging in debates about the extent to which museums can and should involve their audiences.[3] Many now seek more far-reaching connections with their communities, as a way of fulfilling their responsibility to the public they serve, strengthening their impact and furthering their educational missions.

Within the museum, discussions about audiences often focus upon issues related to diversity and access. While often referred to separately, they are closely linked. For increasing access to a museum, making it more welcoming and usable, increases the diversity of the audiences that it serves. In this context, *diversity* is commonly used to refer to the ethnic, cultural, and social mix of an institution's board, staff, and visitors. *Access* conventionally meant the availability of collections for reference or research, and while this use is still common, *access* also has come to have a much broader meaning. In the most expansive sense, it can refer to the approachability of a museum—the ease with which the public can enter a museum and navigate its spaces. Is the museum's front door forbidding or off-putting to those not familiar with the institution? Are its front desk and security staff welcoming? *Access* can also refer to the hours of operation. Is the museum open at times that are convenient for its audiences? Does it have evening and/or weekend hours to afford access to those unable to visit during the weekdays? Are its weekend hours flexible enough to include people of all faiths? Since the enactment of the Americans with Disabilities legislation in 1990, it also refers to accessibility for people with physical and cognitive challenges, encompassing both physical access and intellectual access for people with visual, auditory, and other impairments. Can wheelchair users easily navigate museum exhibitions? Do labels and text panels use fonts that are legible by people with visual impairments? Can individuals with different learning abilities understand them? How will the deaf and people with hearing loss participate in the museum's programs?

Access can also refer to social inclusion. As Mark O'Neill notes, this "is not about simplifying difficult things. It is about providing points of entry for people whose education or background has not equipped them to approach difficult works that they might in fact be interested in."[4] And, finally, *access* can also be used to mean affordability, especially as museum entrance fees rise and income disparities increase.

What are the ethical issues that museums face relating to these questions? Interestingly, the American Alliance of Museums' Code of Ethics addresses diversity and access in only the most general terms. It notes that the governance of a museum must ensure that all of the institution's resources "support the museum's mission, respond to the pluralism of society, and respect the diversity of the natural and cultural common wealth." Further, "the governing authority ensures that . . . it [the museum] is responsive to and represents the interests of society."[5]

On the issue of a museum's collections, the Code notes, "Stewardship of collections entails the highest public trust and carries with it the presumption of rightful ownership, permanence, care, documentation, accessibility and responsible disposal." It goes on to specify that "access to the collections and related information is permitted and regulated." The AAM Code also states that "programs [e.g., exhibitions, publications, educational activities] . . . are responsive to the concerns, interests and needs of society," thus they are "accessible and encourage participation of the widest possible audience consistent with its [i.e., the museum's] mission and resources." They also "respect pluralistic values, traditions and concerns."[6]

Nonetheless, AAM considers diversity and access to be core standards. They are articulated in the "Characteristics of Excellence for U.S. Museums," which emphasizes their importance in maintaining the public trust and the museum's accountability. The Characteristics state:

- The museum identifies the communities it serves, and makes appropriate decisions on how it serves them.
- Regardless of its self-identified communities, the museum strives to be a good neighbor in its geographic area.

- The museum strives to be inclusive and offers opportunities for diverse participation.
- The museum asserts its public service role and places education at the center of that role.
- The museum demonstrates a commitment to providing the public with physical and intellectual access to the museum and its resources.[7]

Given this emphasis within the core standards, it could be argued that AAM might consider it unethical if a museum were not to take these responsibilities to its audiences into account.

Issues related to access and diversity underpin the ICOM Code of Ethics for Museums. Five of its eight principles mention access and the remaining three mention it implicitly or indirectly. The ICOM Code of Ethics places the responsibility for a museum's accessibility, first and foremost, with its governing body. In outlining the elements that make up its first ethical principle, the Code states, "The governing body should ensure that the museum and its collections are available to all during reasonable hours and for regular periods. Particular regard should be given to those persons with special needs." And "the governing body should ensure that institution standards of health, safety and accessibility apply to its personnel and visitors."[8]

In discussing ethical principles related to a museum's collections, ICOM notes that "inherent in this public trust is the notion of stewardship that includes rightful ownership, permanence, documentation, accessibility and responsible disposal"; that "museums have particular responsibilities to all for the care, accessibility and interpretation of primary evidence collected and held in their collections"; and that "museums have a particular responsibility for making collections and all relevant information available as freely as possible, having regard to restraints arising for reasons of confidentiality and security."[9]

AASLH devotes a section of its Statement of Professional Standards and Ethics to Access, "Access to historical resources is what gives preservation activities their meaning. Providing non-discriminatory access to historical resources through exhibitions, tours, educational programs, publication, electronic media and research is critical in fulfilling the public trust and mission of historical organizations. Access and limitations of access are governed by institutional policies and by applicable rights of privacy, ownership and intellectual freedom."

In its discussion of interpretation, this Statement notes, "Interpretation must use a method of delivery that takes into consideration both the intended audience and the resources of sound scholarship and thorough research. Historical organizations shall work towards inclusiveness with the goals of social responsibility and respect for different cultures and peoples."

All of these codes and standards for professional practice, then, focus upon the responsibility of museums to serve their public audiences, to provide accessible facilities and programs for all, and to ensure that their collections, either on exhibition or in storage, are available. But they are also very general in scope and may not give adequate assistance to a museum in handling problems related to access. Consequently, guidance in dealing with these issues needs to be and is often covered in a museum's policies and procedures (e.g., the institutional code of ethics should be more detailed and the collection management policy usually specifies terms for access to collections not on exhibition); nonetheless, these documents provide only general direction, and museum staff must weigh alternative actions to determine the ethically appropriate way to proceed. The following case studies illustrate how issues related to diversity, collections access, and accessibility for individuals with special needs might create ethical dilemmas.

ETHICS IN ACTION

With the exception of the Musée D'Orsay, the people and institutions in the following cases are fictional. The hypothetical situations combine real and imaginary circumstances and reflect actual issues faced by museums. Any resemblance to a real museum is purely coincidental.

A Disadvantaged Family Visits a Museum

While museums may pride themselves in being "open to all," they are, nonetheless, public institutions and must make sure that they maintain a safe, welcoming, and pleasant environment. Consider the case of a large urban art museum that is reaching out to poor families, encouraging them to visit. The museum works in partnership with a number of community service organizations in this effort to broaden its audience base and to allow for greater diverse participation in the museum's activities. One Saturday afternoon, a family (mother, father, and son) visits the museum, accompanied by a volunteer from the social service organization with which the family is affiliated. As they walk through one well-populated gallery, some visitors begin to discretely cover their noses and leave the gallery, and a number of others approach the museum guard in the room, complaining about the family's odor. Museum regulations mention nothing about suitable dress, physical appearance, or personal hygiene. What is the appropriate response to this situation? Would it be unethical for the museum guard to ask the visitors to leave? Are there alternatives that might be pursued?

Would the situation be different if some of the visitors who complained were major donors to the museum or museum trustees? How can the museum demonstrate that it respects all of its visitors?

At the Musée d'Orsay in Paris in 2013, in a situation not unlike that of the poor family described above, a museum guard asked the family to leave. On behalf of the family, the accompanying volunteer refused, noting that the family was decently dressed and they were not bothering anyone. He added that the family was not in breach of the regulations of the museum. When the family moved to an empty gallery in another part of the museum, several guards approached them and escorted them to the exit, refunding their admission fee. While the guards treated the family respectfully and did not call attention to them, the representative of the organization accompanying the family was deeply offended by the incident. He complained to the museum and to the media, which then widely circulated his complaint, embellishing upon the story.[10] In response, the museum issued a press release explaining its perspective on the incident, saying that the museum had responded appropriately and discretely, respecting the dignity of the poor visitors. The museum also expressed chagrin over the inaccuracies that had cropped up in the reports by the press. One month later, the social service organization, which represents an international movement to fight poverty and social exclusion, sued the museum.

Later in the year, the case was mediated by the Défenseur des droits (the Defender of Rights), a French independent constitutional authority responsible for ensuring the protection of rights and freedoms and promoting equality.[11] The Defender found that no legal or ethical wrongs had been committed by the museum and invited the museum and the human rights organization to continue to work together to raise the awareness of caregivers, staff, and managers so that the museum might be a host to all members of the public without stigmatization or difference in treatment.[12]

Considering again the basic situation in the museum, would your response have been different if the offending visitors were wearing heavy perfume that aggravated others in the galleries? Or if the visitors were tall teenage boys, wearing t-shirts with offensive slogans, who were making their presence known to other visitors without directly engaging them verbally or touching them?

Small Fry

Sometimes when a museum welcomes one group, it may have to limit the use of its spaces by other groups. For example, a new exhibition at an aquarium tested the institution's ability to balance the needs of two visitor groups. The aquarium was interested in developing a new exhibition for a very young audience, for they had noticed that these toddlers were often intimidated by crowds of older and bigger children that congregated in their hands-on exhibit areas. As a result they developed *Fishscapes*, an exhibition for children aged three and under that includes a range of hands-on activities. With its fanciful environment mimicking the undersea world, it is a space in which children and their caregivers can explore and play together. Fish Guides, specially trained staff, are posted in the gallery to facilitate the use of the exhibition, and one of them guards the entrance to make sure that the toddlers don't run off to other unsupervised parts of the aquarium.

When the exhibit was in development, aquarium staff became aware that its activities would be appropriate not only for toddlers but also for older children with learning disabilities. But they knew that the presence of these older children could be distracting to the toddlers. They consulted with several organizations that work with children with learning disabilities to see if they might have objections to the aquarium creating an exhibition that would be restricted to a younger age group and that would prohibit their groups from entering. These groups, frequent visitors to the aquarium, understood the issues involved and saw no issues with the restrictions. Thus, to ensure that toddlers can enjoy *Fishscapes* without interruption, the aquarium restricted the space, posting signs explaining that *Fishscapes* is only open to for children aged three and under, accompanied by an adult. It falls upon the Fish Guide who monitors the entrance to the exhibition to enforce the restrictive policy and make sure that older children who might overpower the toddlers do not use the area.

Fishscape's colorful graphics and engaging activities make it one of the most attractive areas in the aquarium and the exhibition has been very successful. Nonetheless, there are times during the day when the space is empty. During those times, the parents or caretakers of older children with learning disabilities have approached the Fish Guides and asked whether these children might play in *Fishscapes*. The exhibition would certainly be appropriate for these older children, since it includes activities that would be suited to their developmental age. But were a group of younger children to arrive while the children with disabilities were in the space, the younger children might be prevented from using it or might not feel comfortable about playing in the area with older and bigger children. The Fish Guides have a difficult time explaining why the children with learning disabilities cannot use the seemingly empty exhibition area. By restricting access to *Fishscapes*, has the aquarium acted unethically? How should the aquarium handle this problem? What kind of guidance could be given to the Fish Guides to help them resolve the issues with visitors?

Child with Autism

The Americans with Disabilities Act (ADA) requires that museums, as places of public accommodation, provide equal access to their facilities to people with disabilities. As a result, museums must ensure that their facilities are accessible to all, including people with disabilities, and that their exhibitions can accommodate individuals with visual, auditory, and learning impairments. While ADA legislation has sensitized museums to some of the issues that arise regarding these groups, problems arise that do not have simple solutions. For example, two parents and their three-year-old autistic son visited a large metropolitan art museum. While they were visiting one exhibition, the young boy saw a ball in a painting. He loved to play with balls and started loudly repeating the word over and over again. The boy's mother approached the museum guard standing in the gallery the family was visiting, identified herself as the child's mother, and explained that her son was *stimming* (from self-stimulatory behavior) or engaging in a repetitive body movement common to many people with autism. She told the guard that both she and the child's father were in the gallery, tending to their son, and she expected that the child would calm down shortly. While some of the other visitors to the gallery looked askance at the child and his parents, none seemed excessively bothered by the child's behavior. The guard, on the other hand, began to pace uncomfortably around the gallery, clearly bothered by the child's behavior and concerned about how best to deal with it. What action, if any, should the guard take? If the child's behavior continues to be disruptive, should the guard intervene and ask the parents and their child to leave? Is this an ethical question or simply an operational problem?

Access to Collections

The American Alliance of Museums Code of Ethics stipulates that access to a museum's collections and related information is permitted and regulated,[13] and taking its resources into account, particularly the availability of its staff to properly oversee the use of the collections, each museum should stipulate in its collection management policy how access will be provided. As Malaro and DeAngelis note, "For the museum, the problem is how to balance a desire to accommodate requests for special access with the need to protect its collections."[14] Sometimes, the urge to protect collections overcomes the duty to provide access, and potential unethical situations result. Consider the case of a local historical society that was given a small purse made from the skin of a convicted murderer after he was executed by hanging. This nineteenth-century oddity has been in the historical society's collections for over one hundred years and has never been exhibited, but recently a television features reporter has called the historical society's registrar asking to see the purse. The reporter is researching the story of the murderer on the occasion of the 175th anniversary of the man's execution and has discovered that the man was flayed after he was killed so that "souvenirs" could be made of his skin.

His research has led him to the historical society, which is rumored to have one of these "souvenirs" in its collections. Although the historical society has known about the wallet in its collections for some time and has even shown it to its board of trustees as an example of some of its more unusual collections items, the staff has been unwilling to make the wallet more broadly known in fear that it will attract a host of inquiries from curiosity seekers that could become disruptive and time consuming. The society has limited staff and the registrar only works three days a week. Consequently, the registrar is reluctant to respond positively to this inquiry, considering it fraught with potential sensationalism. Is it unethical for the historical society to deny access to the skin wallet because of the registrar's fear that he will be overwhelmed with requests to view it? Or that potential negative publicity might result from providing access? Would the case be different if the query were from a member of the public who simply wishes to see the skin wallet? Or, more generally, would it be ethical for a museum to limit access to items in its collections to people who have what the museum considers an appropriate purpose in examining them (e.g., education, research)?

Consider the case of a museum with a valuable coin collection. Previously when the museum provided access to coin collectors, pieces were stolen from the collection. As a result, the museum restricts access to its coins and does not allow coin collectors to have access to them. Is this ethical?

In another case, two individuals independently approach a museum with a modest but exquisite collection of Greek and Roman antiquities and request access to the collections not on display. The museum's collection management policy stipulates that such access is permissible for "serious inquiries." The individuals are a high school student working on a term paper about Poseidon and a well-known art historian finishing an article for a scholarly journal. Would it be ethical for the museum to allow the scholar and not the high school student to have access for their research?

Access to Collections Records

Collections records, developed to document the objects in a museum's care, provide important information about the objects. Without these records, many items in a museum's collection would have limited value for use in exhibitions and research. Yet some of the information in the records is private (e.g., information about donors and collectors as well as the assessed value of objects) and should be protected especially from commercial use. Other information, for example, research notes for future publications or exhibitions, could be considered proprietary. An institution's collection management policy should demonstrate knowledge of relevant legislation and privacy laws in stipulating terms of access for collections records.[15] Nonetheless, even the best collection management policies do not cover all the possible situations that might arise. For example, a regional art museum has an important collection of early twentieth-century paintings that include works by several artists who have recently become popular. The museum has both registration and curatorial archives related to these paintings. The registration records include accession data, condition reports, donor information, the conservation and exhibition history of the paintings since they were donated to the museum, and their assessed value at that time. The latter was information given to the museum by the painting's previous owner, a friend of one of the artists.

The curator of the museum is working on an exhibition highlighting the museum's works by these painters, which she hopes will bring renewed attention to the museum's collection. She has uncovered some previously unknown correspondence between one of the artists and his patron which sheds new light onto the artist's work as well as on the relationships among the group of painters. She has also developed relationships with several collectors who own paintings by members of the group which have not previously been exhibited. All of her notes are part of the curatorial records relating to the collection of paintings.

An art dealer, known to the museum as a specialist in early twentieth-century art, is researching subjects related to the museum's painting collection for an exhibition he is organizing in his gallery. He has requested access to the museum's collections records. While the museum has a detailed collection management policy for its collections, its section on access merely states that reasonable access will be given to the collections. It does not specifically mention the collection records. Would it be unethical for the museum to deny the dealer access to the collections records? What options might the museum have?

FINAL THOUGHTS

As information about museum collections becomes more readily available through museums' own websites as well as aggregate sites like Google Art Project, demands on access to collections objects could increase significantly. These demands could also intensify the tension between the museum's need to preserve its holdings and its desire to provide public access. Creative solutions may be needed to give visitors adequate access to their cultural heritage while still ensuring the museum collections are safeguarded for future generations.

Museums are by their very nature socially responsible institutions. They hold, preserve, and exhibit collections for the edification of the public and in so doing can benefit society. But their success and vitality rely not just upon their ability to care for their resources but also upon the quality of their relationships with people. In order to maintain their significance amidst the demographic and technological changes that we are witnessing today, museums must continually make a case for their relevance and speak to increasingly diverse audiences with different needs. An aging population, increased awareness of special needs of young learners, the obligation to provide equal access for people with disabilities place greater demands upon museums to provide appropriate accommodations in their facilities, exhibitions, and programs. Ethical issues related to diversity and access will come more and more to the fore as museums grapple with their proper role in our changing society. A commitment to diversity and access will be critical. It helps broaden a museum's audiences, encourages existing visitors to return more often, and opens the possibility for fruitful partnerships with other institutions. The greater a museum's dedication to access, the stronger its connections with the people it serves will be.

NOTES

1. American Alliance of Museums, "Code of Ethics for Museums," American Alliance of Museums website, amended 2000, http://www.aam-us.org/resources/ ethics-standards-and-best-practices/code-of-ethics.
2. Ellen Cochran Hirzy, ed., *Excellence and Equity: Education and the Public Dimension of Museums* (Washington, DC: American Association of Museums, 1992), 11.
3. See for example, James Cuno, ed., *Whose Muse? Art Museums and the Public Trust* (Princeton, NJ: Princeton University Press, 2004) on the universal or encyclopedic museum versus the volumes on a museum's social responsibility, for example, Richard Sandell and Eithne Nightingale, eds., *Museums, Society, Inequality* (New York: Routledge, 2002), and Elizabeth Crooke, *Museums and Community: Ideas, Issues and Challenges* (New York: Routledge, 2007).
4. Mark O'Neill, "Commentary 4. John Holden's *Capturing Cultural Value: How Culture has become a tool of Government Policy*," *Cultural Trends* 14:1, no. 53 (2005): 123.
5. Ibid.
6. Ibid.
7. American Alliance of Museums, "Characteristics of Excellence for U.S. Museums," American Alliance of Museums website, accessed January 3, 2014. http://www.aam-us.org/resources/ethics-standards-and-best-practices/ characteristics-of-excellence-for-u-s-museums.
8. International Council of Museums, "ICOM Code of Ethics for Museums," International Council of Museums website, revised 2004, http://icom.museum/ the-vision/code-of-ethics/.
9. Ibid.

10. Alexandra Michot, "Une Famille défavorisée expulse du Musée d'Orsay," LE FIGARO.fr, 29/01/2013, http://www.lefigaro.fr/actualite-france/2013/01/29/01016-20130129ARTFIG00323-une-famille-defavorisee-expulsee-du-musee-d-orsay.php.

11. Le Défenseur des Droits, "Qui sommes nous?" Le Défenseur des Droits website, accessed January 6, 2014, http://www.defenseurdesdroits.fr/sinformer-sur-le-defenseur-des-droits/linstitution/actualites/litige-atd-quart-monde-contre-musee.

12. Dominique Baudis, Décision du Défenseur des droits no.MSP 2013-223, Le Défenseur de Droits website, accessed January 6, 2014, http://www.defenseurdesdroits.fr/sinformer-sur-le-defenseur-des-droits/linstitution/actualites/litige-atd-quart-monde-contre-musee.

13. American Alliance of Museums, "Code of Ethics for Museums."

14. Marie C. Malaro and Ildiko Pogány DeAngelis, *A Legal Primer on Managing Museum Collections*, 3rd ed. (Washington, DC: Smithsonian Books, 2012), 476.

15. Ibid., 477–86.

ADDITIONAL RESOURCES

Crooke, Elizabeth. *Museums and Community: Ideas, Issues and Challenges.* New York: Routledge, 2007.

Sandell, Richard and Eithne Nightingale, eds. *Museums, Equality and Social Justice.* New York: Routledge, 2012.

Appendix 1

American Alliance of Museums

Code of Ethics for Museums

Adopted 1994, amended 2000

Please note that the Code of Ethics for Museums references the American Association of Museums (AAM), now called the American Alliance of Museums.

Ethical codes evolve in response to changing conditions, values, and ideas. A professional code of ethics must, therefore, be periodically updated. It must also rest upon widely shared values. Although the operating environment of museums grows more complex each year, the root value for museums, the tie that connects all of us together despite our diversity, is the commitment to serving people, both present and future generations. This value guided the creation of and remains the most fundamental principle in the following Code of Ethics for Museums.

CODE OF ETHICS FOR MUSEUMS

Museums make their unique contribution to the public by collecting, preserving and interpreting the things of this world. Historically, they have owned and used natural objects, living and nonliving, and all manner of human artifacts to advance knowledge and nourish the human spirit. Today, the range of their special interests reflects the scope of human vision. Their missions include collecting and preserving, as well as exhibiting and educating with materials not only owned but also borrowed and fabricated for these ends. Their numbers include both governmental and private museums of anthropology, art history and natural history, aquariums, arboreta, art centers, botanical gardens, children's museums, historic sites, nature centers, planetariums, science and technology centers, and zoos. The museum universe in the United States includes both collecting and noncollecting institutions. Although diverse in their missions, they have in common their nonprofit form of organization and a commitment of service to the public. Their collections and/or the objects they borrow or fabricate are the basis for research, exhibits, and programs that invite public participation.

Taken as a whole, museum collections and exhibition materials represent the world's natural and cultural common wealth. As stewards of that wealth, museums are compelled to advance an understanding of all natural forms and of the human experience. It is incumbent on museums to be resources for humankind and in all their activities to foster an informed appreciation of the rich and diverse world we have inherited. It is also incumbent upon them to preserve that inheritance for posterity.

Museums in the United States are grounded in the tradition of public service. They are organized as public trusts, holding their collections and information as a benefit for those they were established to serve. Members of their governing authority, employees and volunteers are committed to the interests of these beneficiaries. The law provides the basic framework for museum operations. As nonprofit institutions, museums comply with applicable local, state, and federal laws and international conventions, as well as with the specific legal standards governing trust responsibilities. This Code of Ethics for Museums takes that compliance as given. But legal standards are a minimum. Museums and those responsible for them must do more than avoid legal liability, they must take affirmative steps to maintain their integrity so as to warrant public confidence. They must act not only legally but also ethically. This Code of Ethics for Museums, therefore, outlines ethical standards that frequently exceed legal minimums.

Loyalty to the mission of the museum and to the public it serves is the essence of museum work, whether volunteer or paid. Where conflicts of interest arise—actual, potential or perceived—the duty of loyalty must never be compromised. No individual may use his or her position in a museum for personal gain or to benefit another at the expense of the museum, its mission, its reputation and the society it serves.

For museums, public service is paramount. To affirm that ethic and to elaborate its application to their governance, collections and programs, the American Association of Museums promulgates this Code of Ethics for Museums. In subscribing to this code, museums assume responsibility for the actions of members of their governing authority, employees and volunteers in the performance of museum-related duties. Museums, thereby, affirm their chartered purpose, ensure the prudent application of their resources, enhance their effectiveness and maintain public confidence. This collective endeavor strengthens museum work and the contributions of museums to society—present and future.

Governance

Museum governance in its various forms is a public trust responsible for the institution's service to society. The governing authority protects and enhances the museum's collections and programs and its physical, human and financial resources. It ensures that all these resources support the museum's mission, respond to the pluralism of society and respect the diversity of the natural and cultural common wealth.

Thus, the governing authority ensures that

- all those who work for or on behalf of a museum understand and support its mission and public trust responsibilities
- its members understand and fulfill their trusteeship and act corporately, not as individuals
- the museum's collections and programs and its physical, human and financial resources are protected, maintained and developed in support of the museum's mission
- it is responsive to and represents the interests of society
- it maintains the relationship with staff in which shared roles are recognized and separate responsibilities respected
- working relationships among trustees, employees and volunteers are based on equity and mutual respect
- professional standards and practices inform and guide museum operations
- policies are articulated and prudent oversight is practiced
- governance promotes the public good rather than individual financial gain.

Collections

The distinctive character of museum ethics derives from the ownership, care and use of objects, specimens, and living collections representing the world's natural and cultural common wealth. This stewardship of collections entails the highest public trust and carries with it the presumption of rightful ownership, permanence, care, documentation, accessibility and responsible disposal.

Thus, the museum ensures that

- collections in its custody support its mission and public trust responsibilities
- collections in its custody are lawfully held, protected, secure, unencumbered, cared for and preserved
- collections in its custody are accounted for and documented
- access to the collections and related information is permitted and regulated
- acquisition, disposal, and loan activities are conducted in a manner that respects the protection and preservation of natural and cultural resources and discourages illicit trade in such materials

- acquisition, disposal, and loan activities conform to its mission and public trust responsibilities
- disposal of collections through sale, trade or research activities is solely for the advancement of the museum's mission. Proceeds from the sale of non-living collections are to be used consistent with the established standards of the museum's discipline; but in no event shall they be used for anything other than acquisition or direct care of collections.
- the unique and special nature of human remains and funerary and sacred objects is recognized as the basis of all decisions concerning such collections
- collections-related activities promote the public good rather than individual financial gain
- competing claims of ownership that may be asserted in connection with objects in its custody should be handled openly, seriously, responsively and with respect for the dignity of all parties involved.

Programs

Museums serve society by advancing an understanding and appreciation of the natural and cultural common wealth through exhibitions, research, scholarship, publications and educational activities. These programs further the museum's mission and are responsive to the concerns, interests and needs of society.

Thus, the museum ensures that:

- programs support its mission and public trust responsibilities
- programs are founded on scholarship and marked by intellectual integrity
- programs are accessible and encourage participation of the widest possible audience consistent with its mission and resources
- programs respect pluralistic values, traditions and concerns
- revenue-producing activities and activities that involve relationships with external entities are compatible with the museum's mission and support its public trust responsibilities
- programs promote the public good rather than individual financial gain.

Promulgation

This Code of Ethics for Museums was adopted by the Board of Directors of the American Association of Museums on November 12, 1993. The AAM Board of Directors recommends that each nonprofit museum member of the American Association of Museums adopt and promulgate its separate code of ethics, applying the Code of Ethics for Museums to its own institutional setting.

A Committee on Ethics, nominated by the president of the AAM and confirmed by the Board of Directors, will be charged with two responsibilities:

- establishing programs of information, education and assistance to guide museums in developing their own codes of ethics
- reviewing the Code of Ethics for Museums and periodically recommending refinements and revisions to the Board of Directors.

Afterword

Each nonprofit museum member of the American Association of Museums should subscribe to the AAM Code of Ethics for Museums. Subsequently, these museums should set about framing their own institutional codes of ethics, which should be in conformance with the AAM code and should expand on it through the elaboration of specific practices. This recommendation is made to these member institutions in the belief that engaging the governing authority, staff and volunteers in applying the AAM code to institutional settings will stimulate the development and maintenance of sound policies and procedures necessary to understanding and ensuring ethical behavior by institutions and by all who work for them or on their behalf.

The Code of Ethics for Museums serves the interests of museums, their constituencies and society. The primary goal of AAM is to encourage institutions to regulate the ethical behavior of members of their governing authority, employees and volunteers. Formal adoption of an institutional code promotes higher and more consistent ethical standards.

International Council of Museums

ICOM Code of Ethics for Museums

PREAMBLE

Status of the ICOM Code of Ethics for Museums

The *ICOM Code of Ethics for Museums* has been prepared by the International Council of Museums. It is the statement of ethics for museums referred to in the ICOM Statutes. The Code reflects principles generally accepted by the international museum community. Membership in ICOM and the payment of the annual subscription to ICOM are an affirmation of the *ICOM Code of Ethics for Museums*.

A Minimum Standard for Museums

The ICOM Code represents a minimum standard for museums. It is presented as a series of principles supported by guidelines for desirable professional practice. In some countries, certain minimum standards are defined by law or government regulation. In others, guidance on and assessment of minimum professional standards may be available in the form of "Accreditation," "Registration," or similar evaluative schemes. Where such standards are not defined, guidance can be obtained through the ICOM Secretariat, a relevant National Committee of ICOM, or the appropriate International Committee of ICOM. It is also intended that individual nations and the specialised subject organisations connected with museums should use this Code as a basis for developing additional standards.

Appendix 2

ICOM CODE OF ETHICS FOR MUSEUMS

1. MUSEUMS PRESERVE, INTERPRET AND PROMOTE THE NATURAL AND CULTURAL INHERITANCE OF HUMANITY

Principle

Museums are responsible for the tangible and intangible natural and cultural heritage. Governing bodies and those concerned with the strategic direction and oversight of museums have a primary responsibility to protect and promote this heritage as well as the human, physical and financial resources made available for that purpose.

INSTITUTIONAL STANDING

1.1 Enabling Documentation

The governing body should ensure that the museum has a written and published constitution, statute, or other public document in accordance with national laws, which clearly states the museum's legal status, mission, permanence and non-profit nature.

1.2 Statement of the Mission, Objectives and Policies

The governing body should prepare, publicise and be guided by a statement of the mission, objectives and policies of the museum and of the role and composition of the governing body.

PHYSICAL RESOURCES

1.3 Premises

The governing body should ensure adequate premises with a suitable environment for the museum to fulfil the basic functions defined in its mission.

1.4 Access

The governing body should ensure that the museum and its collections are available to all during reasonable hours and for regular periods. Particular regard should be given to those persons with special needs.

1.5 Health and Safety

The governing body should ensure that institutional standards of health, safety and accessibility apply to its personnel and visitors.

1.6 Protection Against Disasters

The governing body should develop and maintain policies to protect the public and personnel, the collections and other resources against natural and human-made disasters.

1.7 Security Requirements

The governing body should ensure appropriate security to protect collections against theft or damage in displays, exhibitions, working or storage areas and while in transit.

1.8 Insurance and Indemnity

Where commercial insurance is used for collections, the governing body should ensure that such cover is adequate and includes objects in transit or on loan and other items that are the responsibility of the museum. When an indemnity scheme is in use, it is necessary that material not in the ownership of the museum be adequately covered.

FINANCIAL RESOURCES

1.9 Funding

The governing body should ensure that there are sufficient funds to carry out and develop the activities of the museum. All funds must be accounted for in a professional manner.

1.10 Income-generating Policy

The governing body should have a written policy regarding sources of income that it may generate through its activities or accept from outside sources. Regardless of funding source, museums should maintain control of the content and integrity of their programmes, exhibitions and activities. Income-generating activities should not compromise the standards of the institution or its public (see 6.6).

PERSONNEL

1.11 Employment Policy

The governing body should ensure that all action concerning personnel is taken in accordance with the policies of the museum as well as the proper and legal procedures.

1.12 Appointment of the Director or Head

The director or head of the museum is a key post and when making an appointment, governing bodies should have regard for the knowledge and skills required to fill the post effectively. These qualities should include adequate intellectual ability and professional knowledge, complemented by a high standard of ethical conduct.

1.13 Access to Governing Bodies

The director or head of a museum should be directly responsible, and have direct access, to the relevant governing bodies.

1.14 Competence of Museum

Personnel

The employment of qualified personnel with the expertise required to meet all responsibilities is necessary (see also 2.19; 2.24; section 8).

1.15 Training of Personnel

Adequate opportunities for the continuing education and professional development of all museum personnel should be arranged to maintain an effective workforce.

1.16 Ethical Conflict

The governing body should never require museum personnel to act in a way that could be considered to conflict with the provisions of this Code of Ethics, or any national law or specialist code of ethics.

1.17 Museum Personnel and Volunteers

The governing body should have a written policy on volunteer work that promotes a positive relationship between volunteers and members of the museum profession.

1.18 Volunteers and Ethics

The governing body should ensure that volunteers, when conducting museum and personal activities, are fully conversant with the ICOM Code of Ethics for Museums and other applicable codes and laws.

2. MUSEUMS THAT MAINTAIN COLLECTIONS HOLD THEM IN TRUST FOR THE BENEFIT OF SOCIETY AND ITS DEVELOPMENT

Principle

Museums have the duty to acquire, preserve and promote their collections as a contribution to safeguarding the natural, cultural and scientific heritage. Their collections are a significant public inheritance, have a special position in law and are protected by international legislation. Inherent in this public trust is the notion of stewardship that includes rightful ownership, permanence, documentation, accessibility and responsible disposal.

ACQUIRING COLLECTIONS

2.1 Collections Policy

The governing body for each museum should adopt and publish a written collections policy that addresses the acquisition, care and use of collections. The policy should clarify the position of any material that will not be catalogued, conserved, or exhibited (see 2.7; 2.8).

2.2 Valid Title

No object or specimen should be acquired by purchase, gift, loan, bequest, or exchange unless the acquiring museum is satisfied that a valid title is held. Evidence of lawful ownership in a country is not necessarily valid title.

2.3 Provenance and Due Diligence

Every effort must be made before acquisition to ensure that any object or specimen offered for purchase, gift, loan, bequest, or exchange has not been illegally obtained in, or exported from its country of origin or any intermediate country in which it might have been owned legally (including the museum's own country). Due diligence in this regard should establish the full history of the item since discovery or production.

2.4 Objects and Specimens from Unauthorised or Unscientific Fieldwork

Museums should not acquire objects where there is reasonable cause to believe their recovery involved unauthorised or unscientific fieldwork, or intentional destruction or damage of monuments, archaeological or geological sites, or of species and natural habitats. In the same way, acquisition should not occur if there has been a failure to disclose the finds to the owner or occupier of the land, or to the proper legal or governmental authorities.

2.5 Culturally Sensitive Material

Collections of human remains and material of sacred significance should be acquired only if they can be housed securely and cared for respectfully. This must be accomplished in a manner consistent with professional standards and the interests and beliefs of members of the community, ethnic or religious groups from which the objects originated, where these are known (see also 3.7; 4.3).

2.6 Protected Biological or Geological Specimens

Museums should not acquire biological or geological specimens that have been collected, sold, or otherwise transferred in contravention of local, national, regional or international law or treaty relating to wildlife protection or natural history conservation.

2.7 Living Collections

When the collections include live botanical or zoological specimens, special consideration should be given to the natural and social environment from which they are derived as well as any local, national, regional or international law or treaty relating to wildlife protection or natural history conservation.

2.8 Working Collections

The collections policy may include special considerations for certain types of working collections where the emphasis is on preserving cultural, scientific, or technical process rather than the object, or where objects or specimens are assembled for regular handling and teaching purposes (see also 2.1).

2.9 Acquisition Outside Collections Policy

The acquisition of objects or specimens outside the museum's stated policy should only be made in exceptional circumstances. The governing body should consider the professional opinions available to it and the views of all interested parties. Consideration will include the significance of the object or specimen, including its context in the cultural or natural heritage, and the special interests of other museums collecting such material. However, even in these circumstances, objects without a valid title should not be acquired (see also 3.4).

2.10 Acquisitions Offered by Members of the Governing Body or Museum Personnel

Special care is required in considering any item, whether for sale, as a donation, or as a tax-benefit gift, from members of governing bodies, museum personnel, or the families and close associates of these persons.

2.11 Repositories of Last Resort

Nothing in this Code of Ethics should prevent a museum from acting as an authorised repository for unprovenanced, illicitly collected or recovered specimens or objects from the territory over which it has lawful responsibility.

REMOVING COLLECTIONS

2.12 Legal or Other Powers of Disposal

Where the museum has legal powers permitting disposals, or has acquired objects subject to conditions of disposal, the legal or other requirements and procedures must be complied with fully. Where the original acquisition was subject to mandatory or other restrictions these conditions must be observed, unless it can be shown clearly that adherence to such restrictions is impossible or substantially detrimental to the institution and, if appropriate, relief may be sought through legal procedures.

2.13 Deaccessioning from Museum Collections

The removal of an object or specimen from a museum collection must only be undertaken with a full understanding of the significance of the item, its character (whether renewable or non-renewable), legal standing, and any loss of public trust that might result from such action.

2.14 Responsibility for Deaccessioning

The decision to deaccession should be the responsibility of the governing body acting in conjunction with the director of the museum and the curator of the collection concerned. Special arrangements may apply to working collections (see 2.7; 2.8).

2.15 Disposal of Objects Removed from the Collections

Each museum should have a policy defining authorised methods for permanently removing an object from the collections through donation, transfer, exchange, sale, repatriation, or destruction, and that allows the transfer of unrestricted title to any receiving agency. Complete records must be kept of all deaccessioning decisions, the objects involved, and the disposal of the object. There will be a strong presumption that a deaccessioned item should first be offered to another museum.

2.16 Income from Disposal of Collections

Museum collections are held in public trust and may not be treated as a realisable asset. Money or compensation received from the deaccessioning and disposal of objects and specimens from a museum collection should be used solely for the benefit of the collection and usually for acquisitions to that same collection.

2.17 Purchase of Deaccessioned Collections

Museum personnel, the governing body, or their families or close associates, should not be permitted to purchase objects that have been deaccessioned from a collection for which they are responsible.

CARE OF COLLECTIONS

2.18 Collection Continuity

The museum should establish and apply policies to ensure that its collections (both permanent and temporary) and associated information, properly recorded, are available for current use and will be passed on to future generations in as good and safe a condition as practicable, having regard to current knowledge and resources.

2.19 Delegation of Collection Responsibility

Professional responsibilities involving the care of the collections should be assigned to persons with appropriate knowledge and skill or who are adequately supervised (see also 8.1).

2.20 Documentation of Collections

Museum collections should be documented according to accepted professional standards. Such documentation should include a full identification and description of each item, its associations, provenance, condition, treatment and present location. Such data should be kept in a secure environment and be supported by retrieval systems providing access to the information by the museum personnel and other legitimate users.

2.21 Protection Against Disasters

Careful attention should be given to the development of policies to protect the collections during armed conflict and other human-made or natural disasters.

2.22 Security of Collection and Associated Data

The museum should exercise control to avoid disclosing sensitive personal or related information and other confidential matters when collection data is made available to the public.

2.23 Preventive Conservation

Preventive conservation is an important element of museum policy and collections care. It is an essential responsibility of members of the museum profession to create and maintain a protective environment for the collections in their care, whether in store, on display, or in transit.

2.24 Collection Conservation and Restoration

The museum should carefully monitor the condition of collections to determine when an object or specimen may require conservation-restoration work and the services of a qualified conservator-restorer. The principal goal should be the stabilisation of the object or specimen. All conservation procedures should be documented and as reversible as possible, and all alterations should be clearly distinguishable from the original object or specimen.

2.25 Welfare of Live Animals

A museum that maintains living animals should assume full responsibility for their health and well-being. It should prepare and implement a safety code for the protection of its personnel and visitors, as well as of the animals, that has been approved by an expert in the veterinary field. Genetic modification should be clearly identifiable.

2.26 Personal Use of Museum Collections

Museum personnel, the governing body, their families, close associates, or others should not be permitted to expropriate items from the museum collections, even temporarily, for any personal use.

3. MUSEUMS HOLD PRIMARY EVIDENCE FOR ESTABLISHING AND FURTHERING KNOWLEDGE

Principle

Museums have particular responsibilities to all for the care, accessibility and interpretation of primary evidence collected and held in their collections.

PRIMARY EVIDENCE

3.1 Collections as Primary Evidence

The museum collections policy should indicate clearly the significance of collections as primary evidence. The policy should not be governed only by current intellectual trends or present museum usage.

3.2 Availability of Collections

Museums have a particular responsibility for making collections and all relevant information available as freely as possible, having regard to restraints arising for reasons of confidentiality and security.

MUSEUM COLLECTING & RESEARCH

3.3 Field Collecting

Museums undertaking field collecting should develop policies consistent with academic standards and applicable national and international laws and treaty obligations. Fieldwork should only be undertaken with respect and consideration for the views of local communities, their environmental resources and cultural practices as well as efforts to enhance the cultural and natural heritage.

3.4 Exceptional Collecting of Primary Evidence

In exceptional cases an item without provenance may have such an inherently outstanding contribution to knowledge that it would be in the public interest to preserve it. The acceptance of such an item into a museum collection should be the subject of a decision by specialists in the discipline concerned and without national or international prejudice (see also 2.11).

3.5 Research

Research by museum personnel should relate to the museum's mission and objectives and conform to established legal, ethical and academic practices.

3.6 Destructive Analysis

When destructive analytical techniques are undertaken, a complete record of the material analysed, the outcome of the analysis and the resulting research, including publications, should become a part of the permanent record of the object.

3.7 Human Remains and Materials of Sacred Significance

Research on human remains and materials of sacred significance must be accomplished in a manner consistent with professional standards and take into account the interests and beliefs of the community, ethnic or religious groups from whom the objects originated, where these are known (see also 2.5; 4.3).

3.8 Retention of Rights to Research Materials

When museum personnel prepare material for presentation or to document field investigation, there must be clear agreement with the sponsoring museum regarding all rights to such work.

3.9 Shared Expertise

Members of the museum profession have an obligation to share their knowledge and experience with colleagues, scholars and students in relevant fields. They should respect and acknowledge those from whom they have learned and should pass on such advancements in techniques and experience that may be of benefit to others.

3.10 Co-operation Between Museums and Other Institutions

Museum personnel should acknowledge and endorse the need for cooperation and consultation between institutions with similar interests and collecting practices. This is particularly so with institutes of higher education and certain public utilities where research may generate important collections for which there is no long-term security.

4. MUSEUMS PROVIDE OPPORTUNITIES FOR THE APPRECIATION, UNDERSTANDING AND MANAGEMENT OF THE NATURAL AND CULTURAL HERITAGE

Principle

Museums have an important duty to develop their educational role and attract wider audiences from the community, locality, or group they serve. Interaction with the constituent community and promotion of their heritage is an integral part of the educational role of the museum.

DISPLAY & EXHIBITION

4.1 Displays, Exhibitions and Special Activities

Displays and temporary exhibitions, physical or electronic, should be in accordance with the stated mission, policy and purpose of the museum. They should not compromise either the quality or the proper care and conservation of the collections.

4.2 Interpretation of Exhibitions

Museums should ensure that the information they present in displays and exhibitions is well-founded, accurate and gives appropriate consideration to represented groups or beliefs.

4.3 Exhibition of Sensitive Materials

Human remains and materials of sacred significance must be displayed in a manner consistent with professional standards and, where known, taking into account the interests and beliefs of members of the community, ethnic or religious groups from whom the objects originated. They must be presented with great tact and respect for the feelings of human dignity held by all peoples.

4.4 Removal from Public Display

Requests for removal from public display of human remains or material of sacred significance from the originating communities must be addressed expeditiously with respect and sensitivity. Requests for the return of such material should be addressed similarly. Museum policies should clearly define the process for responding to such requests.

4.5 Display of Unprovenanced Material

Museums should avoid displaying or otherwise using material of questionable origin or lacking provenance. They should be aware that such displays or usage can be seen to condone and contribute to the illicit trade in cultural property.

OTHER RESOURCES

4.6 Publication

Information published by museums, by whatever means, should be well-founded, accurate and give responsible consideration to the academic disciplines, societies, or beliefs presented. Museum publications should not compromise the standards of the institution.

4.7 Reproductions

Museums should respect the integrity of the original when replicas, reproductions, or copies of items in the collection are made. All such copies should be permanently marked as facsimiles.

5. MUSEUMS HOLD RESOURCES THAT PROVIDE OPPORTUNITIES FOR OTHER PUBLIC SERVICES AND BENEFITS

Principle

Museums utilise a wide variety of specialisms, skills and physical resources that have a far broader application than in the museum. This may lead to shared resources or the provision of services as an extension of the museum's activities. These should be organised in such a way that they do not compromise the museum's stated mission.

IDENTIFICATION SERVICES

5.1 Identification of Illegally or Illicitly Acquired Objects

Where museums provide an identification service, they should not act in any way that could be regarded as benefiting from such activity, directly or indirectly. The identification and authentication of objects that are believed or suspected to have been illegally or illicitly acquired, transferred, imported or exported, should not be made public until the appropriate authorities have been notified.

5.2 Authentication and Valuation (Appraisal)

Valuations may be made for the purposes of insurance of museum collections. Opinions on the monetary value of other objects should only be given on official request from other museums or competent legal, governmental or other responsible public authorities. However, when the museum itself may be the beneficiary, appraisal of an object or specimen must be undertaken independently.

6. MUSEUMS WORK IN CLOSE COLLABORATION WITH THE COMMUNITIES FROM WHICH THEIR COLLECTIONS ORIGINATE AS WELL AS THOSE THEY SERVE

Principle

Museum collections reflect the cultural and natural heritage of the communities from which they have been derived. As such, they have a character beyond that of ordinary property, which may include strong affinities with national, regional, local, ethnic, religious or political identity. It is important therefore that museum policy is responsive to this situation.

ORIGIN OF COLLECTIONS

6.1 Co-operation

Museums should promote the sharing of knowledge, documentation and collections with museums and cultural organisations in the countries and communities of origin. The possibility of developing partnerships with museums in countries or areas that have lost a significant part of their heritage should be explored.

6.2 Return of Cultural Property

Museums should be prepared to initiate dialogues for the return of cultural property to a country or people of origin. This should be undertaken in an impartial manner, based on scientific, professional and humanitarian principles as well as applicable local, national and international legislation, in preference to action at a governmental or political level.

6.3 Restitution of Cultural Property

When a country or people of origin seeks the restitution of an object or specimen that can be demonstrated to have been exported or otherwise transferred in violation of the principles of international and national conventions, and shown to be part of that country's or people's cultural or natural heritage, the museum concerned should, if legally free to do so, take prompt and responsible steps to cooperate in its return.

6.4 Cultural Objects from an Occupied Country

Museums should abstain from purchasing or acquiring cultural objects from an occupied territory and respect fully all laws and conventions that regulate the import, export and transfer of cultural or natural materials.

RESPECT FOR COMMUNITIES SERVED

6.5 Contemporary Communities

Where museum activities involve a contemporary community or its heritage, acquisitions should only be made based on informed and mutual consent without exploitation of the owner or informants. Respect for the wishes of the community involved should be paramount.

6.6 Funding of Community Activities

When seeking funds for activities involving contemporary communities, their interests should not be compromised (see 1.10).

6.7 Use of Collections from Contemporary Communities

Museum usage of collections from contemporary communities requires respect for human dignity and the traditions and cultures that use such material. Such collections should be used to promote human well-being, social development, tolerance, and respect by advocating multisocial, multicultural and multilingual expression (see 4.3).

6.8 Supporting Organisations in the Community

Museums should create a favourable environment for community support (e.g., Friends of Museums and other supporting organisations), recognise their contribution and promote a harmonious relationship between the community and museum personnel.

7. MUSEUMS OPERATE IN A LEGAL MANNER.

Principle

Museums must conform fully to international, regional, national and local legislation and treaty obligations. In addition, the governing body should comply with any legally binding trusts or conditions relating to any aspect of the museum, its collections and operations.

LEGAL FRAMEWORK

7.1 National and Local Legislation

Museums should conform to all national and local laws and respect the legislation of other states as they affect their operation.

7.2 International Legislation

Museum policy should acknowledge the following international legislation that is taken as a standard in interpreting the *ICOM Code of Ethics for Museums*:

- *Convention for the Protection of Cultural Property in the Event of Armed Conflict* ("The Hague Convention" First Protocol, 1954, and Second Protocol, 1999);
- *Convention on the Means of Prohibiting and Preventing the Illicit Import, Export and Transfer of Ownership of Cultural Property* (UNESCO, 1970);
- *Convention on International Trade in Endangered Species of Wild Fauna and Flora* (Washington, 1973);
- *Convention on Biological Diversity* (UN, 1992);
- *Convention on Stolen and Illicitly Exported Cultural Objects* (UNIDROIT, 1995);
- *Convention on the Protection of the Underwater Cultural Heritage* (UNESCO, 2001);
- *Convention for the Safeguarding of the Intangible Cultural Heritage* (UNESCO, 2003).

8. MUSEUMS OPERATE IN A PROFESSIONAL MANNER

Principle

Members of the museum profession should observe accepted standards and laws and uphold the dignity and honour of their profession. They should safeguard the public against illegal or unethical professional conduct. Every opportunity should be used to inform and educate the public about the aims, purposes, and aspirations of the profession to develop a better public understanding of the contributions of museums to society.

PROFESSIONAL CONDUCT

8.1 Familiarity with Relevant Legislation

Every member of the museum profession should be conversant with relevant international, national and local legislation and the conditions of their employment. They should avoid situations that could be construed as improper conduct.

8.2 Professional Responsibility

Members of the museum profession have an obligation to follow the policies and procedures of their employing institution. However, they may properly object to practices that are perceived to be damaging to a museum, to the profession, or to matters of professional ethics.

8.3 Professional Conduct

Loyalty to colleagues and to the employing museum is an important professional responsibility and must be based on allegiance to fundamental ethical principles applicable to the profession as a whole. These principles should comply with the terms of the ICOM Code of Ethics for Museums and be aware of any other codes or policies relevant to museum work.

8.4 Academic and Scientific Responsibilities

Members of the museum profession should promote the investigation, preservation, and use of information inherent in collections. They should, therefore, refrain from any activity or circumstance that might result in the loss of such academic and scientific data.

8.5 The Illicit Market

Members of the museum profession should not support the illicit traffic or market in natural or cultural property, directly or indirectly.

8.6 Confidentiality

Members of the museum profession must protect confidential information obtained during their work. In addition, information about items brought to the museum for identification is confidential and should not be published or passed to any other institution or person without specific authorisation from the owner.

8.7 Museum and Collection Security

Information about the security of the museum or of private collections and locations visited during official duties must be held in strict confidence by museum personnel.

8.8 Exception to the Obligation for Confidentiality

Confidentiality is subject to a legal obligation to assist the police or other proper authorities in investigating possible stolen, illicitly acquired, or illegally transferred property.

8.9 Personal Independence

While members of a profession are entitled to a measure of personal independence, they must realise that no private business or professional interest can be wholly separated from their employing institution.

8.10 Professional Relationships

Members of the museum profession form working relationships with numerous other persons within and outside the museum in which they are employed. They are expected to render their professional services to others efficiently and to a high standard.

8.11 Professional Consultation

It is a professional responsibility to consult other colleagues within or outside the museum when the expertise available in the museum is insufficient to ensure good decision-making.

CONFLICTS OF INTEREST

8.12 Gifts, Favours, Loans, or Other Personal Benefits

Museum employees must not accept gifts, favours, loans, or other personal benefits that may be offered to them in connection with their duties for the museum. Occasionally professional courtesy may include the giving and receiving of gifts, but this should always take place in the name of the institution concerned.

8.13 Outside Employment or Business Interests

Members of the museum profession, although entitled to a measure of personal independence, must realise that no private business or professional interest can be wholly separated from their employing institution. They should not undertake other paid employment or accept outside com- missions that are in conflict, or may be viewed as being in conflict, with the interests of the museum.

8.14 Dealing in Natural or Cultural Heritage

Members of the museum profession should not participate directly or indirectly in dealing (buying or selling for profit) in the natural or cultural heritage.

8.15 Interaction with Dealers

Museum professionals should not accept any gift, hospitality, or any form of reward from a dealer, auctioneer, or other person as an inducement to purchase or dis- pose of museum items, or to take or refrain from taking official action. Furthermore, a museum professional should not recommend a particular dealer, auctioneer, or appraiser to a member of the public.

8.16 Private Collecting

Members of the museum profession should not compete with their institution either in the acquisition of objects or in any personal collecting activity. An agreement between the museum professional and the governing body concerning any private collecting must be formulated and scrupulously followed.

8.17 Use of the Name and Logo of ICOM

The name of the organisation, its acronym or its logo may not be used to promote or endorse any for-profit operation or product.

8.18 Other Conflicts of Interest

Should any other conflict of interest develop between an individual and the museum, the interests of the museum should prevail.

Appendix 3

American Association of State and Local History

Statement of Professional Standards and Ethics

(June 2012)

INTRODUCTION

The American Association for State and Local History is a membership organization comprising individuals, agencies, and organizations acting in the public trust, engaged in the practice of history and representing its many disciplines and professions. The Association expects its members, employees, and elected officials to abide by the ethical and performance standards adopted by all appropriate discipline-based and professional organizations.[1] The association and its members are to comply with all laws, regulations, and applicable international conventions. The association and its members are expected to take affirmative steps to maintain their integrity so as to warrant public confidence. The following ethical statements and related professional standards are provided for the guidance of all members of the Association.

HISTORICAL RESOURCES

Historical resources, including collections, built environment, cultural landscapes, archaeological sites, and other evidence of the past, provide the tools through which we interact with the past and are the bedrock upon which the practice of history rests. In fulfillment of their public trust, historical organizations and those associated with them must be responsible stewards and advocates on behalf of the historical resources within their care and throughout their communities.

A. Association members shall give priority to the care and management of the historical resources within their care and always shall act to preserve their physical and intellectual integrity.
B. Institutions shall manage historical resources, in accord with comprehensive policies officially adopted by their governing authorities.
C. Historical resources shall not be capitalized or treated as financial assets.
D. Collections shall not be deaccessioned or disposed of in order to provide financial support for institutional operations, facilities maintenance, or any reason other than preservation or acquisition of collections, as defined by institutional policy.
E. Historical resources shall be acquired, cared for, and interpreted with sensitivity to their cultural origins.
F. It is important to document the physical condition of historical resources, including past treatment of objects, and to take appropriate steps to mitigate potential hazards to people and property.

ACCESS

Access to historical resources is what gives preservation activities their meaning. Providing non-discriminatory access to historical resources through exhibitions, tours, educational programs, publications, electronic media, and research is critical in fulfilling the public trust and mission of historical organizations. Access and limitations of access are governed by institutional policies and by applicable rights of privacy, ownership, and intellectual freedom.

INTERPRETATION

Historical interpretation may be presented in a variety of formats.

A. All interpretation must be based upon sound scholarship and thorough research.
B. Intellectually and scholarly honest interpretation reflects the cultural and temporal context of the subject matter and recognizes the potential for multiple interpretations.
C. Interpretation must use a method of delivery (historic marker, exhibit, book, program, etc.) that takes into consideration both the intended audience and the results of sound scholarship and thorough research.
D. Historical organizations and agencies shall act to ensure that the breadth of American cultural experiences and perspectives is represented accurately in all programming and interpretations.

E. Historical organizations shall work toward inclusiveness with the goals of social responsibility and respect for different cultures and peoples.

MANAGEMENT

The primary responsibility for governance, institutional policies, financial stability and legal accountability of a historical organization rests with the governing authority.

A. The governing authority has the responsibility to hold safe the assets of its organization, including, but not limited to: the good name of the organization, the human resources, collections, facilities, property, membership, donors, finances, etc.
B. The governing authority has the responsibility to secure resources for the benefit of their organization, including, but not limited to: finances, partnerships, human resources, etc.
C. The governing authority must ensure proper delegation of responsibility.
D. The governing authority must establish policies that reflect current legal, ethical, and professional practices.
E. The governing authority must consistently review application of policies established for the organization.
F. Institutions shall maintain financial records from which accurate information can be generated to manage in a fiscally sound manner.

HUMAN RESOURCES

Operational responsibility rests with the staff, paid or volunteer.

A. Individuals employed in the practice of history deserve respect, pay and benefits commensurate with their training, dedication, and contribution to society. Volunteers deserve the same consideration as their paid colleagues.
B. Institutions shall maintain personnel policies, adopted by the governing authority and distributed to all staff, documenting the terms of employment.
C. Institutions have the responsibility to engage personnel, including volunteers, who have appropriate training and expertise and to provide them with opportunities for additional training necessary to continue to meet their responsibilities.
D. If the governing authority employs an administrator, that person alone is responsible for the employment, discipline, and release of all other staff, subject to established personnel policies.

E. An employee or volunteer is never wholly separable from the institution and actions by an employee or volunteer may reflect upon the organization or be attributed to it. Therefore, the employee or volunteer must be concerned not only with his or her motivations as he or she sees them, but also with the way those actions could be perceived by others.

F. Institutions have the responsibility to respect the privacy of their members, volunteers and employees and act in their best interests.

G. Institutions shall not discriminate against anyone on the basis of race, color, creed, age, sex, religion, nationality, or sexual orientation.

H. Employers and volunteer managers shall not engage in or condone any type of harassment or discrimination.

I. Institutions and individuals working and volunteering in the history field shall observe confidentiality and treat colleagues with respect, fairness, courtesy and good faith, avoiding relationships with others which could compromise professional judgment or their reputation.

REVENUE-PRODUCING ACTIVITIES

Activities that involve the marketing and sale of products, programs, services, and facilities are acceptable ways to produce support revenues and increase public awareness of, and participation in, historical activities.

A. No such activities shall be undertaken that violate or compromise the integrity of an institution's mission, the ability of an institution or individual to meet professional standards or an institution's not-for-profit status.

B. Control of products (e.g., exhibitions, publications, collections, programs) shall neither be delegated nor abrogated to outside parties in order to obtain financial support.

C. Historical organizations shall review the potential cultural sensitivity of materials considered for commercial use with representatives of the appropriate affiliated communities.

CONFLICT OF INTEREST

Historical organizations and agencies exist to serve the public interest and must always act in such a way as to maintain public confidence and trust.

A. All governing authority members, employees, and volunteers shall be careful to avoid the appearance and the reality of using their positions or the information and access gained from their positions for personal gain or for the benefit of another organization. They must exercise discretion and maintain the confidential nature of proprietary information.

B. Board members, volunteers, and employees shall refrain from personal collecting in any manner that conflicts with the interests or credibility of the institution and its policies. Institutions are encouraged to obtain statements of personal collecting interests before individuals become associated with them.

C. Collections shall not be made available to any individual on any basis for personal use, either on or off the premises or for any other purpose and contrary to the adopted collections policies.

D. Historical organizations and their representatives must protect the integrity of their institutions from both the reality and the appearance of undue influence by donors, sponsors, and other sources of financial support.

SOCIAL RESPONSIBILITY

A. Historical organizations and agencies shall act to ensure that the breadth of American experiences and perspectives is represented accurately in staffing and operational activities.

B. Historical organizations shall provide leadership to the field in becoming representative of our diverse society through equity in staffing, training, collecting, programming, and marketing.

INTELLECTUAL FREEDOM

Historical scholarship and interpretation depend upon free and open exploration and interpretation of the human experience.

A. Historical institutions must respect other legal, ethical, and cultural standards regarding individual privacy, human-based research and access to and use of sensitive cultural materials.

B. Historical institutions and their representatives shall respect the rights and authority of individuals and cultures that had no voice in the disposition of those collections related to them.

C. AASLH recognizes the diversity and variety of historical interpretation and therefore supports open and thoughtful scholarly debates.

D. Once employed or engaged, all persons deserve the professional respect and support necessary for professional growth and advancement. Such respect precludes unequal treatment based on any nonprofessional criteria. In particular, it precludes any harassment or discrimination, which is unethical, unprofessional, and threatening to intellectual freedom.

NOTE

1. A bibliography of ethical standards can be obtained from the AASLH executive offices.

Appendix 4

Association of Art Museum Directors

Professional Practices in Art Museums

2011

STATEMENT OF MISSION

Adopted by the Membership of the AAMD, June 2009

The Association of Art Museum Directors (AAMD) promotes the vital role of art museums throughout North America and advances the profession by cultivating leadership and communicating standards of excellence in museum practice.

PREFACE TO THE 2011 EDITION

Professional Practices in Art Museums was first published by the AAMD in 1971 and has been revised every ten years thereafter. Museum directors and others responsible for museum governance are urged to review carefully and be guided by the professional principles outlined herein.

This edition of *Professional Practices in Art Museums* represents a multi-year effort on the part of the AAMD to revise and update the 2001 edition. Special thanks go to the following committee members, each of whom has participated in the writing and editing of this edition:

- William U. Eiland, Georgia Museum of Art (chair)
- James K. Ballinger, Phoenix Art Museum
- Graham W. J. Beal, Detroit Institute of Arts
- Brent Benjamin, Saint Louis Art Museum
- James H. Duff, Brandywine River Museum

- Charles Loving, Snite Museum of Art
- Mary Sue Sweeney Price, Newark Museum
- Susan Taylor, New Orleans Museum of Art
- Matthew Teitelbaum, Art Gallery of Ontario
- James A. Welu, Worcester Art Museum
- Sylvia Wolf, Henry Art Gallery (incoming chair)

For their contributions to the preparation and editing of the manuscript, gratitude also goes to Christine Anagnos, Deputy Director, AAMD; Leslie Green Bowman, Director, Thomas Jefferson Foundation, Inc.; Sharon Cott, General Counsel, The Metropolitan Museum of Art; Josh Knerly, Hahn Loeser & Parks LLP; and Michaelyn Mitchell, Director of Publications, American Federation of Arts. The chairman wants to thank particularly Janet Landay, formerly Executive Director, AAMD, for her work on this document and her counsel to the committee.

INTRODUCTION

An art museum is a permanent, not-for-profit institution—essentially educational and humanistic in purpose—which studies and cares for works of art and on some regular schedule exhibits and interprets them to the public. Most, but not all, art museums have permanent collections from which exhibitions are drawn and upon which educational programs are based.

Directors of art museums have particular obligations and responsibilities to their staffs, their governing bodies, and the communities they serve. *Professional Practices in Art Museums* provides a set of principles to guide directors in their administration of these obligations.

The principles set forth here are deemed by the AAMD as fundamental and applicable to all art museums. Circumstances, however, can affect the manner in which such principles apply. Recognizing this fact, the AAMD, through its officers and staff, is prepared to consult with any member, or any nonmember representing an art museum, about the application of these principles in particular circumstances. Advance consultation can help avoid infractions of principles of professional practices and the imposition of sanctions such as those indicated in the Appendix A Code of Ethics for Art Museum Directors.

Art museums that are part of larger educational entities, such as universities or colleges, have grown in number and importance. Traditionally, they have had different administrative patterns from museums that are constituted as independent corporations, but their broad goals and responsibilities are essentially the same. The relatively few differences are considered in the appendix University and College Art Museums.

From time to time, the AAMD issues statements concerning aspects of the art museum profession, such as AAMD Policy on Deaccessioning and Disposal, Report of the AAMD Task Force on Nazi Looted Art, Report of the AAMD Task Force on the Acquisition and Stewardship of Sacred Objects, and Report of the AAMD Task Force on the Acquisition of Archaeological Materials and Ancient Art. These documents can be found on aamd.org

For the first time, this edition of *Professional Practices in Art Museums* is being produced in electronic form only and will be updated as necessary.

GOVERNANCE

1. The museum is governed by a body such as a board of trustees. (Hereafter, the term *board* is used to refer to any form of governing body and its appointees or designated committees legally responsible for a museum). The board adopts and updates the mission, the bylaws and policies that guide its function, and the museum's operations.
2. The board must be informed of, and active in overseeing, the museum's operations, plans, and finances. The board should meet frequently and clearly communicate its decisions and should include members with the skills, backgrounds, expertise, and experience necessary to enhance the museum's ability to fulfill its mission. Board members should receive no compensation for their service. Boards should represent the diverse communities the museum serves.
3. The museum must be administered by a professional staff. The board and staff must be united in their commitment to the institution's mission and responsibilities and clear in the distinctions among their various roles.
4. Together, the board and director must set the direction of the museum, develop its long-range plan, and secure the resources needed to fulfill its mission. The board approves the policies that govern the museum's operations. These policies should be a reflection of the goals established in the museum's statement of mission. The board has fiduciary responsibility for the museum's resources, including its collections, physical plant, financial assets, and staff. The board acts collectively, generally by majority vote. Within established policy, it can delegate to board-appointed committees that also act collectively. The board should make clear the types of issues that must be brought before it.
5. The board should appoint the director—to whom it delegates responsibility for day-to-day operations—to be the chief executive officer of the museum. The administration of an art museum requires connoisseurship, discernment, and knowledge in dealing with works of art, as well as the judgment and experience necessary for the operation of a complex

organization. Achieving an appropriate balance among these requirements is essential. Without such a balance, problems that could undermine the museum's professional performance and public service could arise.

6. The director should nurture the intellectual and aesthetic philosophy of the museum. The director is responsible for administration that is consistent with established policy and enables staff members to perform to the full extent of their abilities. The director should foster such values and practices as collaboration, communication, respect, and delegation of duties. (Hereafter, references to the director mean the director in consultation with staff, as appropriate.) (See also Appendix A.)

7. In certain cases, a paid president or equivalent administrative post may also be appointed. Such an appointment may, however, result in ambiguity, especially if the positions are defined as equal by the board. A clear definition of the responsibilities of each position is essential, and the director should carry the ultimate responsibility for advancing the institution's mission, including its artistic direction, collections, scholarship, and programs.

8. Museum directors, trustees, and others in positions of responsibility should make every effort to anticipate and address situations in which a conflict of interest or the appearance of a conflict exists. The board must establish and maintain polices regarding conflicts of interest and ethics and ensure that they are transparent and reviewed regularly by the board, staff, and volunteers.

9. Appropriate policies guide a museum and help avoid misunderstandings. In addition to policies regarding conflicts of interest and ethical conduct, the following issues should be addressed: collections management; human resources; finance, audit, and investment management; and fundraising. In order to serve the needs of a particular museum, other issues not mentioned here may be appropriate subjects of policies.

MISSION, POLICY, AND LONG-RANGE PLAN

10. The purposes of most art museums are set forth broadly in their charters, articles of incorporation, and bylaws, as well as in their statements of mission adopted by the board. The statement of mission should define the museum's purpose and its benefit to the public.

    The museum's policy is the aggregate of the decisions and actions taken by the board to implement the mission. All policy development, changes, and additions should result from thorough discussions between the board and the director. Through its policies, the museum establishes a covenant with its constituency; with past, present, and future donors; with succeeding groups of board members; and with the staff. Such policies should be recorded in the minutes of board meetings, or a policy manual, and be periodically reviewed.

11. Every museum should have a clearly articulated long-range plan that is approved by the board and reviewed periodically. The long-range plan is an instrument by which an art museum reflects its mission, assesses its current resources, defines its goals, identifies future needs, and formulates strategies. The director is responsible for organizing the planning process and implementing the plan.

THE COLLECTION

12. The development, preservation, conservation, documentation, study, presentation, and explication of the collection are essential responsibilities of a collecting museum and should be reflected in its policies.

13. The collection exists for the benefit of present and future generations. It should be made as accessible as is prudent for the protection of each object. Every effort should be made to provide information about the collection, document it visually, and respond appropriately to serious inquiries.

14. Member museums must have clear, written collections management policies, including collection goals and acquisition and deaccession principles, procedures, and processes, as well as policies that address preservation, conservation, and collection care.

15. The director and the curatorial staff are responsible for identifying possible acquisitions. No work of art may be considered for acquisition without the recommendation of the director. Except as set forth below, the board, as a whole or through an authorized committee, must approve recommendations for all acquisitions. The board may grant authority to the director to approve purchases and accept gifts and bequests within prescribed limits; the director must report these acquisitions to the board or the authorized committee.

16. Joint ownership of works of art, whether acquired by gift or purchase, may be appropriate and desirable. Such arrangements should have the approval of the board of each museum. In such instances, terms governing the parties' respective interests should be documented in writing, with consideration given to such issues as custodianship, stewardship, display, conservation, publication, research, scholarship, copyright, insurance, possible deaccession, and intellectual control.

17. Gifts and bequests should be unrestricted whenever possible. No work of art should be accepted or acquired with conditions that restrict or otherwise interfere with the museum's obligation to apply the most

reliable scholarly and scientific information available to questions of attribution, dating, iconography, provenance, conservation, and related matters.

18. When accepting gifts, and where required by law or regulation, the museum must stipulate that the responsibility for securing (and paying for) appraisals and furnishing this information to the appropriate government authorities rests with the donor.

19. The director must ensure that best efforts are made to determine the ownership history of a work of art considered for acquisition. The director must not knowingly allow to be recommended for acquisition—or permit the museum to acquire—any work of art that has been stolen (without appropriate resolution of such theft) or illegally imported into the jurisdiction in which the museum is located.

20. Cataloguing and documenting works of art in the collection are basic responsibilities of the museum staff. The information should represent sound scholarship and the staff's informed judgment, independent of any external pressures. Other scholarly opinions, including dissenting opinions concerning a work of art, should be recorded. Major changes in attribution and dating, as well as any serious questions concerning authenticity, should be reported to the board and made available to the public.

21. The ultimate responsibility for protecting the collection rests with the board while the daily preservation, conservation, handling, storing, and presentation of works of art in the collection are the responsibility of the director. To assure the board's full awareness of preservation and conservation as primary museum functions, the director should report periodically on the state of the collection.

22. Museums rely on one another for loans to exhibitions, and a spirit of cooperation and collegiality should inform decisions relative to such loans and the setting of charges and fees. In any decision about a proposed loan from a collection, however, the protection of the work of art, the intellectual merit, and the educational benefits must be primary considerations. The director should advise the board and recommend or approve loans according to established policies.

23. Deaccessioning and disposal of works of art from the collection by sale, exchange, or other means require particularly rigorous examination and should be pursued with great prudence. There are circumstances in which the deaccessioning of works of art from the collection is justified; however, such deaccessioning must be governed by the museum's written policy rather than by exigencies of the moment. The museum's policy must conform to the requirements of the AAMD's policy on deaccessioning and disposal (see Appendix B).

24. No work of art in the collection may be considered for deaccessioning without the recommendation of the director to the board with whom the final decision must rest (see Appendix B).

25. Funds received from the disposal of a deaccessioned work shall not be used for operations or capital expenses. Such funds, including any earnings and appreciation thereon, may be used only for the acquisition of works of art in a manner consistent with the museum's policy on the use of restricted acquisition funds. In order to account properly for their use, the AAMD recommends that such funds, including any earnings and appreciation, be tracked separately from other acquisition funds.

26. Private collecting of works of art by the director and other members of the museum staff is appropriate and can enhance expertise to the benefit of the museum, provided that no private collecting by the director or other members of the museum's staff conflicts in any way with the collecting interests of the museum (see also Appendix A and Appendix B, Paragraph E.).

27. The museum must have the opportunity to acquire for its own collection any work of art related to the museum's collections offered as a gift or sale to the director or any member of the museum staff. When prompt action must be taken to secure a work before it can be considered by the museum, the work in question must be offered to the museum at the earliest opportunity by the director or staff member who has acquired it. The terms of the museum's acquisition of any such work must be at least as favorable to the museum as the terms offered to the director or other staff member. In order to preclude any conflict of interest, the museum should have clear, written guidelines for the director and the museum staff about private collecting and accepting art as a gift.

PUBLIC PROGRAMS

28. The museum's public programs serve its mission, reflect the goals of its long-range plan, and offer its audience edification and enrichment. Such programs, including, among others, exhibitions, publications, lectures, workshops, films, and performances, should present and interpret works of art and expand public understanding of the scope of human creativity.

29. Artistic and educational excellence and public engagement and accessibility must be primary considerations when planning a museum's public programs. Other valid considerations include attendance, revenue potential, and media response.

30. Within the context of its mission, the museum should serve as broad and diverse a public as possible by offering a range of programs that provide

experiences with works of art. Ideas and information must be based on principles of sound scholarship, respect for artistic expression, and the ability to engage the public.

31. On occasion, museums may present programs in which works of art are available for sale. Except in the case of presentations specifically organized and clearly identified for fundraising purposes, no commission from the sale of a borrowed work of art should be accepted by the museum.

FINANCES

32. The board carries full responsibility for financial and investment policies and approves the budget of the museum. Any significant change in the museum's financial condition must be addressed by the board in consultation with the director, who must, therefore, regularly inform the board of any actual or anticipated changes in income or expenditures.

33. The director has the responsibility to identify priorities of the museum that are consistent with its board-approved policy and to recommend the allocation of funds required to support them. The director prepares the budget of the museum and is responsible for submitting it to the board for approval before the commencement of each fiscal year.

34. In approving the budget, the board should recognize that expenditures consistent with the budget and subject to the availability of funds may be made by the director without further action by the board. The latitude permitted the director within this structure should be defined by policy.

35. If it becomes necessary to alter the approved budget or to act outside its provisions, the board and the director must be jointly engaged in the decision-making process.

36. Expenditures for purposes that are not part of the budget, such as acquisitions and capital programs, must be approved by the board. Exceptions, such as discretionary funds, should be governed by procedures defined in board-approved policy.

37. While the museum may generate income to support its operations and programs, the museum is first and foremost a not-for-profit institution. In developing the museum's fiscal policy, income-producing activity must not compromise the museum's mission or standards.

38. The collections the museum holds in public trust are not financial assets and may not be converted to cash for operating or capital needs. No collection or portion thereof may be pledged as collateral for a loan, except that a museum may grant a security interest in a work that it is acquiring in order to secure the payment of the balance of the purchase price. To present fairly the museum's financial position, collections should not be

capitalized. (For further guidance and reference to applicable accounting standards, see Appendix B, Paragraph D.) Likewise, no funds established for future art acquisitions (endowment or otherwise) should be pledged as collateral for loans. Member organizations should follow applicable accounting standards regarding the use of restricted funds and honor donor intent regarding the establishment and use of such funds.

39. The museum should make available financial statements sufficient to allow the public to make well-informed decisions regarding the appropriateness and effectiveness of the museum's use of contributed funds and other financial assets.

FUNDRAISING AND EARNED INCOME

40. As part of its fiduciary responsibility, the board secures and provides the funds needed to satisfy the financial requirements of the museum. The director must be prepared to play a significant role in that effort.

41. Particular care must be taken to assure that fundraising is conducted in a manner consistent with professional standards. The museum should avoid any fundraising practices that could damage the community's trust or its respect for the institution. The concept of public benefit rather than private benefit to individuals or taxable entities should apply while recognizing that a variety of stakeholders may incidentally benefit from fundraising activities.

42. Sources of financial support should be publicly disclosed whenever possible. Requests for anonymity should be respected, except where doing so would conceal a real or perceived conflict of interest. The museum must retain artistic control at all times; sources of financial support must not be allowed to compromise or unduly influence the integrity of any program.

43. Fundraising goals of volunteer and auxiliary groups must be approved by the board and the activity monitored by the director. When such groups operate as a separate legal entity but have a mission of providing support to the museum, the group's governing body and the museum's board should approve a document that codifies the relationship.

LEGAL MATTERS

44. Although ultimate fiduciary responsibility rests with the board, the director is responsible for the daily monitoring of the institution's compliance with laws and regulations. Appropriate legal counsel must be available

to advise on general matters, as well as specific issues. Legal matters arising in the operation of the museum include those pertaining to collections, exhibitions, personnel and labor relations, contracts, governance, finances, facilities, taxes, rights and reproductions, and events. The board, the director, and counsel should share current information about legal issues and legislation relevant to the institution and museum standards.

THE PHYSICAL PLANT

45. The physical plant is among the assets of the museum for which the board assumes ultimate responsibility. Attention must be given to the preservation and security of the plant and its contents, including collections. The museum must provide a secure, safe, and accessible environment for its visitors and staff.
46. When the museum is used for ancillary activities, the director must assure that these activities do not endanger facilities or collections or compromise the integrity of programs.
47. The director should submit for board review and approval such matters as revisions to a comprehensive facilities plan, the selection of architects or other professional consultants, plan objectives, development concepts, schematic and final designs, and the awarding of major construction contracts.
48. The director is responsible for the construction, operation, maintenance, security, repair, renovation, and alteration of the physical plant; for planning capital improvements and related budgets; for public safety; and for such general facilities policies as the board may adopt.
49. The museum must protect its facilities against potential risk and loss through appropriate measures, including a comprehensive, board-approved emergency-preparedness plan that includes regular staff training. The museum must comply with all applicable federal, state and local laws, rules, and regulations.

The Staff

50. The director is responsible for the appointment of the staff of the museum. The staff should comprise employees with the skills, backgrounds, professional expertise, and experience necessary to advance the museum's mission. The director should build and sustain a high level of morale and productivity.
51. The staff is one of the museum's most valued resources. In order to build a strong institutional culture, the staff should be provided with

competitive compensation and benefits, a supportive working environment, and opportunities for professional development.

52. The board is responsible for establishing policy relating to the rights and benefits of museum employees. The director is responsible for developing and implementing personnel practices in conformity with established policy. Such practices include providing all employees with job descriptions, setting goals, and conducting regular performance evaluations with processes that are fair, consistent, and clear.

53. In the event that a labor union is a recognized bargaining agent for certain museum employees, the board must establish clear roles and responsibilities for negotiating agreements. Whether or not the director takes a direct role in the negotiations, he or she is responsible for the final contract. The board should review any labor union agreements recommended by the director.

54. Any employee's personnel disputes and grievances not covered by a bargaining agreement should be settled through an established dispute-resolution procedure. Employees must be protected by a policy that provides for reporting in confidence, and without retaliation, any suspected improprieties or misuse of the museum's resources.

THE DIRECTOR

55. In order to be qualified professionally for the position, the director should possess an appropriate balance of training in art history and/or knowledge of art, museum experience, administrative skills, and demonstrated leadership ability.

56. The responsibility for appointing the director should be exercised by the full board although the search for the director and negotiations with the candidates may be delegated to a board-appointed committee. During the hiring process, the board should provide complete and accurate information relevant to the management of the museum. (For university and college art museum procedures, see Appendix C.)

57. The director must have a clear understanding of the museum's mission, policies, long-range plan, programs, and finances and is responsible for their implementation and for making accurate information about them publicly available.

58. The board should confirm its selection and appointment of the director by delivering to the appointee a formal document such as a letter or contract signed as authorized by the board. This document should describe all components of the compensation package. The document should be accepted in writing by the appointee. The total compensation package should be in keeping with professional indices.

59. The director should be present at all meetings of the board and its executive committee, although with prior notice these meetings may include sessions without the director. The director has the right to be present at all meetings of the board's permanent standing committees. The director is responsible for informing the staff of board decisions; likewise, the ideas, concerns, and requests of the staff are communicated to the board by the director.

60. The director should have the full support of the board. Should this support become seriously diminished, every effort should be made to restore the relationship as soon as possible for the well-being of the museum.

61. Disagreements serious enough to result in erosion of board support for the director might be resolved by such successive efforts as a conference between officers of the board and the director, a special meeting of the full board, and involvement of an outside mediator.

62. The director's employment may be terminated only by a vote of the full board. Notice of termination should be delivered to the director in writing. Consideration should be given to appropriate notice and/ or severance. Agreed-upon arrangements should be recognized in any employment contract or letter of agreement. Confidentiality in such matters should be maintained. (For university and college art museum procedures, see Appendix C.)

63. In a period of transition between directors, procedures should be established to assure that the museum's operation continues in as orderly a manner as possible. The board should determine which staff member or members will assume responsibilities customarily borne by the director. Without such a clearly defined procedure, departures from policy could occur.

APPENDIX A

A Code of Ethics for Art Museum Directors

Adopted by the membership of the AAMD, June 1966; amended 1971, 1973, 1974, 1991, 2001, and 2011.

The position of the museum director is one of trust. The director should act with integrity and in accordance with the highest ethical principles. The director should avoid any and all activities that could compromise his or her position or the institution. The professional integrity of the director should set a standard for the staff. The director is responsible for implementing the policy of the governing board for the benefit of the museum and the public. The director is responsible for ensuring that the museum adopts and disseminates a code of ethics for the board, staff, and volunteers.

The director must not use his or her influence or position for personal gain. The director must not function as a commercial dealer in works of art nor be party to the recommendation for purchase by museums or collectors of works of art in which the director has any undisclosed financial interest. The director must not accept any commission or compromising gift from any seller or buyer of works of art. The director must not provide any statement as to the monetary value, authenticity, or attribution of a work of art.

If the director collects art, extraordinary discretion is required to assure that no conflict of interest arises between the director's personal collecting activity and the concerns of the museum. If there is a perception of a conflict, the museum's governing board must be granted the first option to acquire the work or works in question for the museum. Gifts of works of art to the director by artists whose work is or may be shown or acquired by the museum can compromise the position of the director and the museum; these should therefore be accepted only in special circumstances and with full disclosure. If there is even the possibility of a perception of a conflict of interest, the museum's governing board must be granted the first option to obtain such gifts for the museum. (See also Paragraph 26 and Appendix B, Paragraph E.)

The director must ensure that best efforts are made to determine the ownership history of a work of art considered for acquisition. The director must not knowingly allow to be recommended for acquisition of—or permit the museum to acquire—any work of art that has been stolen (without appropriate resolution of such theft) or illegally imported into the jurisdiction in which the museum is located.

In accordance with the AAMD's policy on deaccessioning and disposal, the director must not dispose of accessioned works of art in order to provide funds for purposes other than acquisitions of works of art for the collection (see Appendix B).

AAMD members who violate this code of ethics will be subject to discipline by reprimand, suspension, or expulsion from the AAMD. Infractions by any art museum may expose that institution to censure and/or sanctions, as determined by the Board of Trustees of the AAMD, that may, in the case of sanctions, include, without limitation, suspension of loans and shared exhibitions between the sanctioned museum and museums of which the AAMD members are directors.

Prior to censuring or recommending suspension or expulsion of a member or censuring or issuing any sanction against an art museum, the Board of Trustees of the AAMD shall provide to the director or museum in question the opportunity to be heard and to explain the reason for the actions considered for censure, suspension, expulsion, or sanction. Such a presentation is to be made by the affected director unless otherwise determined by the Board of Trustees of the AAMD or, in the case of a museum, by the director or any member of the board of trustees or governing board of the museum, as determined by the museum with the concurrence of the Board of Trustees of the AAMD. If the Board of Trustees of the AAMD determines to censure or recommend suspension or expulsion of a member or to censure or sanction a museum, the Board of Trustees of the AAMD shall, contemporaneously with the issuance of a censure or sanctions or the recommendation of suspension or expulsion, determine and advise the affected director or museum of the process that may be followed, as the case may require, to allow the censure to be rescinded or modified, the suspension to be lifted, the expulsion to not bar a subsequent application for admission, or the sanction to be lifted.

In the event that the museum is not a legal entity but rather is part of an entity or controlled by another entity, any censure or sanction may be issued against the museum, the entity of which the museum is part, the entity controlling the museum, or, as applicable, all or any combination of the foregoing as the Board of Trustees of the AAMD shall determine.

APPENDIX B

Deaccessioning and Disposal

Adopted by the membership of the AAMD, June 2010.

Deaccessioning is defined as the process by which a work of art or other object (collectively, a "work"), wholly or in part, is permanently removed from a museum's collection. *Disposal* is defined as the transfer of ownership by the museum after a work has been deaccessioned; in the case of false or fraudulent works, or works that have been irreparably damaged or cannot practically be restored, removal from the collection and disposition are determined by the museum and may include destruction of the work.

The AAMD recognizes the unique challenges museums face in managing and developing collections largely built through gift and bequest by private donors. Most art museums continue to build and shape their collections over time to realize their mission more fully and effectively. Acquisitions to or deaccessions from the museum's collection must be guided by well-defined, written collecting goals and acquisition and deaccession principles, procedures, and processes approved by a museum's board of trustees or governing body. These goals, principles, procedures, and processes must conform to the

AAMD's *Professional Practices in Art Museums* and policy on deaccession-ing and disposal.[1]

Deaccession decisions must be made with great thoughtfulness, care, and prudence. In making such decisions, expressions of donor intent should always be respected; and the interests of the public, for whose benefit collections are maintained, must always be foremost.

Policy Statement

A. The AAMD requires member museums[2] to develop clear, written collections management policies, including collection goals and acquisition and deaccession principles, procedures, and processes, as well as those that address preservation, conservation, and collection care.

B. The AAMD encourages member museums to accept into their collections only gifts of works that support the mission of the institution and to be thoughtful about accepting gifts of works with restrictions.

C. Member museums must comply with all applicable laws—including, if applicable to the AAMD member museum, the filing of required Internal Revenue Service forms—in deaccessioning and disposing of works from the collection.

D. Member museums should not capitalize or collateralize collections or recognize as revenue the value of donated works. In 1992, following proceedings involving the museum profession, the Financial Accounting Standards Board (FASB) established standards regarding how museums (and other entities) subject to FASB[3] may account for their collections, assuming certain conditions are met. As a result, in 1993, FASB issued Statement Number 116. As amended, the statement provides that contributions of works of art, historical treasures, and similar assets need not be recognized as revenue or capitalized if the donated items are added to collections that are (a) held for public exhibition, education, or research in furtherance of public service; (b) protected, kept unencumbered, cared for, and preserved; and (c) subject to an organizational policy that requires the proceeds from sales of collection items to be used to acquire other items for the collection.

E. When recommending a work to the museum's board of trustees for deaccessioning, a member museum's staff should provide thorough research on prior ownership history, an explanation of expressed donor intent (if any), current scholarly evaluation, and relevance to the existing collection and future collecting goals.

F. A member museum should publish on its website and within a reasonable period of time works that have been deaccessioned and disposed of.

Application

I. Purpose of Deaccessioning and Disposal

A. Deaccessioning is a legitimate part of the formation and care of collections and, if practiced, should be done in order to refine and improve the quality and appropriateness of the collections, the better to serve the museum's mission.
B. Funds received from the disposal of a deaccessioned work shall not be used for operations or capital expenses. Such funds, including any earnings and appreciation thereon, may be used only for the acquisition of works in a manner consistent with the museum's policy on the use of restricted acquisition funds. In order to account properly for their use, the AAMD recommends that such funds, including any earnings and appreciation, be tracked separately from other acquisition funds.

II. Criteria for Deaccessioning and Disposal

There are a number of reasons why deaccessioning might be contemplated. Primary among these are the following:

A. The work is of poor quality and lacks value for exhibition or study purposes.
B. The work is a duplicate that has no value as part of a series.
C. The museum's possession of the work is not consistent with applicable law, for example, the work may have been stolen or illegally imported in violation of applicable laws of the jurisdiction in which the museum is located, or the work may be subject to other legal claims.
D. The authenticity or attribution of the work is determined to be false or fraudulent, and the object lacks sufficient aesthetic merit or art historical importance to warrant retention. In disposing of or retaining a presumed forgery, the museum shall consider all related ethical issues including the consequences of returning the work to the market.
E. The physical condition of the work is so poor that restoration is not practicable or would compromise the work's integrity or the artist's intent. Works that are damaged beyond reasonable repair and are of no use for study or teaching purposes may be destroyed.
F. The work is no longer consistent with the mission or collecting goals of the museum. The board of trustees or governing body of the museum must exercise great care in revising a museum's mission or reformulating collecting goals.
G. The work is being sold as part of the museum's effort to refine and improve its collections, in keeping with the collecting goals reviewed and approved by the museum's board of trustees or governing body.

H. The museum is unable to care adequately for the work because of the work's particular requirements for storage or display or its continuing need for special treatment.

III. Authority and Process

A. Deaccessioning and disposal must comply with all applicable laws of the jurisdiction in which the museum is located and must observe any terms or obligations that pertain to the acquisition of the work by the museum.
B. The final authority for the deaccessioning and disposal of works rests with the board of trustees or governing body or its designee.
C. The process of deaccessioning and disposal must be initiated by the appropriate professional staff and any recommendations, with full justification, presented to the director, who will review the facts and circumstances of the proposed deaccession and disposal. As part of this process, the staff must undertake a thorough review of all records to determine donor intent, clear title, donor restrictions, and current market value. If the director determines that deaccessioning is appropriate, the proposal shall be presented to the board of trustees or governing body or its designee in accordance with the steps outlined in the museum's collection policy with regard to deaccessioning.
  1. The director shall exercise care to assure that the recommendations are based on authoritative expertise.
  2. Third-party review and appraisal may be considered in the case of objects of substantial value.
  3. In the case of work(s) by a living artist, special considerations may apply.
D. The timing and method of disposal should be consistent with the museum's collection policy. Attention must be given to transparency throughout the process.
E. No member of a museum's board or staff, or anyone whose association with the museum might give them an advantage in acquiring the work, shall be permitted to acquire directly or indirectly a work deaccessioned, wholly or in part, by the museum, or otherwise benefit from its sale or trade. The foregoing, however, shall not apply to a sale by a museum of its interest in a work to one or more of any co-owners of such work.
F. If a museum proposes to dispose of less than all of its interest (sometimes known as fractional deaccessioning) in a deaccessioned work (unless the interest to be retained is insubstantial[4]), the disposal should only be made to an organization[5] or organizations that are open to the public.

IV. Selection of Methods of Disposal

The following may be taken into account in selecting a method of disposal:

A. Preferred methods of disposal are sale or transfer to, or exchange with, another public institution; sale through publicly advertised auction; and sale to, or exchange with, or through a reputable, established dealer. Every reasonable effort should be taken to identify and evaluate the various advantages and yields available through different means of disposal.
B. In the case of a work of art by a living artist, consideration may be given to an exchange with the artist.
C. While it is understood that museums must fulfill their fiduciary responsibilities and act in the museum's best interests, museums may give consideration to keeping a deaccessioned work in the public domain.

V. Interests of Donors and Living Artists/Notifications

A. When practicable, museums should notify the donor of a work that is under consideration for deaccessioning and disposal. Circumstances may warrant extending similar courtesy to the heirs of a donor.
B. When a work by a living artist is deaccessioned, consideration must be given to notifying the artist.

VI. Documentation

When a work is deaccessioned, all electronic and paper records must be updated. Prior to disposal, an image should be taken of the work and retained in the museum's records. As works are disposed of, the method of disposition—including possible consignee, new owner, sale price, and location, if known—should be recorded according to the museum's collection management policy.

VII. Special Circumstances

The AAMD recognizes that part of the mandate of a contemporary arts organization is to expand the definition of what constitutes a work of art, as well as to question traditional exhibition practices. Therefore, if the organization's written policy provides for the sale of deaccessioned works, the funds derived from such sales may in exceptional cases be used for purposes analogous to the purchase or commission of works of art, specifically the creation of new works, including some that may not be collectible. Expenditure of these funds for operations or capital expenses is, however, precluded.

VIII. Sanctions

In the event an AAMD member or museum violates one or more of the provisions of this policy, the member may be subject to censure, suspension, and/or expulsion; and the museum may be subject to censure and/or sanctions in accordance with the relevant provisions of the code of ethics of the AAMD, which have been amended consistent with the following:

Infractions by any art museum may expose that institution to censure and/or sanctions, as determined by the Board of Trustees of the AAMD, that may, in the case of sanctions, include, without limitation, suspension of loans and shared exhibitions between the sanctioned museum and museums of which the AAMD members are directors.

Prior to censuring or recommending suspension or expulsion of a member or censuring or issuing any sanction against an art museum, the Board of Trustees of the AAMD shall provide to the director or museum in question the opportunity to be heard and to explain the reason for the actions considered for censure, suspension, expulsion, or sanction; such presentation to be by the affected director unless otherwise determined by the Board of Trustees of the AAMD or, in the case of a museum, the director or any member of the board of trustees or governing board of the museum, as determined by the museum with the concurrence of the Board of Trustees of the AAMD. If the Board of Trustees of the AAMD determines to censure or recommend suspension or expulsion of a member or to censure or sanction a museum, the Board of Trustees of the AAMD shall, contemporaneously with the issuance of a censure or sanctions or the recommendation of suspension or expulsion, determine and advise the affected director or museum of the process that may be followed, as the case may require, to allow the censure to be rescinded or modified, the suspension to be lifted, the expulsion to not bar a subsequent application for admission or the sanction to be lifted.

In the event that the museum is not a legal entity but rather part of an entity or controlled by another entity,[6] any censure or sanction may be issued against the museum, the entity of which the museum is a part, the entity controlling the museum, or, as applicable, all of the foregoing as the Board of Trustees of the AAMD shall determine.

IX. University and College Museums

University and college museums play a significant role in acquiring, preserving, and presenting collections. While the primary focus of the university or college is education, the university or college must also adhere to professional standards and ethics when operating a museum.

A. The director is responsible for the development and implementation of policy related to all aspects of the museum's collections, including acquisition, deaccessioning and disposal, preservation, conservation, and exhibition, as well as scholarly research and interpretation. The director is responsible for ensuring that the university or college is aware of its ethical responsibilities to the museum's collection, including issues around its deaccessioning, use, and the physical conditions under which it is maintained.

B. Deaccessioning and disposal from the collection must result from clear museum policies that are in keeping with the AAMD's professional practices (see also the section on the collection and Appendix B). Deaccessioning and disposal from the museum's collection must never be for the purpose of providing financial support or benefit for other goals of the university or college or its foundation. In no event should the funds received from disposal of a deaccessioned work be used for operations or capital expenditures.

C. Policies developed by the director with regard to acquisition and deaccession should be adopted or ratified by the central governing authority of the university or college.

APPENDIX C

University and College Art Museums

Adopted by the membership of the AAMD, 1991; amended 2001 and 2011

University and college museums are an important part of the spectrum of art museums in the United States. These institutions arose from the belief that the benefits of education should be made available to all citizens and that the opportunity to experience art is a vital part of education. University and college art museums often have responsibility for significant collections; in some communities, they are the major, or sole, art museum for the municipality or the region. University and college art museums serve as links between their campuses and surrounding communities and play important roles in the public service and missions of the parent universities or colleges. At the same time, university and college art museums must be part of the central academic missions of the institutions and must participate fully in the education of students and the advancement of scholarship. The museum within a university or college functions best when this dual role is acknowledged and appreciated by the university or college and by the community.

Operating within a university or college setting may offer advantages and protections to directors that might not be available to directors in other museums, among them, sabbaticals, tenure policies, and traditions of academic freedom. Other advantages may include access to university or college faculty, libraries, legal counsel, human resource specialists, risk managers, and institutional support for facilities and grounds maintenance. The director of a university or college museum should receive all of the rights and privileges of tenured faculty. Because of their positions within academic institutions, university and college museum directors may face issues that are significantly different from other museums. This appendix recognizes some of those issues and offers professional practices appropriate for most art museums within a university or college structure. Although not all-inclusive, these practices address issues of special concern to university and college art museum directors at the time of the revision of this document.

I. Appointment

A. The director should be appointed by the president, chief academic officer, or his or her designee and ratified, according to the practice of the institution, by the governing body of the university or college or appointed by whatever procedure is consistent with deans or directors at the university or college.

B. Salaries of university or college art museum directors (and all staff) should be consistent not only with faculty and administrative salaries within the institution but also with professional salaries at comparable museums throughout the country.

II. Performance, Review and Dismissal

The director's performance should be reviewed regularly according to professional museum standards. The director is subject to dismissal only after due process, which is offered according to the statutes of the university or college. In addition, best practice suggests that the university or college commission an external review of the art museum every seven to ten years. Such a review should be conducted by a committee of peer university or college art museum directors.

III. Reporting Structure

A. The director should report to the governing board of the university or college via the central academic administration of the university or college rather than to a school, department, division, program, or other unit of the university or college. While recognizing that some university or college art museums operate satisfactorily under different reporting arrangements, reporting to the central academic officer is preferred. The position of the art museum within the central academic structure reconfirms and emphasizes the relevance of its collections and programs to all of the university or college rather than to any one part and recognizes the public service and outreach mission of the museum. If faculty or other university or college advisory committees for the art museum exist, it must be clear that they are not its governing body.

B. The public role of the museum within the community should be acknowledged. The director is more likely to be supported in that role if he or she reports to a senior officer who understands the relationship of the university or college to the community and the role the museum can play in strengthening that relationship. Equally, the central role the museum plays in the research mission of the university or college and in the education of students at the university or college must be acknowledged and supported. In many university and college museums, the office of the president, provost, executive vice president, vice president for academic affairs, or some similar office is the one most likely to understand and support both the academic and public-service mission of the museum.

IV. Responsibilities and Authority

A. As in other museums, the university or college art museum director is responsible for the artistic direction and vision for the museum, as well as management and direction of the staff and the budget.

B. While the museum must be the director's primary responsibility, the director may also teach academic courses. The teaching of such courses should be mutually agreed upon by the director and the relevant academic unit. The director or the director's designee should participate centrally in the design and/or implementation of any art museum training curriculum offered by the university or college.

C. The director provides artistic leadership to the community and participates in community artistic affairs at his or her discretion. Participation on boards and committees of community arts organizations is part of the public-service responsibility of the director, so long as such participation does not involve a conflict of interest in fundraising, artistic affairs, or any other part of the director's responsibilities to the museum or the university or college.

D. The director is a leader and spokesperson for art museum issues within the university or college and in the community.

E. The director is responsible for the development and implementation of policy related to all aspects of the museum's collections, including acquisition, deaccessioning and disposal, preservation, conservation, and exhibition, as well as scholarly research and interpretation. Recognizing that the university, college, or related foundation owns the museum's collection, the director is responsible for making the governing authority of the university or college aware of its legal and ethical responsibilities to the art museum's collection, including issues of its use and the physical conditions under which it is maintained.

F. Deaccessioning and disposal from the collection must adhere to clear, written museum policies that are in keeping with the AAMD's professional practices (see also the section on the collection and Appendix B). Deaccessioning and disposal from the art museum's collection must never be for the purpose of providing general operating support or other benefit to the parent university, college, or related foundation. The university or college museum must have written policies on deaccessioning that define the director's role and responsibilities and clearly specify which university or college office or body has the final authority to approve deaccessioning.

G. Policies developed by the director with regard to acquisition and deaccession should be adopted or ratified by the central governing authority of the university or college.

H. Art outside the museum's collection may be acquired by the university or college, but the museum should be offered the right of first refusal for such acquisitions. If the university, college, or related foundation disposes of art outside the museum's collection, the museum should be offered the right of first refusal to acquire the art for the museum's collection. Should the university or college desire that its museum document and manage such university collections, the university or college should provide necessary staff and funds.

I. The director is responsible for using the museum's collections for teaching and research, without exposing the objects to undue risk. The director must have sole discretion as to how, when, and where objects from the museum's collection are used and under what conditions they are stored and exhibited. Policies and practices covering the foregoing should be included in the institution's written collection management plan.

J. While the museum's spaces may be made available to the university, college, or community for entertaining or other purposes, the director is responsible for determining what constitutes appropriate use of museum spaces, in keeping with his or her responsibilities for the safekeeping of the museum's collection, exhibitions, and programs. The director should develop a written policy for use of museum spaces consistent with the physical limitations of the space and the safeguarding of the collections, exhibitions, and programs. If the museum rents some of its spaces to university, college, or community groups, the museum—rather than the central offices of the university, college, or any related foundation or another collegiate unit—should receive the financial benefits. Likewise, if the university or college art museum operates a museum store, financial benefits should accrue directly to the museum.

K. The director must be a central participant in any project that involves alteration, enlargement, or renovation of the museum's facilities. The director must be involved with the selection of an architect and the determination of the final building program and design.

L. While joint appointments of art museum staff with other departments are desirable in some cases, the director should have sole discretion for hiring, reviewing, and dismissing art museum employees within the existing personnel policies of the university or college.

M. Advisory groups are often central to building relationships and support. If the museum has such groups, whether community, alumni, or otherwise constituted, the director should work closely with them to ensure that their goals and priorities are in keeping with those of the museum. The director should select, or be principally involved with the selection of, members of such groups and their officers. If groups assist with fundraising for the museum, all fundraising must be done with the approval of the director and for priorities established with the director.

APPENDIX D

Reproductions of Works of Art

Adopted by the membership of the AAMD, January 1979; amended 2001 and 2011.

Art museums legitimately generate income through the sale of such educational materials as catalogues, books, postcards, and reproductions. The manufacture and knowledgeable use of reproductions for teaching purposes or in a decorative context is appropriate.

The proliferation of "art-derived" materials, coupled with misleading marketing of reproductions, has created such widespread confusion as to require clarification and disclosure in order to maintain professional standards. When producing and/or selling reproductions, museums must clearly indicate, through the use of integral markings on the objects, as well as signs, labels, and advertising, that these items are reproductions. Signatures, print edition numbers, and printers' symbols or titles must not appear in the reproduction if in the original they occur outside the borders of the image. Similarly, signatures, edition numbers, and/or foundry marks on sculpture must not appear on the reproduction.

Reproductions must be in materials and/or sizes other than those used by the artist in the original works of art. Although reproductions of decorative arts serving functional purposes may pose special problems in this regard, the fact that they are reproductions should be clearly indicated on the object.

The touting of exaggerated investment value of reproductions must be avoided because the object or work being offered for purchase is not original and the resale value is highly in doubt.

When advertising reproductions, museums should not use language implying that there is any identity of quality between the copy and the original or that would lead the potential buyer to believe that by purchasing any such reproduction, he or she is acquiring an original work of art.

NOTES

1. Canadian and Mexican member museums should follow applicable legal restrictions and policies of national associations and, to the extent not inconsistent with either of the foregoing, the AAMD's *Professional Practices in Art Museums* and policy on deaccessioning and disposal.

2. A *member museum* is one whose director is a member of the AAMD.

3. Museums that follow other accounting rules, such as those of the Government Accounting Standards Board (GASB), or are subject to a legal restrictions may be required to treat collections for financial statement purposes in a different manner, but museums still should not collateralize their collections.

4. For example, rights of reproduction or the right to borrow the work.

5. "Organization" means a museum or institution exempt from federal income tax and classified as a public charity or a private operating foundation (or substantially similar organization in Canada or Mexico) or governmental entity or agency.

6. An example of a museum that is part of another entity would be a museum that is not separate legal entity but is part of a college or university. An example of a museum that is controlled by another entity would be a separately incorporated museum the sole member of which is a trust or foundation.

.

Bibliography

Akinsha, Konstantin and Grigorii Kozlov. *Beautiful Loot: The Soviet Plunder of Europe's Art Treasures.* New York: Random House, 1995.

Alaimo, Michelle. "Meteorite Mission: Tribal members visit Tomanowos in New York City." *Smoke Signals.* July 1, 2014. http://www.grandronde.org/news/smoke-signals/2014/07/01/meteorite-mission-tribal-members-visit-tomanowos-in-new-york-city/#sthash.MfQ1mvjb.dpbs.

Albright-Knox Art Gallery. "About the Albright-Knox." Albright-Knox Art Gallery website. Accessed February 5, 2014. http://www.albrightknox.org/about-ak/.

American Alliance of Museums. "Characteristics of Excellence for U.S. Museums." American Alliance of Museums website. Accessed January 3, 2014. http://www.aam-us.org/resources/ethics-standards-and-best-practices/characteristics-of-excellence-for-u-s-museums.

———. "Code of Ethics for Museums." American Alliance of Museums website. Amended 2000. http://www.aam-us.org/resources/ethics-standards-and-best-practices/code-of-ethics.

———. "Core Documents." American Alliance of Museums website. Accessed September 27, 2015. http://www.aam-us.org/resources/assessment-programs/core-documents/documents.

———. "Financial Stability." American Alliance of Museums website. Accessed February 21, 2014. http://www.aam-us.org/resources/ethics-standards-and-best-practices/financial-stability.

———. "Recommended Procedures for Providing Information to the Public about Objects Transferred in Europe during the Nazi Era." 2001. American Alliance of Museums website. http://www.aam-us.org/docs/default-source/professional-resources/nepip-recommended-procedures.

———. "Standards Regarding Archaeological Material and Ancient Art." American Alliance of Museums website. Accessed March 6, 2015. http://www.aam-us.org/resources/ethics-standards-and-best-practices/collections-stewardship/archaeological-material-and-ancient-art.

———. "Standards Regarding Exhibiting Borrowed Objects." American Alliance of Museums website. Accessed November 14, 2014. http://www.aam-us.org/resources/ethics-standards-and-best-practices/education-and-interpretation.

———. "Standards Regarding Developing and Managing Business and Individual Donor Support." American Alliance of Museums website. Accessed November 14, 2014. http://www.aam-us.org/resources/ethics-standards-and-best-practices/financial-stability.

———. "Standards Regarding the Unlawful Appropriation of Objects During the Nazi Era." 1998. American Alliance of Museums website. http://www.aam-us.org/resources/ethics-standards-and-best-practices/collections-stewardship/objects-during-the-nazi-era.

———. "What are Ethics? Relevant Ethics." American Alliance of Museums website. Accessed March 6, 2014. http://www.aam-us.org/resources/ethics-standards-and-best-practices/ethics.

American Alliance of Museums Curators Committee (CurCom). "A Code of Ethics for Curators." 2009. American Association of Museums website. http://www.aam-us.org/docs/continuum/curcomethics.pdf?sfvrsn=0.

American Association for State and Local History. "Publication: AALH Statement of Professional Standards and Ethics." American Association for State and Local History website. Updated June 2012. http://resource.aaslh.org/view/aaslh-statement-of-professional-standards-and-ethics/.

———. "Technical Leaflet: Ethics Position Paper: The Capitalization of Collections." American Association of State and Local History website. Fall 2003. http://resource.aaslh.org/view/ethics-position-paper-the-capitalization-of-collections/.

American Institute for Conservation of Historic and Artistic Works. "About Us, Code of Ethics and Guidelines for Practice." American Institute for Conservation of Historic and Artistic Works. Revised August 1994. http://www.conservation-us.org/about-us/core-documents/code-of-ethics#.U8ASu1ZcUso.

———. "Commentaries to the Guidelines for Practice." American Institute for Conservation of Historic and Artistic Works website, Accessed July 11, 2014. http://www.conservation-us.org/about-us/core-documents/guidelines-for-practice#.U8ATd1ZcUso.

American Museum of Natural History. "Willamette Meteorite Agreement." June 22, 2000. American Museum of Natural History website. http://www.amnh.org/exhibitions/permanent-exhibitions/rose-center-for-earth-and-space/dorothy-and-lewis-b.-cullman-hall-of-the-universe/willamette-meteorite-agreement.

———. "The Willamette Meteorite, Exhibition Text." American Museum of Natural History website. Accessed May 6, 2015. http://www.amnh.org/exhibitions/permanent-exhibitions/rose-center-for-earth-and-space/dorothy-and-lewis-b.-cullman-hall-of-the-universe/planets/planetary-impacts/the-willamette-meteorite.

Anderson, Gail, ed. *Museum Mission Statements: Building a Distinct Identity*, 2nd ed. Washington, DC: American Association of Museums, 1998.

Anderson, Terri. "Too Museum of a Good Thing: Lessons from Deaccessioning at National Trust Historic Sites." In *Museums and the Disposals Debate*. Edited by Peter Davies, 230–53. Edinburgh: MuseumsEtc, 2011.

Art Museum Subdist. of the Metro. Zoo. Park v United States, 4:11-cv-00291-HEA, E.D. Mo. Complaint for Declaratory Judgment, February 15, 2011.

Associated Press. "NY court revives suit over Nazi stolen art at Oklahoma Univ." newsok.com. March 14, 2015. http://newsok.com/court-revives-lawsuit-of-nazi-stolen-art-displayed-at-university-of-oklahoma/article/feed/811703?custom_click=rss&utm_source=feedburner&utm_medium=feed&utm_campaign=Feed%3A+newsok%2Fhome+(NewsOK.com+RSS+-+Home).

Association of Art Museum Directors. "AAMD Policy on Deaccessioning." 2010. Association of Art Museum Directors website. https://aamd.org/standards-and-practices.

———. "Art Museums and the Identification and Restitution of Works Stolen by the Nazis." May 2007. Association of Art Museum Directors website, https://aamd.org/standards-and-practices.

———. "Code of Ethics for Art Museum Directors." In "Professional Practices in Art Museums." 2011, 17–18. Association of Art Museum Directors website. https://aamd.org/sites/default/files/document/2011ProfessionalPracticesinArtMuseums.pdf.

———. "Introduction to the Revisions to the 2008 Guidelines on the Acquisition of Archaeological Material and Ancient Art." In "2013 Guidelines on the Acquisition of Archaeological Material and Ancient Art." January 29, 2013. Association of Art Museum Directors website. https://aamd.org/standards-and-practices.

———. "Managing the Relationship Between Art Museums and Corporate Sponsors." 2007. Association of Art Museum Directors website. https://aamd.org/standards-and-practices.

———. "Professional Practices in Art Museums," 2011, Association of Art Museum Directors website. https://aamd.org/sites/default/files/document/2011ProfessionalPracitiesinArtMuseums.pdf.

———. "Protocols for Safe Havens for Works of Cultural Significance from Countries in Crisis." Association of Art Museum Directors website. September 28, 2015. https://www.aamd.org/document/aamd-protocols-for-safe-havens-for-works-of-cultural-significance-from-countries-in-crisis.

———. "Report of the AAMD Task Force on the Spoliation of Art during the Nazi/World War II Era (1933–1945), June 4, 1998." Association of Art Museum Directors website. https://aamd.org/standards-and-practices.

———. "Revenue Generation: An Investment in the Public Service of Art Museums." 2007. Association of Art Museum Directors website. https://aamd.org/standards-and-practices.

Association of Fundraising Professionals. "Guidelines, Codes, Standards: Code of Ethical Standards." Amended October 2014. Association of Fundraising Professionals website. http://www.afpnet.org/files/ContentDocuments/CodeofEthicsLong.pdf.

Badiou, Alain. *Ethics: An Essay on the Understanding of Evil.* Translated by Peter Hallward. New York: Verso, 2001.

Bandle, Anne Laure and Raphael Contel. "Reparation Art: Finding Common Ground in the Resolution of Disputes on Russian War Spoils and Nazi-Looted Art." In *Art, Cultural Heritage and the Market: Ethical and Legal Issues.* Edited by Valentina Vadi and Hildegard E.G.S. Schneider. New York: Springer, 2014.

Barker, Alex W. "Archaeological Ethics: Museums and Collections." In *Ethical Issues in Archaeology*. Edited by Larry J. Zimmerman, Karen D. Vitelli, and Julie Hollowell-Zimmer. New York: AltaMira Press, 2003.

Bator, Paul M. "An Essay on the International Trade in Art." *Stanford Law Review,* Vol. 34, No. 2 (Jan. 1982): 275–384.

Baudis, Dominique. Décision du Défenseur des droits n.MSP 2013–223.

Besterman, Terence. "Museum Ethics." In *Companion to Museum Studies*. Edited by Sharon Macdonald, 431–441. Oxford: Blackwell Publishing, 2006.

Bradsher, Greg. "Documenting Nazi Plunder of European Art." *The Record*. November 1997. Washington, DC: National Archives and Records Administration. http://www.archives.gov/research/holocaust/records-and-research/documenting-nazi-plunder-of-european-art.html.

Brooks, Mary M. and Dinah Eastop. "Matter Out of Place: Paradigms for Analyzing Textile Cleaning." *Journal of the American Institute for Conservation* Vol. 45, No. 3 (2006):171–81.

Buck, Rebecca A. and Jean Allman Gilmore, eds. *MRM5: Museum Registration Methods, 5th Edition*. Washington, DC: American Alliance of Museums, 2010.

Burke Museum. "About Us." The Burke Museum of Natural History and Culture website, updated May 2010. https://www.burkemuseum.org/info/about#mision.

Campbell, Thomas P. "Opening of the Met's New David H. Koch Plaza." September 10, 2014. Metropolitan Museum of Art website. http://www.metmuseum.org/about-the-museum/now-at-the-met/2014/opening-of-the-mets-new-david-h-koch-plaza.

Canaday, John. "Very Quiet and Very Dangerous." *The New York Times*. February 27, 1972, p.175. http://timesmachine.nytimes.com/timesmachine/1972/02/27/91321031.html?pageNumber=175.

Coggins, Clemency C. "A Proposal for Museum Acquisitions in the Future." *International Journal of Cultural Property*, 7 (1998): 434–37.

———. "United States Cultural Property Legislation: Observations of a Combatant." *International Journal of Cultural Property*, Vol. 7, No. 1 (1998): 52–68.

College Art Association. "Statement Concerning the Deaccession of Works of Art." Revised October 27, 2013. College Art Association website. http://www.collegeart.org/guidelines/sales.

Committee for Cultural Policy. "St. Louis Art Museum Prevails in Ka Nefer Nefer Mummy Mask Case." Committee for Cultural Property website. June 15, 2014. http://committeeforculturalpolicy.org/st-louis-art-museum-prevails-in-ka-nefer-nefer-mummy-mask-case/.

Cossman, Brenda. *Censorship and The Arts: Law, Controversy, Debate, Facts*. Toronto, Ontario: Ontario Association of Art Galleries, 1995.

Cott, Sharon H. and Stephen J. Knerly, Jr. "Comparison of the Report of the AAMD Task Force on the Acquisition of Archaeological Material and Ancient Art (revised 2008) and The American Association of Museum Standards Regarding Archaeological Material and Ancient Art (July 2008)." ALI-ABA Course of Study, Legal Issues in Museum Administration, April 1–3, 2009, Boston, MA.

Crooke, Elizabeth. *Museums and Community: Ideas, Issues and Challenges,* New York: Routledge, 2007.

Cuno, James. *Museums Matter: In Praise of the Encyclopedic Museum.* Chicago: The University of Chicago Press, 2011.

———. *Who Owns Antiquity? Museums and the Battle over Our Ancient Heritage.* Princeton: Princeton University Press, 2008.

———, ed. *Whose Muse? Art Museums and the Public Trust.* Princeton, NJ: Princeton University Press, 2004.

Davies, Peter, ed. *Museums and the Disposals Debate.* Edinburgh: MuseumsEtc, 2011.

Dennis v Buffalo Fine Arts Academy NY Slip Op 50520(U). Accessed January 31, 2014. http://law.justia.com/cases/new-york/other-courts/2007/2007–50520.html.

Dubin, S.C. *Displays of Power: Controversy in the American Museum from the Enola Gay to Sensation.* New York: New York University Press, 1999.

Donnelly-Smith, Laura. "Blessings and Curses of Doorstep Donations." *Museum.* May/June 2011, 48–53. http://aam-us.org/resources/publications/museum-magazine/archive/doorstep-donations.

Eastop, Dina. "Conservation practice as enacted ethics." In *The Routledge Companion to Museum Ethics: Redefining Ethics for the Twenty-First-Century Museum.* Edited by Janet Marstine, 426–444. New York: Routledge, 2010.

Edgar, Heather J.H. and Anna L.M. Rautman. "Contemporary Museum Policies and the Ethics of Accepting Human Remains." *Curator: The Museum Journal,* Vol. 57, No. 2 (April 2014): 244.

Feliciano, Hector. *The Lost Museum: The Nazi Conspiracy to Steal the World's Greatest Works of Art.* New York: Basic Books, 1997.

Financial Accounting Standards Board. Statement No. 116: Accounting for Contributions Received and Contributions Made." FAS116–4, 1993. Financial Accounting Standards Board website. http://www.fasb.org/jsp/FASB/Document_C/DocumentPage?cid=1218220128831&acceptedDisclaimer=true.

———. "Summary of Statement No. 116: Accounting for Contributions Received and Contributions Made." 1993. Financial Accounting Standards Board website. http://www.fasb.org/jsp/FASB/Pronouncement_C/SummaryPage&cid=900000010226.

Fishman, Margie. "Museum to sell art to pay debt." *The News Journal.* March 27, 2014. http://www.delawareonline.com/story/entertainment/arts/2014/03/26/delaware-art-museum-sell-four-works/6913117/.

Francisco, Courtney. "UPDATE: Lawmaker telling patrons to avoid OU until famous art stolen by Nazis is returned." KFOR.com. February 7, 2014. http://kfor.com/2014/01/29/could-could-artwork-that-became-nazi-loot-be-hanging-in-ous-museum/.

Galerie Nationale du Jeu de Paume. *Ahlam Shibli Phantom Home [Foyer Fantome], #104.* Galerie Nationale du Jeu de Paume website. Accessed December 9, 2013. http://www.jeudepaume.org/index.php?page=article&idArt=1837.

Gay, Malcolm. "Out of Egypt. From a long-buried pyramid to the Saint Louis Art Museum: The Mysterious voyage of the Ka-Nefer-Nefer mask." *Riverfront Times.* February 15, 2006. http://www.riverfronttimes.com/2006–02-15/news/out-of-egypt/full/.

Gerstenblith, Patty. "The Meaning of 1970 for the Acquisition of Archaeological Objects." *Journal of Field Archaeology,* Vol. 38, No. 4 (2013): 262–66.

———. "Museum Practice: Legal Issues." In *Companion to Museum Studies.* Edited by Sharon Macdonald, 442–56. Oxford: Blackwell Publishing, 2006.

———. "Ownership And Protection Of Heritage: Cultural Property Rights for the 21st Century: The Public Interest in the Restitution of Cultural Objects." *Connecticut Journal of International Law* 16 (Spring 2001): 197–246.

———, ed. "Special Issue: Ethical Considerations and Cultural Property." *International Journal of Cultural Property*, Vol. 7, No. 1 (1998).

Getty Conservation Institute. "Ethical Dilemmas in the Conservation of Modern and Contemporary Art," an event organized by the Getty Conservation Institute on April 29, 2009. https://www.getty.edu/conservation/publications_resources/videos/public_lecture_videos_audio/ethical_dilemmas.html.

Gili, Marta, Carles Guerra, Joao Fernandes, and Isabel Sousa Braga in *Ahlam Shibli Phantom Home [Foyer Fantome], #104.* Galerie Nationale de Jeu de Paume website, accessed December 9, 2013. http://www.jeudepaume.org/index.php?page=article&idArt=1837.

Goneim, M. Zakaria. *The Lost Pyramid.* New York: Reinhart & Company, 1956.

———. *Excavations at Saqqara Horus Sekhem-khet—The Unfinished Step Pyramid at Saqqara.* Vol. I. Cairo: Impremerie L'Institute Français D'Archéologie Orientale, 1957.

Graham, Martha and Nell Murphy. "NAGPRA at 20: Museum Collections and Reconnections." *Museum Anthropology.* Vol. 33, No. 2 (2010): 105–124.

Greenfield, Jeanette. *The Return of Cultural Treasures.* 3rd Edition. New York: Cambridge University Press, 2007.

Hatchfield, Pamela, ed. *Ethics and Critical Thinking in Conservation.* Washington, DC: American Institute for Conservation of Historic & Artistic Works, 2013.

Heddaya, Mostafa. "São Paulo Biennial Curators Join Artists in Repudiating Israeli Sponsorship." *Hyperallergic.* August 28, 2014. http://hyperallergic.com/146308/sao-paulo-biennial-curators-join-artists-in-repudiating-israeli-sponsorship/.

Hirzy, Ellen Cochran, ed. *Excellence and Equity: Education and the Public Dimension of Museums.* Washington, DC: American Association of Museums, 1992.

Holocaust-Era Assets Conference. "Terezin Declaration." June 30, 2009. Holocaust-Era Assets Conference website. http://www.holocausteraassets.eu/program/conference-proceedings/.

Illustrated London News. "The Discovery of a New Step Pyramid: A Third Dynasty Find at Sakkara." June 7, 1952, No. 5903, 980–81.

Internal Revenue Service. Publication 598 (03/2012). Tax on Unrelated Business Income of Exempt Organizations. Internal Revenue Service website. http://www.irs.gov/publications/p598/ch03.html.

International Council of Museums, "ICOM Code of Ethics for Museums," International Council of Museums website, revised 2004, http://icom.museum/the-vision/code-of-ethics/.

———. "ICOM Recommendations concerning the Return of Works of Art Belonging to Jewish Owners." January 14, 1999. International Council of Museums website. http://archives.icom.museum/worldwar2.html.

International Council of Museums—Committee on Conservation (ICOM-CC), "The Conservator-Restorer: A Definition of the Profession." August 1984.

International Council of Museums website. http://www.icom-cc.org/47/#.U80r9l-ZcUsp Accessed July 21, 2014.

Journal of the American Institute for Conservation. Vol. 45, No. 3 (Fall/Winter 2006). Maney Publishing. Special Issue on Cleaning.

Kennicott, Philip. "An art loan from Bill Cosby draws the Smithsonian into a national debate." *The Washington Post.* November 20, 2014, http://www.washingtonpost.com/lifestyle/style/an-art-loan-from-bill-cosby-draws-the-smithsonian-into-a-national-debate/2014/11/20/bde2794a-70e5-11e4-ad12-3734c461eab6_story.html.

———. "Passing Judgment: What does it Mean When Smithsonian Shows 'American Idol' Desk?" *Washington Post.* August 30, 2009. http://www.washingtonpost.com/wp-dyn/content/article/2009/08/27/AR2009082704411.html.

King, Elaine A. and Gail Levin, eds. *Ethics and the Visual Arts.* New York: Allworth Press, 2006.

Landes, Richard. "Notice at the Jeu de Paume in Response to the Controversy about 'Phantom Homes,'" The Augean Stables, July 21, 2012, www.theaugeanstables.com.

Lane, Mary M. "The Dutch Stedelijk Museum Questions Origins of Some of its Art." *The Wall Street Journal.* February 26, 2015. http://www.wsj.com/articles/the-dutch-stedelijk-museum-questions-ownership-of-its-art-1424977203.

Laurie, Marilyn. "Corporate Funding for the Arts," in *The Arts in the World Economy: Public Policy and Private Philanthropy for a Global Cultural Community.* Edited by Olin Robison, Robert Freeman and Charles A. Riley II, 67–76. Hanover, NH: University Press of New England, 1994.

Legal Information Institute, Cornell University Law School. Wex Legal Dictionary. Cornell University Law School website. Accessed May 22, 2015. https://www.law.cornell.edu/wex/forfeiture.

Litt, Steven. "Cleveland Museum of Art returns Hanuman sculpture to Cambodia, saying new evidence indicates it was probably looted." *The Plain Dealer.* May 11, 2015. http://www.cleveland.com/arts/index.ssf/2015/05/cleveland_museum_of_art_return.html.

Lonshein, Alison and Marsha S. Shaines, "Charitable Contributions 101," The American Law Institute Continuing Legal Education, Legal Issues in Museum Administration, March 19–21, 2014.

Malaro, Marie. *Museum Governance: Mission, Ethics, Policy.* Washington, DC: Smithsonian Institution Press, 1994.

Malaro, Marie and Ildiko Pogány DeAngelis. *A Legal Primer on Managing Museum Collections*, 3rd ed. Washington, DC: Smithsonian Books, 2012.

Marstine, Janet, ed. *The Routledge Companion to Museum Ethics: Redefining Ethics for the Twenty-First Century Museum.* New York: Routledge, 2012.

Marstine, Janet, Alexander Bauer and Chelsea Haines, eds. *New Directions in Museum Ethics.* New York: Routledge, 2014

Mashberg, Tom and Graham Bowley. "Islamic State Destruction Renews Debate Over Repatriation of Antiquities." *The New York Times*, March 31, 2015. http://www.nytimes.com/2015/03/31/arts/design/islamic-state-destruction-renews-debate-over-repatriation-of-antiquities.html.

Matassa, Freda, "Creating Your Acquisition Policy," *ICOM News,* No. 1–2, 2014, pp. 8–9.

Matero, Frank. "Ethics and Policy in Conservation." *The Getty Conservation Institute Newsletter,* Vol. 15, No. 1 (Spring 2000). http://www.getty.edu/conservation/publications_resources/newsletters/15_1/feature1_2.html

Merryman, John Henry, Albert E. Elsen, and Stephen K. Urice. *Law, Ethics and the Visual Arts,* 5th Ed. The Netherlands: Kluwer Law International, 2007.

Merryman, John Henry. "Museum Ethics." Address given at the American Law Institute – American Bar Association Continuing Legal Education ALI-ADA Course of Study. Legal Issues in Museum Administration, March 29–31, 2006. http://www.law.harvard.edu/faculty/martin/art_law/museum_ethics.html.

Metropolitan Museum of Art. Charter of The Metropolitan Museum of Art. State of New York, Laws of 1870, Chapter 197, passed April 13, 1870 and amended L. 1898, ch. 34; L. 1908, ch. 219.

———. "Collections Management Policy." Last revised June 10, 2014. Metropolitan Museum of Art website. http://www.metmuseum.org/about-the-museum/collections-management-policy#care.

———. "Ethical Guidelines for Trustees, Officers and Key Employees of The Metropolitan Museum of Art As Approved by the Board of Trustees on May 13, 2014," 4.

———. "Jewels by JAR, November 20, 2013-March 9, 2014." Metropolitan Museum of Art website. Accessed March 6, 2014. http://www.metmuseum.org/exhibitions/listings/2013/jewels-by-jar.

———. "Museum Mission Statement." Metropolitan Museum of Art website. Amended January 15, 2015. Metropolitan Museum of Art website. http://www.metmuseum.org/about-the-museum/mission-statement.

Michot, Alexandra. "Une Famille défavorisée expulse du Musée d'Orsay." LE FIGARO.fr, 29/01/2013. http://www.lefigaro.fr/actualite-france/2013/01/29/01016–20130129ARTFIG00323-une-famille-defavorisee-expulsee-du-musee-d-orsay.php.

Museum Security Network. "Info and Contact." Museum Security Network website. http://www.museum-security.org.

Museum Store Association. "Museum Store Association Code of Ethics." Museum Store Association Website. Revised 2014. https://museumstoreassociation.org/code-of-ethics/.

National Coalition Against Censorship. "Museum Best Practices for Managing Controversy." National Coalition Against Censorship website. Issued May 7, 2012. http://ncac.org/resource/museum-best-practices-for-managing-controversy/.

National Museum of African Art website. Accessed December 8, 2014. http://africa.si.edu.

National Park Service, United States Department of the Interior. "Native American Graves Protection and Repatriation Act (NAGPRA): A Quick Guide for Preserving Native American Cultural Resources." Draft 2012. http://www.nps.gov/history/tribes/Quick_Guides.htm.

———. "National NAGPRA, Native American Graves Protection and Repatriation Act." Accessed July 30, 2015. http://www.nps.gov/nagpra/MANDATES/25USC3001etseq.htm.

———. "National NAGPRA, Native American Graves Protection and Repatriation Review Committee, About the Review Committee." Accessed May 1, 2015. http://www.nps.gov/NAGPRA/REVIEW/.

Nazi-Era Provenance Internet Portal. Accessed July 5, 2015. Nazi-Era Provenance Internet Portal website. http://nepip.org/index.cfm?menu_type=.

The New York Times. "Museum Ethics." December 29, 1902, 6. http://timesmachine. nytimes.com/timesmachine/1902/12/29/101095197.html?pageNumber=6.

Nicholas, Lynn H. *The Rape of Europa: The Fate of Europe's Treasure in the Third Reich and the Second World War.* New York: Vintage Books, 1995.

Nicholas Stanley-Price, M. Kirby Talley, Jr., and Alessandra Melucco Vaccaro, eds. *Readings in Conservation: Historical and Philosophical Issues in the Conservation of Cultural Heritage.* Los Angeles: The Getty Conservation Institute, 1996.

Norton, Bryan G., Michael Hutchins, Elizabeth Stevens, and Terry L. Maple, eds. *Ethics in the Ark: Zoos, Animal Welfare and Wildlife Conservation.* Washington, DC: Smithsonian Books, 1995.

Oddy, Andrew, ed. *Restoration: Is it Acceptable?* Occasional Paper 99, British Museum Occasional Papers. London: The British Museum, 1994.

O'Hara, Mary Emily. "Should Oil Barons Like David Koch Be Funding Our Museums?" VICE. September 12, 2014. http://www.vice.com/read/should-oil-barons-like-david-koch-be-funding-our-museums-912.

O'Neill, Mark. "Commentary 4. John Holden's *Capturing Cultural Value: How Culture has become a tool of Government Policy.*" *Cultural Trends* 14:1, No. 53, 2005.

Perrot, Paul N. "Museum ethics and collecting principles." In *Museum Ethics.* Edited by Gary Edson, 171–77. New York: Routledge, 1997.

Phelan, Marilyn. "Legal and Ethical Considerations in the Repatriation of Illegally Exported and Stolen Cultural Property: Is There a Means to Settle the Disputes?" INTERCOM. Accessed March 20, 2015. http://www.intercom.museum/conferences/2004/phelan.html.

Preston, Douglas J. "The Willamette Meteorite." In *Dinosaurs in the Attic: an Excursion into the American Museum of Natural History.* New York: Ballantine Books, 1986. http://www.usgennet.org/alhnorus/ahorclak/MeteorTreasures.html.

Registrars Committee of the American Alliance of Museums. "A Code of Ethics for Registrars, 1984." In *RC-AAM History: History of the Registrars Committee 25 Years.* Edited by Rebecca Buck. Registrars Committee of the American Alliance of Museums website. 2002. http://www.rcaam.org/about/about-rc-aam/rc-aam-history/.

République Française, Les Défenseur Des Droits. "Une institution independent." Accessed January 6, 2014. http://www.defenseurdesdroits.fr/sinformer-sur-le-defenseur-des-droits/linstitution/actualites/litige-atd-quart-monde-contre-musee.

Richmond, Alison and Alison Bracker, eds. *Conservation: Principles, Dilemmas and Uncomfortable Truths.* New York: Elsevier published in Association with the Victoria and Albert Museum London, 2009.

Rosenthal, Lesley. *Good Counsel: Meeting the Legal Needs of Nonprofits.* New York: John Wiley & Sons, Inc., 2012.

Saint Louis Art Museum, Ancient Art Collections. "Mummy Mask of the Lady Ka-nefer-nefer." Accessed February 23, 2015. http://slam.org:8080/emuseum/view/objects/asitem/6827/65/displayDate-esc?t:state:flow=90f5ef23-a8ca-4c38-a593-7dcfc9fc42d2.

Sandell, Richard and Eithne Nightingale, eds. *Museums, Equality and Social Justice.* New York: Routledge, 2012.

Sarbanes-Oxley Act 2002, "The Sarbanes-Oxley Act." Sarbaanes-Oxley Act 2002 website. http://www.soxlaw.com/index.htm.

Schubert, Jessica. "Prisoners of War: Nazi-Era Looted Art and the Need for Reform in the United States." *Truro Law Review,* Vol. 30, No. 3 (2010): 675–95.

Smithsonian Institution. "Report of the Regents Advisory Panel." Smithsonian Institution website. January 31, 2011. http://newsdesk.si.edu/releases/report-regents-advisory-panel-january-31-2011.

Smithsonian National Museum of African Art. *"Conversations: African and African American Artworks in Dialogue* from the Collections of the Smithsonian National Museum of African Art and Camille O. and William H. Cosby Jr." Accessed November 24, 2014. http://conversations.africa.si.edu.

Spence, Rachel. "Who funds the arts and why we should care." *Financial Times.* September 19, 2014. http://www.ft.com/intl/cms/s/2/4313691c-3513–11e4-aa47–00144feabdc0.html.

Starr, Penny. "Smithsonian Christmas-Season Exhibit Features Ant-Covered Jesus, Naked Brothers Kissing, Genitalia, and Ellen DeGeneres Grabbing her Breasts." CNS News, November 29, 2010. http://www.cnsnews.com/news/article/smithsonian-christmas-season-exhibit-fea.

Starr, Penny. "Boehner and Cantor to Smithsonian: Pull Exhibit Featuring Ant-Covered Jesus or Else." November 30, 2010. http://www.cnsnews.com/news/article/boehner-and-cantor-smithsonian-pull-exhibit-featuring-ant-covered-jesus-or-else.

Stayton, Kevin. "The Brooklyn Museum Costume Collection." Metropolitan Museum of Art website. Accessed October 24, 2014. http://www.metmuseum.org/research/curatorial-research/the-costume-institute/american-woman-symposium/collection-sharing/brooklyn-museum-costume-collection.

St. Hilaire, Rick. "Two Court Battles Raise Questions of Liability for AAM, AAMD, and Other Cultural Property Organizations." Cultural Heritage Lawyer. February 5, 2015. http://culturalheritagelawyer.blogspot.com/2014/02/two-court-battles-raise-questions-of.html.

Stedelijk Museum. "The Stedelijk Museum in the Second World War." Stedelijk Museum website. Accessed April 10, 2015. http://www.stedelijk.nl/en/exhibitions/the-stedelijk-museum-the-second-world-war.

Steiner, Christopher B. "Museum Censorship." In *The Routledge Companion to Museum Ethics: Redefining Ethics for the Twenty-First-Century Museum.* Edited by Janet Marstine, 393–413. New York: Routledge, 2011.

Trope, Jack F. and Walter R. Echo-Hawk. "The Native American Graves Protection and Repatriation Act: Background and Legislative History." *Arizona State Law Journal* 24 (1992): 35–73.

UNESCO. "Convention on the Means of Prohibiting and Preventing the Illicit Import, Export and Transfer of Ownership of Cultural Property." UNESCO website. November 14, 1970. http://portal.unesco.org/en/ev.php-URL_ID=13039&URL_DO=DO_TOPIC&URL_SECTION=201.html.

United States Department of Agriculture. "Animal Welfare Act." United States Department of Agriculture website. 2008. http://awic.nal.usda.gov/government-and-professional-resources/federal-laws/animal-welfare-act.

United States Department of State. "Washington Conference Principles on Nazi-Confiscated Art." December 3, 1998. http://www.state.gov/p/eur/rt/hlcst/122038.htm.

United States v. Mask of Ka-Nefer-Nefer, No. 12–2578 (8th Cir. June 12, 2014).

Urice, Stephen K. "Deaccessioning: A Few Observations." American Law Institute— American Bar Association Continuing Legal Education. Legal Issues in Museum Administration Course, SR005 ALI-ABA 207 (2010).

Vadi, Valentina and Hildegard E.G.S. Schneider, eds. *Art, Cultural Heritage and the Market: Ethical and Legal Issues.* New York: Springer, 2014.

Vilnius International Forum on Holocaust-Era Looted Cultural Assets. "Vilnius Forum Declaration." Commission for Looted Art in Europe website. October 5, 2000. http://www.lootedartcommission.com/vilnius-forum.

Weil, Stephen E. Beauty and the Beasts: On Museums, Art, the Law and the Market. Washington, DC: Smithsonian Institution Press, 1983.

———. Cabinet of Curiosities: Inquiries into Museums and their Prospects. Washington, DC: Smithsonian Institution Press, 1995.

———. "Deaccession Practices in American Museums." In *Rethinking the Museum and Other Meditations.* Washington, DC: Smithsonian Institution Press, 1990.

———, ed. *A Deaccession Reader.* Washington, DC: American Association of Museums, 1997.

———. *Rethinking the Museum and Other Meditations.* Washington, DC: Smithsonian Institution Press, 1990.

Weiser, Benjamin. "Museum Sues to Keep Meteorite Sought by Indian Group." *The New York Times.* February 29, 2000. http://www.nytimes.com/2000/02/29/nyregion/museum-sues-to-keep-meteorite-sought-by-indian-group.html.

Wikipedia. David H. Koch. Accessed December 10, 2014. http://en.wikipedia.org/wiki/David_H._Koch.

Williams, Stephen L. "Preventative conservation: The evolution of a museum ethic." in *Museum Ethics.* Edited by Gary Edson. New York: Routledge, 1997. Pp. 198–206.

Wuichet, John and Bryan Norton, "Differing conceptions of Animal Welfare." In *Ethics on the Ark: Zoos, Animal Welfare, and Wildlife Conservation.* Edited by Bryan G. Norton, Michael Hutchins, Elizabeth Stevens, and Terry L. Maple. Washington, DC: Smithsonian Books, 1995.

Wylie, Alison. "On Ethics." In *Ethical Issues in Archaeology.* Edited by Larry J. Zimmerman, Karen D. Vitelli, and Julie Hollowell-Zimmer. New York: AltaMira Press, 2003.

Yerkovich, Sally. "Is There a Future for Museum Ethics?" Paper presented at "Museums, Politics, and Power," a joint conference of the International Council of Museums-US, ICOM-Russia, and ICOM-Germany, September 2014.

Young, Laura Elizabeth. "A Framework for Resolution of Claims for Cultural Property." MA thesis, University of Oregon, 2007.

YouTube. Accessed December 9, 2013. http://www.youtube.com/verify_age?next_url=http%3A//www.youtube.com/watch%3Fv%3D0fC3sUDtR7U.

Index

AAM. *See* American Alliance of Museums

AAMD. *See* Association of Art Museum Directors

AASLH. *See* American Association of State and Local History

AIC. *See* American Institute for Conservation of Historic and Artistic Works

Albright Knox Art Gallery, 2

American Alliance of Museums (AAM), ix, x, 51, 66–67, 69, 75, 113–14, 121, 123, 135, 140n65;
"Characteristics of Excellence for U.S. Museums," 144–45;
"Code of Ethics for Museums," 1, 3–4, 8–9, 21, 32, 50, 66–67, 80–81, 101, 113, 144, 155–59;
core documents, 9;
"Direct Care of Collections: Ethics, Guidelines and Recommendations," 76n9;
"Recommended Procedures for Providing Information to the Public about Objects Transferred in Europe during the Nazi Era," 121–22;
"Standards Regarding Archaeological Material and Ancient Art," 114;

"Standards Regarding Developing and Managing Business and Individual Donor Support," 81–82;
"Standards Regarding Exhibiting Borrowed Objects," 82;
"Standards Regarding Unlawful Appropriation of Objects During the Nazi Era," 121

American Association for State and Local History (AASLH), x, 22, 123, 135;
"Ethics Position Paper on the Capitalization of Collections," 67;
Professional Standards and Ethics, 9–10, 32–33, 50, 67, 83–84, 101–2, 145, 181–85

American Institute for Conservation of Historic and Artistic Works (AIC), 51

American Museum of Natural History, 85, 125–26

Americans with Disabilities Act (ADA), 13, 144, 148–49

archaeological objects and ancient art, 113–19

Association of Art Museum Directors (AAMD), x, 22, 69, 121, 123, 135, 140n65;

About the Author

Sally Yerkovich is an internationally known speaker and museum leader. She is director of the Institute of Museum Ethics at Seton Hall University and adjunct professor in the Museum Professions Program at Seton Hall as well as in the Museum Anthropology Program at Columbia University. She also teaches in the Bank Street Graduate School's Leadership in Museum Education Program. A member of the Ethics Committee for the International Council of Museums (ICOM), the only international organization representing museums and museum professionals, she worked extensively with museums in Central and Eastern Europe as President of the Fund for Arts and Culture.

A cultural anthropologist with over thirty years of experience in high profile cultural institutions in New York and Washington, DC, she held leadership positions at the National Endowment for the Humanities, National Endowment for the Arts, South Street Seaport Museum and Museum of the City of New York. She was president and CEO of The New Jersey Historical Society, interim executive director at the Museum for African Art, and first president of the Tribute NYC Center. She served as chair of the American Alliance of Museums Task Force charged with clarifying the ethical principles involved in the use of funds realized from the sale of deaccessioned objects and is a member of the American Association of State and Local History Standards and Ethics Committee.

Printed in Great
Britain
by Amazon

31247815R00147